WRITING
PRACTICE

**Longman Series in
College Composition and Communication**

Advisory Editor: Harvey Wiener
LaGuardia Community College
The City University of New York

WRITING PRACTICE

A Rhetoric

of the

Writing Process

BEN W. McCLELLAND

Rhode Island College

Longman

New York & London

Writing Practice

Longman Inc., 1560 Broadway, New York, N.Y. 10036
Associated companies, branches, and representatives
throughout the world.

Developmental Editor: Gordon T. R. Anderson
Editorial and Production Supervisor: Ferne Y. Kawahara
Interior Design: Antler & Baldwin
Manufacturing Supervisor: Marion Hess
Composition: Kingsport Press
Printing and Binding: Haddon Craftsmen

Library of Congress Cataloging in Publication Data

McClelland, Ben W., 1943–
  Writing Practice

    (Longman series in college composition and communication)
    Includes index.
    1. English language—Rhetoric. I. Title. II. Series.
PE1408.M3936 1984   808'.042   83–12000
ISBN 0–582–28362–0

Manufactured in the United States of America
Printing: 9 8 7 6 5 4 3 2 1   Year: 92 91 90 89 88 87 86 85 84

For
Ben L., who grows through practice and performance,
and
Susan, who nurtures that growth

CONTENTS

ACKNOWLEDGMENTS

This book evolved from ideas which grew with writing. Many people contributed to that growth. William E. Coles, Jr. presented me with a teaching style that initiated a search for my own. Harvey Wiener enabled me to see the making of a book out of my teaching and started me on the way. Barbara Cambridge read an early draft of the first chapter and responded helpfully. William E. Smith, a close friend, served faithfully as well as a reader of drafts, making especially useful suggestions on sentence combining. Rosemary Herring read proof, bringing an experienced teacher's view to the text.

The Rhode Island College Faculty Research Fund awarded me grants in the early stages of writing. Rhode Island College granted me a sabbatical leave for the final months of composition.

Anonymous reviewers worked with me and the publisher over several months through successive drafts, providing expertise and common sense.

My colleagues Ellen Gardiner, Kathryn Kalinak, and John Roche had the energy (and courage) to try out an untried book in their classes.

Those at Longman Inc. who were associated with this project—Harvey Wiener, Tren Anderson, and Ferne Kawahara—brought humane care and professional concern to all of our dealings.

I owe all of these people—and I express it now—a deep debt of gratitude.

I also want to thank some who experienced the growth of this book with me daily: my students for what they have contributed directly to the text and for what they have taught me about the learning and teaching of writing; Ellen Gardiner for careful manuscript reading and thoughtful response; Arlene Robertson and Natalie DiRissio for professional typing services which transformed my tedious script into typescript; and, especially, my wife Susan and my family for abiding with me (and frequently without me) through the two-year process during which this book grew.

Chapter Three from *THE GRAPES OF WRATH* by John Steinbeck. Copyright 1939 by John Steinbeck. Copyright renewed (c) 1967 by John Steinbeck. Reprinted by permission of Viking Penguin Inc.
"Pitchers' Duel" by Pat Jordan originally appeared in PLAYBOY Magazine. Copyright (c) 1981 by Playboy. Reprinted by permission of The Sterling Lord Agency, Inc.
Mortal Lessons by Richard Selzer copyright (c) 1974, 1975, 1976 by Richard Selzer. Reprinted by permission of Simon & Shuster, Inc.
"Shall the University Become a Business Corporation?" by Henry S. Pritchett originally published in *The Atlantic Monthly*. Reprinted by permission of the author and *The Atlantic Monthly*.
"The Spider and the Wasp" by Alexander Petrunkevitch from *Scientific American* (August 1952). Copyright (c) 1952 by Scientific American, Inc. All rights reserved.
"Uptight and Loose" originally appeared in PLAYBOY Magazine. Copyright (c) 1981 by Playboy.
"Instant Techie Handbook" by Lindsay Van Gelder reprinted by permission of Ms. Magazine Corp.
Excerpts on champagne by Raymond Oliver from *LaCuisine: Secrets of Modern French Cooking*, edited by Nika Stauden and Jack Van Bibber, 1969. Reprinted with permission of Tudor Publishing Company, New York.
"The Lessons of Beekeeping" by Michael J. Kelly originally appeared in *The Chronicle of Higher Education*. Reprinted by permission of *The Chronicle of Higher Education* and the author.
"Voltaire and Frederick the Great" from *Two Cheers for Democracy* by E. M. Forster. Reprinted by permission of Harcourt Brace Jovanovich, Inc.
"A Close Marriage Should Not Mean Individuality's End" © 1983 by Barbara Lazear. Reprinted by special permission of the Rhoda Weyr Agency, New York.
"Men and Madness: Some Thoughts on the Violence Factor" by Philip Slater reprinted by permission of Ms. Magazine Corp.
Excerpts from "Among School Children" reprinted with permission of Macmillan Publishing Company from *Collected Poems* by William Butler Yeats. Copyright 1928 by Macmillan Publishing Co., Inc., renewed 1956 by Georgie Yeats.

1

PRACTICING:
Write Only on the
Days You Eat

*A Single Good Performance Requires Days
of Regular Practice.*

Your English composition course differs in a significant way from most other college courses. In a typical course you read about a subject, listen to lectures, discuss ideas, study your reading and class notes, and demonstrate your understanding of the subject by completing tests and writing papers. Your English composition course differs because, in addition to having you study writing as a subject, it requires that you practice the activity of writing. In this way, taking a composition course is more like playing a varsity sport or taking a course in dance, music performance, or studio art. If you have taken such a dance, music, or art course or have played a varsity sport, you know that to do well you must develop the habit of practicing the activity daily.

You may also recall your teacher or coach urging, "Practice! Practice!" So don't be surprised if you find your composition teacher behaving more like a coach or a performance or studio teacher than a teacher of a subject-matter course, because a composition teacher asks students to keep in shape, practice, and perform writing acts. In fact, I have adapted this chapter's title

1

from a violin teacher's maxim. Much of Shinichi Suzuki's success with very young students lay in his ability to motivate them to practice daily.

When my first-grade son, Ben, began studying the violin, I demanded that he follow the rigorous practice schedule Mr. Suzuki required of his pupils. Ben excelled, practicing an hour a day, memorizing and performing this gavotte and that sonata. He learned to express ideas and feelings through music. Within a few months his teacher and I knew that Ben could become an accomplished young violinist, if only he would maintain the habit of practicing. My son's trial of will—to practice daily bowing exercises, rhythmic games, scales, and full pieces—has been going on for nine years. To be sure, he has had dark days; I recall when comic books, girlfriends, roller disco, and Fleetwood Mac beckoned him to sights and sounds more enticing than pulling a well-rosined bow over taut metal wires. But after a few months the sight of a soundless violin was more than he could bear: he resumed daily practice because he wanted to feel again the power of being a performing musician. He wanted to express himself musically.

You may have had a similar experience as a youngster with music or dance lessons or with Little League sports. If so, you know that to perform an activity effectively and gracefully, you must practice it regularly. In order to use your body and mind to accomplish demanding actions, you must be physically and mentally in shape. Like artistic performers and athletes, writers must practice consistently to develop muscle tone and endurance so that fingers, hands, arms, eyes, and brains can function long and effectively at their peak.

Shortly, I will offer some writing exercises to help you begin developing habits of effective writers. But before doing so, I want to give you a few reasons for becoming a writer who practices. Have you ever marveled at Mikhail Baryshnikov leaping effortlessly and touching down light-as-a-feather? Anyone who has can see aesthetic beauty as well as physical prowess in these motions. Similarly, anyone seeing a Wyeth painting or hearing Itzak Perlman play the violin enjoys sensuous delight as well as intellectual stimulation. Daily practice is essential to the works these people perform. Yet one doesn't have to be an accomplished professional to move someone else by artistic performance. Even my son, who is not precocious, transports me with music.

Handing him the bow for his daily practice, I watch quietly as he adjusts the tension of its horsehair strands. He peers intently at the music sheet, a page of dots and circles, lines and spaces, all nonsense to me; shortly he begins, playing with ease, as if the violin and bow were natural appendages. He takes me musically to another time and place. In this special moment I am his child, not old enough to read the words from a storybook,

Photograph by Martha Swope

so he reads them for me, leading me to a world of warmth and light, of fear and brooding, of failure and triumph.

Just as athletes and artists, professional or amateur, move us with their performances, so writers move us with their words. Reading the written word can move us as powerfully as listening to music or watching dance. My students and I regularly move each other with our writing: We are persuaded to act, moved to laughter and tears, jostled to question our beliefs, or compelled to make rejoinders.

Many of my students, however, lack the desire to perform as athletes, musicians, and dancers do. So, why do they practice writing? For different reasons: many students simply want to learn how to express themselves more effectively in words; some of them want to write dramatic poems or amusing stories; others want to write better examinations or academic papers; and still others want to transmit clear instructions or logical reasoning in reports. The aim of the practicing writer, after all, is to gain control over language and to move others with words. Doing so, a writer may become a more effective problem solver and a more resourceful thinker as well as a more successful writer. To write effectively means practicing daily—or at least on the days you eat. Here is a plan of finger (and brain) exercises to help you become a practicing writer.

WRITING PRACTICE SCHEDULE

First, schedule a time for a writing workout each day. If you keep a daily schedule of your college class meetings, record on it your daily writing practice time. If you have no such class schedule, then make one for your writing regimen. How much time should you allot each day to writing? Many of you should attempt to work gradually up to an hour daily. Some of you may be able to warm up effectively with less practice; others of you will need more time, just as different athletes and artists vary the amounts of time for practicing to keep in shape.

Setting and adhering to a schedule of regular writing workouts is essential to your writing improvement. Through these daily practice sessions you get in and stay in shape to write more effectively. For example, you develop writing endurance, the ability to write for longer periods of time before tiring, mentally or physically. If you work rigorously through the exercises below, you should begin to develop new patterns of thinking, new ways of seeing, and eventually new ways of expressing yourself. Furthermore, the writing you produce during workouts can serve as sources of ideas for the papers you will write for class.

Here are some exercises for your writing workouts. By practicing them regularly for the first month of the course, you will begin to feel the power of the practicing writer. Even though you may falter once or twice (everybody has a bad day now and then), you will return to the regimen because, even if seeing blank pages will not be more than you can bear, you will regain an interest in expressing yourself in written words.

EXERCISES

Exercise 1: Freewriting

Have you ever gotten writer's cramp when completing an essay exam or taking notes on a fast-moving lecture? Freewriting builds up your endurance for fast writing and for quick thinking. Select a topic and write continuously for a set period of time. Ten minutes is a reasonable period at first. (After a week or so increase the period gradually to 20 minutes.) Keep writing words across the page nonstop for the full period. If during the exercise you can think of no more to write on the topic, continue writing nonetheless. Simply recopy words, phrases, or sentences until your mind lights up with new ones again. At the end of the period, stop writing and count the number of words you produced. Your only purpose in this exercise is to write as many words on a topic as you can in a given period. (Note: After you have determined how many words you write per line on average, you may estimate the total number of words rather than counting every one.)

Are you looking for some topics for freewriting? Why not begin with an idea from this chapter: for example, the comparison of writing with playing sports and music; or how, as an athlete or a musician, you mustered up the discipline required to practice daily. Looking for more topics? Perhaps you and your classmates can draw up a list of possible topics to which you may refer from time to time.

Try this freewriting exercise every day for a month. Record

MONTH: _____

	S	M	T	W	T	F
DATE TIME WORDCOUNT						
DATE TIME WORDCOUNT						
DATE TIME WORDCOUNT						
DATE TIME WORDCOUNT						
DATE TIME WORDCOUNT						

Figure 1.1

on the chart above the length of exercise periods, word totals, name of the month, and the days' dates. Discuss with your classmates your experiences with this exercise.

Examples of Freewriting

Let's look at some examples of my students' freewriting exercises. Freewriting is a novel kind of writing assignment for students because it is free and unstructured. For that reason, students' first few attempts are very taxing and the initial results often are disappointing. For example, here's all that Pat could write during a tension-filled, 10-minute freewriting period in the first week of class when I suggested that students write about why they were in the class and what they wanted to get out of it:

I am taking this course cause I was told I have to improve my English. I thought I was going to get help learning how to write, now the teacher tells me to write without giving any help. I'm stuck, he says not to stop writing, this is stupid. I can't think of anymore to say. I know he's going to look at me. What can I say? The sign on the wall says No Smoking. The teacher wrote his office number and telephone number on the board. Is he going to make us write like this everyday?

WORDCOUNT: 98

Beginning-of-the-course freewriting exercises often look like Pat's. It takes practice to develop the ability to think through an idea spontaneously and to write out that thinking. Before developing control over that ability, students often get very tense, feel stupid and on-the-spot, as Pat did. Many write little more than 75 words, and their writing rambles, containing few focused ideas.

It is surprising, therefore, to see how rapidly students begin to improve their ability to write more words and to create more connected and focused ideas during timed writing periods. The following are exercises written in the last month of classes. The freewriting periods were 15 minutes each. Among others, Matilda and Alison selected "If next week were my last week to live. . . ." Matilda's response reflects the two lines of thinking explored by all the students who chose this topic: whether to do things they had never dared to do or to maintain the same routine activities to the end.

IF NEXT WEEK IS MY VERY LAST WEEK OF LIFE

I wouldn't be sitting here right now. I'd be acting out all my wildly perverted fantasies! Singing atop restaurant tables, between the soup spoon and salad fork; riding naked upon horseback against the rolling waves on the beach; skiing down the white, ravenous alps. That's where I would be—doing things I had never done before.

Or maybe I'd be out in the quiet, peaceful country with my family, enjoying the sights and sounds of spring. Looking at things I'd seen a hundred times before, only now through different eyes—observing each patch of moss upon a growing tree, noticing each tiny wrinkle upon my mother's lovely face, enjoying my nephew's wild screaming for the first time— that's what I'd be doing, probably.

Or I might choose to just sit down with a good book and read. Read of the foreign, distant places where I've never been; read of the famous people I have never met; read of the wonders in outer space that I'll never see. I might just sit down and think of things I'll never do, experiences I'll never feel, children I'll never have.

Or would I do any of that? Most unlikely. I'd probably just live each day as I normally would, only this time more joyously.

WORDCOUNT: 201

Alison took the occasion to write something considerably more daring than she ever had.

UNTITLED

If next week were my last one on this complicated earth, I would be devastated. My goodness, it would mean giving up the things I enjoy most in life: decorating my bedroom; eating, rock 'n roll, and term paper deadlines. These may seem trivial to some, but how I enjoy them. What would life be like without three papers due on the same day? Could I actually survive without "pigging out"? Can I leave these luxuries behind?

Ending my life would not be easy. It means getting things ready; moreover, it means getting myself ready. The first thing I'd do is eat all my Easter candy. Who cares about being fat in heaven—everyone floats anyway. The second thing I'd do is pick out a real tacky outfit to wear at my wake. It would be something I wouldn't have the nerve to wear normally—maybe a hot pink tube top and some black leather pants. The third thing I'd engage in would be fulfilling my fantasies, sexual and otherwise (maybe even wear the tacky outfit for the sexual fantasies). Next, I'd make love to the man I'll leave behind, until I breathe my last breath. Finally, if next week were my last one alive, I'd set my lingering thoughts to music—creating a song sure to make you cry (just to reveal the seriousness and sensitivity I *really* possess).

WORDCOUNT: 222

This exercise gave Alison the idea for later writing a satire, poking fun at "proper thoughts and proper behavior for young ladies." In the next selection Edith discusses struggling with a certain kind of goal which should sound familiar to us pudgy folks.

MY GOAL FOR 1982

Every year I set some goal for myself, sometimes I attain that goal and sometimes I don't. This year I have set the goal to lose 20 pounds. Now, that doesn't sound too difficult does it? Well, let me tell you, it isn't as easy as it sounds.

In January I began my campaign to lose 20 pounds in 1982. I began going to exercise class four and sometimes five times a week. I was sure this would do something for me besides take up my time, which I must admit I have little of. It wasn't very successful. Three months of toil for approximately eight pounds which return in a month if I don't exercise.

In order to reach my goal I will have to diet. This is something I try to do on a regular basis but I find it hard to be consistent. I do really well for about a week or two and then I blow it all in two days.

I really want to lose this 20 pounds before I get any older. It seems that the older I get, the more difficult this twenty pounds will be to lose. I am also afraid that if I don't lose it now it will start creeping higher and higher until before I know it I'll be so fat that I won't be able to do anything.

So this year's goal is to lose 20 pounds. Presently I am trying to follow Weight Watchers diet and exercise regularly. It is a slow process but I think I can do it.

WORDCOUNT: 262

While it is quite long, Edith's exercise contains a lot of repetition. It demonstrates that even though she has been practicing for several weeks, impromptu writing stimulates just the beginning of her thinking on a topic; if she is stalled on one spot, she can simply "write out of it" without feeling panicked, tense, or stupid, as beginning students sometimes do.

In the following exercise Mura, a bright, 35-year-old, faces squarely the writer's dilemma that plagued her and a number of her classmates during the course:

WHAT KEEPS ME FROM WRITING MY VERY BEST: OR PRIORITIES OF LIFE

Initially, a wave of enthusiasm engulfs my being, and I can't wait to set my earth-shattering thoughts onto paper. The ink flows unceasingly in an effort to keep pace with the plethora of ideas crying to be heard. During this first phase of writing I am absolutely positive no one has ever composed a more perfect sentence, paragraph, or paper. Completing the first impetus of the procedure, I set aside my masterpiece, to be proofread at a later date.

A few days later, the excitement completely gone from the project, I attempt to correct my mistakes and type out my scribbling. At this point my only hope is to be able to make as few typographical errors as possible and get the thing in on time. The first typed draft is normally such a mess it has to be typed again.

By now I have gone into "writer's shock" and no longer recognize the meaning of the words, but only if they are spelled correctly. As hours dwindle down to a precious few (sounds like a song) inertia sets in and mundane things take on grandiose importance. Such as cleaning the bathroom, matching socks, changing the litter-box, watering the plants or sweeping the back steps. It is at this time I should be examining sentence structure and paragraphs, but unconsciously I know that might mean a whole rewrite. By procrastinating it is possible to let the clock run out, thereby making it impossible to complete another draft.

On my last paper I played a dirty trick on myself. Because of the snowstorm we had an extra week to spend, but I had it prepared for last Tuesday. On Sunday night, I took a little peek. This was my undoing. The only solution to the horrible sentence structures was another draft. I am thankful spring is around the corner and the likelihood of another snow storm is minimal. I wouldn't want to make it a habit.

WORDCOUNT: 297

Exercise 2: Write a Journal

In a journal jot down your thoughts on current events, ideas about your reading, ideas brought up in class or in discussions with your friends. Although many people prefer to set aside a certain time for journal writing, I suggest that you keep your journal handy to jot down your ideas while they're still clearly in your mind. Unless you get them down quickly, they'll be out of mind and out of sight. Bits of information that you store in your journal may serve you well later when you begin composing essays. For this type of journal writing some entries may be as short as 20 or 30 words, while others may be as long as 75 or 100. The length depends on the complexity of the idea, the amount of thought you have given it, how much time you have to write, and so on.

You may also want to use your journal as a workbook for expanding freewriting exercises, or for drafting longer pieces— parts of essays, for example. If that's the case, you may want to develop a system of marking the types of entries you write. In any case, you will probably find it helpful to get a special notebook or journal book for these purposes and, of course, you will find it useful to date each entry as you write it.

Examples of Journal Writing

There are many published journals of professional writers. For example, you may find in your college library the journals of such diverse writers as Ralph Waldo Emerson, Henry David Thoreau, May Sarton, Joan Didion, and Woody Allen.

Here are several entries from my students' journals. A part-time student in his mid-20s who also worked full-time, John wrote in the evenings on some topics about which he thought during the day.

DEATH

As far as I'm concerned there are two stages of life. The first being a time of fun with only a minimal amount of worries. The second is reached at some undetermined point in a person's life when fun decreases and worrying increases. This worrying ranges everywhere from financial stability to death and dying. Many people accept death as a part of life. Others fear death because the feeling and experience is unknown. A person by the name of Kubler-Ross has a theory of how to accept death and deal with it. She is a firm believer that death should and will be accepted by all. There is another theory that states, people who constantly fear death seem to live longer. An example would be Russia, where there are reports of people living as long as 140 years. The theory also states that those people who do accept death seem to die sooner. I would assume that this theory is driving at a conclusion that the willingness to live or die is in our minds. If this theory is true it has been proven by my grandmother, she is 87 years old and fears death.

TAKING CRITICISM

The ability to accept criticism is good, for the reason that it can get used as an advantage. People who do things on their own are less apt to complete something to perfection. The person who accepts criticism on the other hand will get a wide range of different ideas from others. It was Thomas Kuhn who believed that in order for a better understanding of a subject, there should be conflicting views. Unfortunately there are people who will not accept criticism. These people become defensive, the thought of another person correcting something of theirs really goes up their skin. Some of these people start feeling sorry for themselves, they begin to figure that they can not make a move without getting instructions first. The initiative of such persons will tend to drop. It is smart for the criticizer to watch a person's reaction, this can guide you to determining what type he or she may be. In a sense the criticizer is acting a lot like a psychiatrist will act.

SONGS AS REMINDERS

Liking a wide range of music lets me recall pleasurable and depressed moments in time. Everywhere I go, radios surround me playing all various beated music. I work, drive, and relax to the sounds of different groups. For the longest time this has been going on. Over the period of years I have encountered fun times and sad times while in the presence of music. Now when I listen to particular albums or tapes I get reminded of certain events. I think of these events and remember that there was something I liked about a thing, maybe I wanted something, or was shocked by an object or person. I feel I can't forget these memories. It is like our minds are stone and this is inscribed on them by a stone cutter.

MEMORIES OF CHILDHOOD RECALLED

For as long as I can remember television has been a main source of entertainment. Recently, I caught a television program I had not seen for a long time. The show was "Ironside." As I watched the program this late night I began to remember when it was aired during prime time hours years ago. I thought back and recalled that the show was on Thursday nights. Thursday nights were special because that was the shopping night. My parents would go out leaving me, my toys, and my grandmother. I can remember playing, having a ball in the livingroom and dining room while the television ran on. For some reason "Ironside" stuck in my mind. Reminiscing of the old times was fun, back when life was easy and no decisions had to be made. Growing older we forget certain times of our lives, until a particular subject is brought up.

You may notice that in the first entry John selected an abstract topic (death), wrote some opening remarks of a general nature about it (some people fear death; others accept it), and then stated a specific example (Elizabeth Kubler-Ross, my grandmother). In the second entry the writing stays on the level of generalization; that is, except for citing Thomas Kuhn as an authority, John does not state any specific examples of people he knows giving or taking criticism. In the last two entries John speaks entirely out of personal experience without generalizing on his experience. His last sentences are conclusions on which wider applications of his ideas could be made. Study these entries and consider how you might develop each more fully.

If sometime during your journal writing you are looking for a topic, consult this list from John's other headings:

people's dedication	stubbornness and pride
car accidents	jealousy

industrial spying

how one thing can bring people together

sleep

eye-openers

self-control

laughing at negative things

music for different occasions

being afraid of the dark

rushing

TV cartoons

TV shows

hypocrites

new cars

working

getting signals crossed

self-fulfilling prophecy

stress

guilt

weather forecasts and the weather

knowing a second language

responsibilities

work overload

Even with a long list of topics to choose from students often run out of good ideas or they just get tired of writing journal entries day after day. So, after a couple of weeks I ask students to turn their journals into "class logs." A log is a record of progress. For example, travelers record the progress of their journeys in logs; researchers record the history of their experiments in logs. Thus, I ask students to write entries on their progress as writers or to record the ideas we discuss in class. Here are entries from the class logs of four students.

Tom, who works full-time and goes to school as well, wrote these remarks about composing a paper:

Selecting a topic was a great challenge. I felt that since I was being given some flexibility, I would write about something important in my life. I have decided to write about, "Communication and Raising Children."

Brainstorming is the strategy I used to compile a list of ideas I wanted to discuss relative to the importance of communication and the way it affects all areas of parenthood.

After compiling my list I wrote each item on the top of individual sheets of lined paper and proceeded to write my heart out on each subject. Words and thoughts are much easier to put down in writing than ever before. My best time to generate material is early in the morning. Last Thursday I had a day off and I wrote 12 pages about my topic in a span of three hours.

Friday morning I was up early again on another day off from work, only instead of writing I was shuffling my pages to put them into an order that made sense. It's surprising how well this technique works. Two hours was spent in deciding how I would join all of my ideas into a meaningful topic.

Saturday I wrote my first draft, painfully trying to develop a flow to my topic. Sunday evening I typed the first draft and that is when Tom the critic began to make revisions. When I type my words I see them and it helps me to rewrite my draft more effectively.

Donna's process differs somewhat from Tom's, but achieves the same goal.

The first night I read over some of the topics I could choose from. I wrote a couple of paragraphs on the two I thought I might be interested in doing. Then I put everything away. But it never leaves me—I just keep thinking about the topics and a few sentences come to mind so I jotted them down.

I decided to particle, wave & field* my topic and as with every other topic I only get so far and then I'm off and writing. That usually gets me going.

I discuss my topics with several people. Usually as a sounding board. By the time I finish talking about it I realize I've said a number of things I could use in my paper.

As far as developing my information, I generally write out everything that comes to mind, then I rewrite a few more times from the beginning. When I finally think I have something to say, enough to write a paper I go back over it and usually rearrange some of the material. Now, I go over it as a critic and see that more information is needed in certain paragraphs. And I just keep rereading it until I'm satisfied with what I've written, how I've said things, etc. I jot down notes, put arrows where I think sentences should be changed to, etc.

Jayne mentions a useful revising strategy:

* This method for getting started on a writing assignment is presented in Chapter 2, pp. 30–34.

I began the final revision on my essay. Again rewriting sentences, although not as much as the last time. I've found the best way for me to understand what I've written is to read it out loud. Otherwise, it's too easy to skim over the paper; I've written it so many times I tend to overlook errors.

While in her second writing class, Ellen chose to revise a paper she originally wrote a year earlier. She discusses her revision in these three entries.

Now that I'm pretty excited about this project, I can't seem to think of anything else. Somehow I think I'm discovering something about my development as a writer now. I'm beginning to see just how far I've come as a writer in the past year or so, especially after reading the article by Sommers.* According to her definition I am a mature writer. Now what I must discover is whether or not I can become more mature, inventive, and sophisticated in my writing of fiction.

The paper is growing by leaps and bounds—how easy it comes for some reason. Though I say a lot more here I am sure there is more for me to say but I won't have time if I am to be able to pass this in on Mon. I want to get started on my Amer. lit. paper, or rather, start putting pen to paper as I've been composing it in my head for a few weeks. Formulating an approach anyway.

It is finished. What relief. An onus off my shoulders but at the same time I cannot stop thinking of it. And how I can make it better the next time I revise it. Somehow as I wrote the paper I felt like I was teaching, that my audience is a bunch of students who don't know how to revise. On the other hand maybe I feel like I am teaching myself. Who'd a thought it? This is the most important writing I've ever done.

Exercise 3: Write What You Eat

Since you are both eating and writing today, personify one of your foods and write an imaginary conversation with it. Here

---

* Ideas on revising are presented in Chapter 4; see the first endnote on p. 135 for a reference to this article.

are some questions to help get you in the mood: What kind of personality would you ascribe to brussel sprouts? How do you think bran cereal feels about your school's sports program? If french fries accompanied you on an evening out, what would they say to each other about you and your date?

Have you ever heard swordfish hold forth on the George's Bank oil-exploration controversy? Swordfish deliver most piercing repartees and have uncanny taste.

Note: My composition-teacher friends have reacted very strongly to this exercise, especially to the wordplay in the last sentence. Some are strongly in favor of it; one asked playfully, "Can swordfish tuna violin?" On the other hand, some are strongly opposed to it; however, even one who opposed it couldn't resist this wordplay in her response: "Are you herring too much negative criticism?" Another opponent said, "Save your sole and throw out this sentence!" Your class might use this exercise and the wordgames it may spawn as the starting point of a discussion of special word usage and reader responses. For example, considering their context and the audience, are such word uses as "piercing," "tuna," "herring," "sole," and "spawn" creative, cute, too cute, corny, or what? Do they add or detract from the purpose of the exercise?

Examples of Writing What You Eat

To give you an idea of what some of my students have written for this exercise, here are two samples of their edible conversationalists:

CASUAL CONVERSATION AT LUNCH

I opened the little box the Big Mac comes in. Have you ever had voices in your head? It started just after I opened the little box. It's a weird feeling. At first I thought the voices were really in my head, but my lunch was talking. It was a private conversation.

"We are two all-beef patties, special sauce, lettuce, cheese, pickles, onions on a sesame seed bun."

"Hey, how come I'm always last in line?"

"Put a lid on it, Bun, you're always complaining."

"That's easy for you to say, Big Cheese, no one argues with you."

"Oh sure, how would you like Onion stuck in your face all day and a hot Burger under your can."

"Get off my back, Big Cheese, you think you got complaints; I have lettuce tickling my belly!"

"Don't get me involved, Burger, I feel like I've been through the shredder with this Pickles' sour personality."

"Shut up, lettuce, if you sat in this mess all day you would be sour too."

" 'Mess,' you call me! McDonald's is famous because of me, Special Sauce. Besides, if that Onion didn't stink so bad, I wouldn't be running all over."

"O.K., Guys, it all boils down that I, the Onion, bring tears to your eyes. Now forget all that. We've got to remember the company."

"All together now; two all-beef patties, special sauce, etc . . ."

People often wonder why their Big Macs are so sloppy. Well, all things considered, they think I'll be out by Christmas.

FRENCH FRIES ON DATING

Here is part of a conversation Sandy and Mike, two french fries, had during my date with Chris last Saturday.

"They do look nervous—just look at him eat!" Mike exclaimed. "I haven't seen anyone chow down so much food since the busboy stuck his head in our freezer trying to swallow down that lasagne before the boss marched through the swinging door. Scrunch down in the basket and maybe we can listen for a bit."

"She looks sort of exasperated. I think it's because he keeps talking about his old flames. That's far from the best way to start out a date. This guy has a major choice to make now—he has to decide whether he considers this girl a best friend or as something more than just a close buddy. He can't do both. Well, if he's chosen, I hope the "something more" came before they stopped to eat. He's been picking the pepperoni off her pizza strips and gobbling it down one piece after another."

"I choose to ignore that tasteless comment. As for this guy, it's my guess that he'll just string her along for as long as he pleases. Same old story—she's filling the Dear Abby role with a little passion play on the side. You men are all alike."

"Think of it this way then, if he's just like me, then as soon as you get past that tough exterior he's all soft inside. He'll straighten out soon enough. Who knows—maybe things will turn out like they did for us. They seem to really understand one another; maybe they can work out all of these surface problems. Here's wishing them the best. I'm glad all of those times are behind us. I'll be content to stretch out and lay back on a bed of ketchup for the rest of my days."

Note: For any of you who find this exercise distasteful, personify something other than food: your car, computer, textbooks, furniture, wristwatch, or telephone, for example.

Exercise 4: Write Summaries

Summarizing is a reading-thinking-writing activity which requires that you distinguish between main ideas and supporting or subordinate ideas. Developing your ability at this activity has great practical value to your learning a subject in addition to your becoming a better writer.

Write brief summaries of your school reading material. For example, summarize each chapter of this text as you read it. Do the same with other course reading assignments. Compare your summaries with those of your classmates.

Exercise 5: Political Cartoons

Open the daily paper to the editorial page or whatever section contains the political cartoons. Describe the situation depicted in the cartoon, including persons, countries, and events, as appropriate. Pay particular attention to the method of depiction. For example, is someone drawn as an animal? Is a metaphor used, that is, a comparison of two dissimilar things? Does the cartoonist employ hyperbole, an exaggeration? After describing the cartoon, state in a sentence or two the main idea of the cartoon. Take relevant notes from any articles in the paper pertaining to the cartoon's subject. Finally, write your response to the situation depicted and to the cartoonist's method of depiction. Attach the cartoon to your notebook page; it may come in handy for later reference.

Exercise 6: Rewrite

Rewrite your class lecture notes. As you do so, look for ways of improving your thoughts; follow your language instincts to expand your notes as appropriate. For example, write out in complete sentences any of the symbols, phrases, shorthand, or abbreviated statements you may have recorded. Did the lecturer use expressions that you understood upon hearing but need to rework for them to make sense in writing? If so, use your general understanding of the material to render them in explicit and complete statements. Later you may wish to check with the lecturer on the accuracy of your version of the lecture.

After a few weeks of daily writing you may also want to rewrite some of the earlier writing you did for Exercises 1–5.

Note: You may soon discover through rewriting class notes and through writing journal entries on course readings or on ideas from class discussion that writing out information from a course is a very effective method of studying. I will be discussing more about learning by writing in later chapters, but you should know now that these are not busywork or empty exercises. You can learn subject matter effectively by writing it out. Not only do these exercises help you form good writing habits, but they can also help you perform better in all of your courses.

SUGGESTIONS FOR LONGER WRITING ASSIGNMENTS

The purpose of the six preceding exercises is to help you practice writing. They are short exercises intended as daily workouts to get you in shape for longer writing assignments. The following are some suggestions for longer writing assignments based on your work on the previous exercises.

1. Reread the examples of student writing for an idea that you could develop into a topic.

A. For example, in their freewriting Matilda and Alison write that they would do socially outrageous things (singing atop restaurant tables, and so on) if the end of the world were near. What would you most want to do or where would you most want to go if next week were your last week of life? What has restrained or prevented you from doing a particular thing or going to a particular place? Would you have to be faced with an end-of-the-world crisis before doing that or going there? Answer these questions and organize and expand your responses into an essay. As you work out your answers, think about your purpose in writing. For example, is your primary purpose to tell about someplace you want to see and to explain why you want to see it? Or is your main interest exploring the idea of why we put off or are prevented from doing things we ought to do until it is too late to enjoy them?

Also, notice that Alison numbers her several things ("The first thing I'd do," "The second thing," "The third thing," and "Finally"); if you have several items to discuss, use some system like Alison's numbering to arrange them in an order for your reader.

B. You might want to write about your problems writing, as Mura did in her freewriting. List the main ideas she mentions; then add some of your own. Perhaps you and your classmates could collaborate in putting together a list of the pros and cons of writing. Select from the list the ideas that relate to you particularly and write an essay on them. You might pretend that you are explaining your writing process and problems to an experienced writing coach who may be able to give you helpful advice on how to use your time more efficiently or how to practice more effectively.

Notice that Mura uses chronological order to develop her idea; that is, she tells us about her writing from beginning to end. Underline her "time markers" in order to see how she uses them to organize her essay. (For example, *Initially, During this first phase, Completing the first impetus, A few days later*, and so on.) You might want to organize your essay this way if it is appropriate.

If your instructor can arrange a time for you and a group of your classmates to read your essay drafts to each other, you will undoubtedly sigh with relief to find that others have difficulties in writing, as you do. Not everyone has the same problem, but sharing ideas and concerns about writing can make the work more bearable. You will also find that the process of sharing drafts with other writers helps you revise your writing. Hearing your paper read aloud and getting responses from an audience help you reformulate ideas more clearly than your original drafting of them.

C. One of the ideas from John's journal may interest you: Should one accept death or fight it? What advice do you have about giving and taking positive criticism? What memories of childhood are "inscribed by a stone cutter" on your mind?

Perhaps you could create a special writing situation in order to write an essay on one of these ideas. For example, you could write a discussion of death for children, or for teenagers who have cancer, or for senior citizens. Or, you could write an essay instructing your classmates on how to give and take positive criticism about each other's essays.

2. Discuss with a small group of your classmates or with your instructor some of the ideas you have written for the exercises in this chapter. Select one of the ideas for developing into an essay. As you discuss the idea and how it might be developed, consider your writing purpose (Just what do you intend to say?) and your audience (To whom are you writing?).

2

DISCOVERING AND INVENTING IDEAS

Making Meaning Is the Writer's First Task.

Getting started on a writing assignment is a problem for many writers: "What do I know about this topic? How can I learn more? How can I begin putting some ideas together?"

When faced with a writing assignment, some beginning writers are passive until an outside agent seems to present them with a starting point. These writers say that they wait for an idea to hit them, or that they cannot begin writing until lightning strikes, or until they become inspired. On the other hand, many experienced writers begin actively writing as soon as a topic is assigned. By employing thinking strategies, these writers jot down all of the ideas they know about the topic, ask questions about what they need to learn, and focus on some part of the topic which interests them.

People who study how writers develop ideas have designed various methods for thinking thoroughly about a topic to help writers discover and create ideas for writing. Following are six methods and some examples and exercises for each.[1] Practice all of them regularly until you develop three or four that work for you consistently. You may discover that you prefer certain methods while some of your classmates prefer others. Also, you may find that one may work well for a certain kind of topic, but not for other kinds. Practice all of the methods so that you may choose the one that best suits you and a particular writing topic. Selecting a single topic and applying each method to it is a good way for you to decide which method is most effective for you and that topic.

BRAINSTORM

As the word implies, this strategy is based on turbulent mind activity. To brainstorm a topic you think intensely but randomly about it, jotting down all of your ideas as rapidly as possible, just as though you were raining ideas down onto the page from your mind's stormclouds.

Directions For Brainstorming

1. Set a time limit of 10 to 15 minutes.
2. Write the topic at the top of a blank page and begin writing as rapidly as possible your ideas on the topic. Write words, phrases, and partial questions. Don't attempt to write out complete sentences unless they flow freely. Just get down the essence of the concept and move on to your next thought.
3. As you write, let one word or phrase suggest another. Follow these word associations as far as they lead you into related ideas.
4. Stop at the end of the time period and review your jottings. Complete fragmentary ideas. While considering your purpose in writing and your intended audience, add writing ideas and organize the entire list according to some system.

Examples of Brainstorming

PART ONE. I assigned "Saving Energy" as a subject for students to write about. I told them to narrow the subject to a manageable topic and then to brainstorm a list of information from which to select ideas for writing.

One student, Martin, narrowed the subject to "Home Insulation." Here's the list of information he brainstormed at his first sitting, a 15-minute session:

Home Insulation

ceiling
walls
windows—caulking

doors—weatherstripping
R-factor
fiberglass blanket in rolls
loose fill
insulation batts
cellulose for walls—contractor
gloves
knife
tape measure
staple gun
hot-water heater
pipes
cost vs. savings

Martin brainstormed more than a dozen items he could use for writing ideas. However, as I told him and his classmates, brainstorming is a random thinking activity. That is, any and all ideas are listed without any concern for sorting them into categories or arranging them in sequences. Also, the time pressure of brainstorming creates a game or performance situation which stimulates our creative faculties to function at a high-activity level, thus producing a number of ideas. On the other hand, the time pressure forces us to rush, preventing us from thinking thoroughly about the relationships between various ideas.

Therefore, for homework I directed the students to read over their lists, first adding new items, then looking for a main or central idea, and finally grouping the information according to some system of their own devising. In this way, I suggested, the students could begin deciding what they intended to say about their topics and could begin considering to what kind of an audience they would be writing.

Martin decided to write an essay telling home owners how to insulate their homes and discussing the costs and savings. He came to the next class meeting with this expanded and re-organized list (new information is italicized):

Home Insulating: How To and How Much
Parts of house to be insulated
ceiling, walls, floor between basement and first floor, windows, doors, heating pipes, and hot-water heater

Materials needed

caulking (*clear silicone*), weatherstripping (*plastic v-channel tape*), fiberglass blankets in rolls (or loose fill, or insulation batts), cellulose for walls, and *pre-formed foam sleeves for pipes*

Tools needed

gloves, knife, tape measure, staple gun, *flashlight, electric drill, pencil or marker*

Technical information needed

R-values (*heat resistance of insulating materials*)

Home energy audit (provided free of charge by utility companies or independent government agencies)

Energy conversion chart (provided free of charge with audit)

How-to-do-it-yourself instruction booklet (provided free of charge with audit)

Cost *vs.* savings

cost estimate of materials

labor contracted out (*cellulose must be blown into walls by professionals*)

Energy savings

Efficiency check

In early winter have house checked with infrared cameras to spot any areas of heat lost. (Cost—$25 to $35)

PART TWO. "Memories of a Summer Place" was one topic I suggested to a writing class for a personal-experience essay. For this assignment I decided to write about my uncle's lodge at Lake O' the Woods, West Virginia, where I had spent several summers as a young boy. Although I was not aware of it when I began brainstorming, I could not settle on a focus for the paper: whether to discuss our activities and family relations or to describe the unique lodge building. My divided mind is revealed in the two separate lists I came up with during the same brainstorming period:

Lake O' the Woods

| uncle's large pine-panelled lodge | all-summer retreat, esp. in 1950–51 polio epidemic |

mother took us to movie;
  uncle angry: fearful of
  exposure to polio virus
40 foot dock (six feet wide)
spring '51 dock painting
  chore on first day at lake
oil-base, white paint
painting all morning in
  shorts; no shirts
sunburn and paint all over
  us
turpentine to remove paint
our cries of "oouch!" at
  turpentine/sunburn pain
locusts
surprise at coming upon
  snake slithering through
  grass
rowboat
fishing
swimming

learning how to dive
  uncle held ankles—told us
  to point head down and
  dive; then he flipped our
  feet in aid to complete
  dive
general store at foot of mtn.
  for groceries, soda and
  popsicles
lodge details: flagstone
  floors, stone fireplace and
  stone chimney, basement
  and driveway—cool;
  snakes resting; large
  schoolhouse bell for
  dinner calls hung on a
  post with circle seat built
  around it; bedrooms on
  second floor; livingroom
  with cathedral ceiling;
  wooden wagon-wheel
  light fixtures

As I read over my brainstorming list (or rather lists) the next day, I realized that I had two competing interests. I was eager to explore the family-relations topic, but as I looked at all of the ideas I had brainstormed about it, I thought it would take too much time to develop that topic well. So I decided to write a descriptive essay, painting the mountain lodge scene for the class. I drafted two paragraphs of description, using the ideas from my shorter list. As I wrote, I recalled many more details than I had when first brainstorming.

LAKE O' THE WOODS
(Draft #1)

It seemed we always went there to play through our childhood summers, to Uncle Tom's cabin in the West Virginia Mountains. Actually more of a lodge, the two-story, frame structure stood poised on a wooded hillside which sloped 150 feet to the edge of a crystal cold lake where a six-foot-wide dock stretched 40 feet into the waters; at its end a massive oak bench seemed to hold its pilings down. Thick tufts of stubby grass served as a lawn running from the shoreline to the sloped-roof lodge; midway an enormous brass dinner bell hung on a post of imposing girth which a two-foot-high loveseat encircled.

The blue-green lakewaters were always visible from the spacious living room or adjoining dining area through the lodge's expansive picture window or glass-paned double doors, which offered a western view. At the northern end of the room rose a masterfully sculptured fireplace and chimney, tribute to a master mason's skill at shaping dumb stones into unspeakable beauty. At the opposite end, near the kitchen, sat a long, picnic-style table crafted out of the same knotty pine with which the entire interior was panelled. Two large wooden wagon-wheel light fixtures hung high overhead from the sloping ceiling; light from electrified, chimneyed "candles" shone weakly down on the varnished flagstones which composed a puzzle-piece floor. The master bedroom and bathroom opened off the livingroom. The stairs at the southern end of the room led to three upstairs bedrooms accessible from a hallway which looked over a railing onto the spacious first floor.

Reading over those two paragraphs, I realized how sterile and boring my summer place was sounding. I decided to scrap the idea to focus on description and, instead, to develop the family-relations idea. In order to sort out my writing ideas more fully for this new writing purpose I used another thinking strategy. (You will see the results on pp. 31–33.)

Brainstorming Exercises

Following the directions on pp. 25 above, develop writing ideas on the following topics:

the computer revolution	popular music trends
cable TV	campus social groups
campus crime	federal aid to education
designer clothes	family pets

SUGGESTIONS. 1. Because the subjects listed are broad, narrow them to smaller, manageable topics for writing. 2. Since initial brainstorming is random and hurried, revise your original list, using your purpose for writing and your intended audience as guides for expanding and organizing your material.

PARTICLE, WAVE, AND FIELD (PWF)

The particle, wave, and field method of thinking is a more formal strategy than brainstorming. PWF enables you to shift perspective by looking at a topic in three ways: first as an activity, thing, or being in and of itself (particle); second, as an activity, thing, or being which changes in a process or over time (wave); and third, as one activity, thing, or being which is part of a larger construct or system (field). Since this method is more complex than some others presented here, take a little extra time to learn how to use it effectively. Applicable to virtually any topic, it can help you produce a lot of useful information. Beginning from the narrowest perspective and moving to the broadest, you may study your topic systematically and thoroughly by looking at it in these ways.

Directions for PWF

1. PARTICLE: View the topic as a particle, an isolated object, or a static entity. Describe its physical characteristics. Identify it as an object.

2. WAVE: View the topic as a changing, dynamic object or event. Examine the process, operation, or function of it over a period of time.

3. FIELD: View the topic as an abstract, or many-sided system. Study the topic in the broad context of its relation to other things and events.

Examples of PWF

PART ONE. Let's say for example that your topic is heating a house by using a woodstove. According to this method, you first (particle phase) describe the stove itself, identifying the model and the manufacturer, stating its price, and so on. You may even want to refer to a diagram to identify its parts and give its dimensions: glass doors, firebricks, grate, flue, etc. You also identify the lengths and kinds of wood you use: two-foot lengths of maple, oak, ash, and so on. Next (wave phase), to examine the process of heating with a woodstove, you discuss where and how to find, cut, and stack the wood; how to start a fire in the stove; how many BTU's each variety of wood yields when it burns; how to regulate the temperature in the house; how, when, and where to dispose of the ashes; when and how to clean the chimney, and so on. Finally (field phase), to discuss heating by this method in relation to other methods (by oil, gas, coal, solar power) you would compare the costs (in time and money), and the types of heat produced, in addition to other variables involved with each method.

PART TWO. I used PWF to develop some ideas for my revised writing purpose for "Lake O' the Woods." While I wanted to retain some descriptive sections to set the scene, I wanted to focus primarily on discussing our family activities and relations while at the lodge. Here's the information I wrote out:

Particle: 1. all-summer retreat at Uncle's cabin at Lake O' the Woods, W. Virginia mountains

- seven years old
- two-story, white-frame lodge called "cabin"
- completely knotty-pine-panelled interior
- finished hardwood floors
- stone fireplace and chimney
- picture window in large livingroom
- glass-paned French doors to outside
- diningroom, long picnic table
- compact, well-equipped kitchen
- wagon-wheel light fixtures
- master bedroom and bathroom off livingroom
- upstairs, three bedrooms; bunkbeds for us
- whole place was filled with antiques

2. the lake itself

- 150 yards down sloping hillside

- midway to lake, a large dinner bell on post; loveseat
- six-foot-wide dock, 20 feet long
- large oak bench at end of dock
- a rowboat tied near the dock
- crystal-clear water, greenish tint
- 10-foot-square float anchored about 20 feet from end of dock

Wave: 1. first day at lake—dock-painting chore for us all

- first time we kids painted anything
- painting with an oil-base, white paint till noon; no shirt, only shorts on
- sunburn, paint all over hands, arms, & legs
- aunt using turpentine to remove paint
- our cries of "oouch!" at turpentine and sunburn sting

2. locust swarm, stripping trees
3. surprise at coming upon a five-foot blacksnake sunning itself; startled, it slithered through the grass
4. rowboating—rowing contests
5. fishing; learning to bait hook with "snakes" (night crawlers) and learning to take bluegills off hook and not get stuck with fins
6. swimming; learning to dive off dock

- uncle encouraged us, he held our ankles, we pointed our heads down, started to fall forward, he flipped feet up in air, we completed a dive, no bellyflops, until he stopped helping

7. large family meals
8. evenings outside listening to the adults tell stories of the old days till mosquito attacks
9. sneaking out of bed to sit on stairs, listening to adults talk by fire
10. one weekend, after several weeks in the mountains, mother got bored

- Took us for a drive down the mountain to the "nearest civilization"; White House—a village with general store, gas station, churches; in the next town was a moviehouse; we bought groceries, had sodas and popsicles; went to the movie matinee and had popcorn. When uncle found out, he became furious, fearful we had been exposed to the disease; they argued, we didn't get polio as we thought we surely would.

Field. 1. Uncles had built the cabin themselves after returning from World War II in which my father was killed.
2. This particular summer (1950) poliomyelitis epidemic; cousin got it; so did my brother's playmate; we children were taken to cabin all summer to escape polio.
3. Uncle sold the cabin when he purchased a new home; at the time we kids took the luxury of the summer lodge for granted; now that it's beyond our financial ability to replace, we appreciate its beauty and the value of those summer days of free play, learning nature lore, and growing up in a loving family that looked after us well.

Working through this PWF exercise brought a big breakthrough in my thinking about this essay: as I wrote out the various ideas, I revived the experiences we had had together at the lodge and I began a long train of inquiry over the next several weeks about what meaning those experiences held for me. In the next chapter I will share with you my work of drafting an essay from this PWF list.

Exercises in Particle, Wave, and Field

1. Incorporate the following items into the woodstove topic for writing. (See pp. 30–31.) Which items belong with particle? Which with wave? Which with field?

P stove body, $\frac{1}{4}''$ plate steel
seasoned oak cordwood,
    F $125/cord
doors are airtight
W aura of romance
    P surrounding a
    woodburning stove

F stove location
W safety practices
    creosote buildup in the
    chimney
savings *vs.* personal labor

2. Write out ideas on the following topics according to the PWF method:

memories of a summerplace in childhood

video games

being a student at your college or university

birth-control practices

training or team rules for varsity sports

religion today

campus housing

gossip

contact lenses

baseball

an important object (thing, activity, person) in your life

3. Select one of your sets of PWF information from the preceding exercise. Write a paragraph from one or from a combination of the perspectives (particle, wave, or field), depending on your primary interest in the topic.

CUBE

A cube is a multidimensional figure having six sides. Using a cube as an aid, you can look at a topic multidimensionally, from six sides. Cubing is similar to brainstorming, but focuses on specific aspects of a subject individually. Therefore, it is less random.

Directions for Cubing

1. Make a cube out of paper; refer to Figure 2.1 and follow these suggestions:

• Draw the sides of each face the same length.

• Cut along solid lines.

• Write the appropriate numbers and words on each of the outer faces:

1. Describe, 2. Compare, 3. Associate, 4. Analyze, 5. Apply, and 6. Argue.

   • Fold along dotted lines.

   • Tape adjoining face seams.

   Note: If you don't want to make a cube, use six cards or slips of paper on which to write the appropriate words.

2. Write your topic at the top of a blank page and, allowing

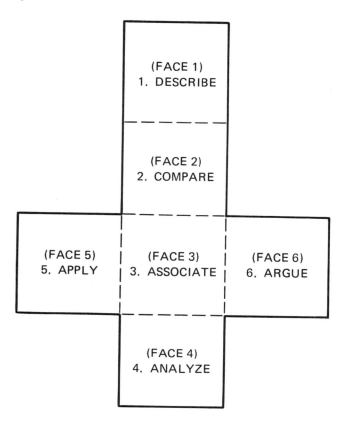

Figure 2.1

yourself three to five minutes for each face of the cube, write about your topic using the words from the cube faces as guides. A stopwatch or an egg timer may help you set consistent time periods.

3. Review and revise your writing ideas. Keeping in mind your purpose in writing and your intended audience, add writing ideas and organize the entire set of information.

ADDITIONAL QUESTIONS AND SUGGESTIONS FOR CUBING. The following questions and suggestions may help you generate writing ideas; modify them as your topic requires.

1. *Describe:* Examine the topic closely. Can it be described physically in colors, shapes, sizes, and so on? List its characteristics, its parts, or its qualities.

2. *Compare:* To what is the topic similar? To what can it

be contrasted? Explain the similarities and differences in particular detail.

3. *Associate:* Of what does the topic make you think? Of what does it remind you? List the things with which you associate it. In what ways is it associated with them?

4. *Analyze:* Identify and categorize the topic's characteristics, its parts or its qualities. Explain how its components fit together.

5. *Apply:* How can the topic be used? What can be done with it? Apply it to some situation, person, or concept.

6. *Argue:* Take a stand for or against the topic. List as many reasons to justify your position as you can. Then take an opposing view and build an argument supporting it.

Examples of Cubing

Here is a set of information on video games which was developed according to the cubing method.

1. *Describe:* Computerized games, TV-like screen, controls, electronic beeps and explosion sounds. Games are timed. Depending on the type of game, player tries to "shoot it out" with attacking troops or to escape fields of meteorites. Cost, generally 25 cents for a few minutes play.

Video dens are darkened rooms. Colored flashes of light coming from game screens, only light. Dens located in shopping malls, near schools and colleges, or in airport terminals.

2. *Compare:* Video games and pinball games. Both games of skill and chance in which player attempts to get a high score. In both games players compete to beat their own best scores or another player's. Video and pinball games are solo adventures; one individual plays at a time. Both challenge the player's eye-hand coordination. Major differences—pinball involves playing with five solid steel balls; video involves no balls, operates on computerized electronic circuitry. Also, pinball slower than video which requires quicker reflexes. Video, more visual and auditory stimuli. Last point leads to a third comparison: like disco or hard-rock music, video games appeal to people who feel action and release of tension in the sights and sounds. Finally, can be compared to gambling; some people become addicted to the activity, spurred by an occasional "win"; "lose their shirts" most of the time.

3. *Associate:* Associated with today's computer or with yes-

terday's pocket-billiard game. Some people see it as a modern, electronic marvel. For others, video games recall the heyday of pocket billiards; video dens, today's version of "pool halls," dens of iniquity in the darkened rooms from which warlike sounds emerge.

4. *Analyze:* Video games appeal to an individual's competitive spirit. Also attract players with outer-space sights and sounds. Players escape from daily pressures into video den; sensory stimuli block worries. Player fantasizes heroic actions in the face of overwhelming odds; if player is "killed off" in one game, another quarter brings back to life.

Adolescent males make up the majority of den customers. Video games combine kids' attraction to TV with their fascination for computer gadgetry. Video-game business is a multimillion-dollar industry. Major game producers invest huge sums of money in development. Fierce competition to create the most popular games. Players enter regional and national competition to vie for championship trophies. Promoters support them.

5. *Apply:* Entrepreneurs have capitalized on attraction to TV and fascination with computer gadgetry; also have located dens where customer traffic is heavy. Some stay open all night, increasing volume of time usage.

6. *Argue:* IN FAVOR. Video games personify life in the high-speed lane: intense pressure, challenge to eye-hand coordination, electronic beeps and booms all part of modern lifestyle. Just as some fine business competitors developed their independence, ingenuity, and mental toughness on the gridiron, some of tomorrow's captains of industry are developing those qualities in video dens. Playing video games not an escape from life, but simulation of a life-and-death challenge. Spending quarters and killing time in video dens are far better than spending dollars and killing yourself with dope. Our fathers and grandfathers frequented pool halls without becoming crooks; video dens won't corrupt our morals.

AGAINST. Video games, a metaphor for all that is life-threatening in today's high-technology world. Like TV and hard-rock music, video games mesmerize young people. Maybe they learn the motor response of pushing a button to destroy an asteroid, but can they read up to their grade level, can they concentrate long enough to solve an algebraic equation, and can they write a poem that resonates with language sense and sound?

How many dollars do people spend in a video den in an hour or two? Perhaps some people mug others or snatch purses in order to get money to play, just as junkies do to pay for drugs.

If watching too much violence on TV isn't good for people, how can games whose whole activity involves killing or being killed be a wholesome activity? At least pocket billiards is a game of people of class, a game that requires skill and finesse. Video games are just a mass of violent sounds and pushbutton panic before the lights go out.

Exercises in Cubing

1. Following the steps on pp. 34–36, develop ideas for writing on the topics below:

American subcompact cars
the fraternity and sorority
  system
jogging shoes
the equal rights amendment
  (ERA)

coed sports teams
junk food
supply-side economics
varsity debate competition

2. Using the set of information you developed by cubing one of the topics in Exercise 1 above, write a paragraph or two on the topic. Before beginning to write, decide which side (or sides) of the topic you wish to emphasize.

STAR

The star method consists of generating information to answer five sets of related questions about human actions and motives; thus, it is appropriate to topics that involve human behavior. Each of the five sets of questions is distinct from but related to the others in that they all probe for information on different aspects of the same act: 1. the action, 2. the actor, 3. the scene, 4. the means, and 5. the purpose. Therefore, this method can be symbolized by the five-pointed star. See Figure 2.2.

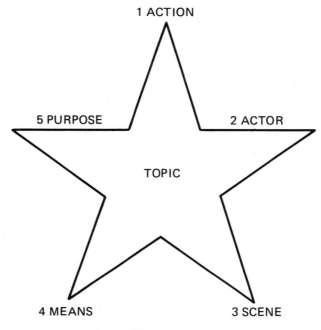

Figure 2.2

Directions for Using the Star Method

Answer each of the following questions as it relates to your topic:

1. Action: What happened? Or, What was done?
2. Actor: Who did it?
3. Scene: Where and when did it happen? Or, Where and when was it done?
4. Means: How did it happen? Or, By what means was it done?
5. Purpose: Why did it happen? Or, What motives did the actor have in doing it? What were the actor's intentions?

Note: As with the questions in other methods, modify these as necessary according to the topic.

Examples of the Star Method

I assigned my students the problem of searching around their home communities for some examples of community action, civic pride, or social concern. Once a student found a subject, she was to present a discussion of it to the class. Linda selected a building-restoration project she knew about. Because Linda had already collected some information and had a pretty good idea of what she wanted to say, this set of information is written out quite fully; it looks more like a draft than just notes for a draft. (But that is not generally the case.)

1. Action: What was done?
A deteriorating, Victorian mansion was restored. Its slate, mansard-style roof was repaired. The exterior was repainted, stained-glass windows repaired or replaced, and doors rehung, as needed. Interior wood was stripped, stained, revealing ornate carvings over doors and windows, on cornices and mantels. Parquet floors were repaired and refinished. New plumbing and heating systems were installed and the building was fully insulated. Fireplaces were opened and put in working order, including repointing the chimneys. All the rooms except for the kitchen were restored to their original style, including draperies, wallpaper, lighting-fixture style and antique furnishings. The kitchen was outfitted with modern commercial appliances.

The first floor is a museum, with an occasional music recital held in the sitting room; banquets are held in the spacious diningroom, and dances take place in the ballroom. The second and third story rooms serve as multipurpose meeting rooms. The grounds behind the building are used as playgrounds. The carriage house was renovated and serves as the recreation center for children and elderly alike.

2. Actor: Who did it?
The restoration work was supervised by the state historical society in cooperation with a neighborhood coalition of families. A plaque at the entranceway lists the names of all of those who worked or contributed to the restoration project.

3. Scene: Where and when did it happen?
The mansion is located just six blocks north of the center of the city (population: 100,000); the neighborhood had once been a well-to-do residential section until the turn of the century brought an industrial boom and mills sprang up nearby. In a period of a few years the wealthy people fled the mills'

noxious fumes, crowded conditions, and rowdy workers. By the 1970s the mills themselves left the city, leaving giant "shells" which the city and private interests renovated for various municipal and business purposes.

Over a 10-year period the historical society had become active in identifying private homes' original owners' names and giving low-interest loans to people for their restoration. In 1980 the historical society looked for a way to stimulate the purchase and restoration of the Brigham mansion, one of the largest private homes in the area. Once the work was begun, it took a year and four months to complete.

4. Means: By what means was it done?

The deed to the house was turned over to the historical society by the city when the absentee owner defaulted on several years' taxes. For two years the society looked for an individual who would purchase the property with a promise to restore it to its original condition. Looking for a multipurpose community hall and recreation center, the coalition of families offered to undertake the project.

The actual labor was done by members of the coalition or their friends, all of whom donated their time. For the several-thousand-dollars' worth of supplies, members of the society and the coalition solicited donations from individuals and businesses. One historical society member, an antique dealer, conducted a "charity auction" at which community members bid on antique furnishings; the winner donated the item to the mansion.

5. Purpose: What motives did the actor have in doing it? What were the actor's intentions?

The historical society's aim was to restore a rare landmark to the area, recalling for residents and visitors the area's architectural heritage. The neighborhood coalition wanted better recreational and social-hall facilities. The city saw a blight removed and neighborhood facilities built without having to foot the bill.

Since she has so much information in each area, Linda could develop an essay from any one of the five perspectives. In fact, because she was interested in the cooperation of the society and the coalition, she told the story from that viewpoint, fitting the other information into that perspective.

Exercises in the Star Method

1. Suppose that you are given this writing assignment: "Write a letter to your congressional representative urging an increase in the tax incentives for energy conservation. Present a specific situation that will demonstrate to your representative that increased incentives are a worthwhile cause." Using the star method, develop some information that would be useful in writing out this assignment. Share your information with a group of students in your class. Draft a letter collaboratively, using the best ideas from the group members' information.

2. Using the topics below, practice developing writing ideas according to the star method. In order to apply the questions of this method to the topics, you will first need to write out a particular, concrete situation for each topic. For example, if the topic is something as broad as "dancing," you would need to make it more specific, as in the following more-defined topics: dancing as a school social activity, or performing in modern-dance competition.

sunbathing
Christmas
campus rituals
health fads
international terrorism
winter sports
wearing orthodontic appliances

METAPHOR

Generally speaking, a metaphor is a comparison of two dissimilar things. For example, look at this sentence in which our country is compared to music: "As a song, America is a loud, discordant chant, a thousand disco bands in an echo chamber."[2]

By comparing your topic to something with which you are familiar you may make observations and ask questions to help you learn more about the topic. For example, if you were asked to write an essay about your experiences at college, you might create one of these metaphors:

My first month at college has been like a visit to the United Nations.

Life in the residence hall is a zoo.

College classes are white-water rafting trips for the intellectually adventurous.

My English professor is the Gloria Steinem of English composition teaching.

Forming a metaphor out of your topic gives you a way of generating ideas about it through a comparison with the qualities and characteristics of the metaphoric base (in these instances, United Nations, zoo, white-water rafting, and Gloria Steinem).

Directions for Developing a Metaphor

1. Create a metaphor, using your topic and a metaphoric base.
2. As in brainstorming, write out in a timed period as many ideas of comparison as you can about your topic and the metaphoric base.
3. After the timed period, review your list of comparisons, adding, revising, and rearranging your list as appropriate.
4. Repeat steps 1, 2, and 3 using the same topic and a different metaphoric base.
5. Discuss with your classmates or instructor which of your comparisons seem useful for your writing assignment.

Examples of Metaphor Making

Here are some examples of metaphors my students made to develop ideas on topics; later they used the metaphors in the opening paragraphs of their essays.

FROM "THE GRAMMAR OF BALLET"

Like writing, ballet is not a natural form of expression; it must be learned or acquired. Starting as a child, one learns to write according to the grammatical rules of one's particular language, and a ballet dancer must also learn to use his or her body according to prescribed rules . . . Barre exercises

[are] the grammar of ballet and must be done daily with few exceptions throughout the life of the dancer . . . The steps must be executed in a precise way; however, each dancer performs a step in his or her own style. . . . No two dancers do a step alike, and no two writers express a thought in the same way. Therefore, the process of learning a new role or a new step is slow, and steps and movements must be repeated and reviewed objectively in the search for purity of line in ballet just as a writer revises words, phrases, and sentences in order to achieve clarity. The exercises, the steps a dancer practices over the years become his or her dance vocabulary, and the way the steps are performed—the ease with which each movement is made—becomes a dancer's technique.

FROM "COMPOSING"

Composing a piece of writing is like writing a piece of music. First, there is the thought process. Ideas and images are to a writer as motifs and sounds are to a music composer. Jottings, ideas, and sentences of thoughts are written on paper; motifs and rhythms are notated, both being the building blocks in their mediums. The physical representation of the thoughts allows the ordering, restructuring and additional comparisons. Again the ideas, or motifs, are rethought and the mind participates in another voyage. Now that jottings and notations are present, there is a freedom to become the audience of previous thoughts and evolve new associations just as a composer may connect another rhythm with a motif and decide on different instrumentation.

FROM "STUDENTS ARE LIKE CIRCUS PERFORMERS"

Students are like circus performers. Just like the big top the classroom is full of entertainers. There is a mixture of talent in every class, whether it be the class clown or the ring leader just waiting to capture his audience's attention. There is also the lion tamer, the one that tames teachers so that they will adhere to his every demand. Then we have the juggler who has to juggle his thoughts around so that they will make some sense. Next we have the tightrope walker walking the borderline between pass and fail.

FROM "EDUCATION: A LUBE JOB FOR THE MIND"

Professors are not like full-service gas station attendants who will uncap your mind and "fill-er-up" with wisdom. Oh sure, they may have the skill to wash an unclear windshield or two, and maybe even help to pump up a deflated ego-belted radial, but that is all they can do. The college station is self-serve; only you possess the key to your mental gas cap. If you only put 50 cents worth of gas in, don't expect to go very far. A conscientious professor may warn you about the hazards of putting regular in a tank marked "unleaded only," and show you how the pump works, but ultimately, your machine is your own responsibility.

Note: By suggesting metaphor making here, I am recommending only that you see the method of comparison as a way of generating information about a topic; I am not necessarily suggesting that you write an essay based on an extended comparison. However, you may wish to discuss the appropriateness of such an essay with your instructor.

Metaphor Exercises

1. Write out several writing ideas based on the metaphor comparing America to music (p. 42).

2. Select one of the following metaphors and develop a list of information for writing. Compare your list with others in your class who selected the same metaphor.

a. Blue-collar laborers are the worker bees of society.

b. A person's emotional stability is like a glass beaker.

c. Learning BASIC is the key to opening the secrets of computer programming.

d. The international nuclear arms race is a global game of Russian roulette.

3. Create metaphors and generate writing ideas from them, using these topics:

Thanksgiving

campus ethics

censorship

U.S. presidential election campaigns

our national resources

being ill   living with roommates
collecting comic books

PERSONIFY

Imagining that a topic is a person or an animal is akin to creating a metaphor, and is another way of generating writing ideas about it. (Of course, this method assumes that the topic is an inanimate object or an abstract concept.) Let's say you are assigned topics such as these: wind, boredom, the American dream, hunger, a car, gossip, illness, and learning. Some possible personifications for these topics are:

The wind is the wolf in "The Three Little Pigs."
To dieters hunger is Napoleon attacking their willpower.
A car is Cheryl Tiegs (or Reggie Jackson).
Gossip is a shark.

There are several ways of proceeding to write out ideas using this thinking strategy.

Directions for Personifying

1. Personify the topic.
2. Interview it. Ask as many questions as occur to you and answer them as you believe the personified topic would.
3. Have your personification deliver a speech to some imagined audience. What would be the main points of the address? How would they be supported? What would be the audience's reaction?
4. Imagine that you are spending a routine day (or perhaps a holiday) with the personified topic in his or her environs. Describe some noteworthy events of the day.
5. Suppose that your personified topic is spending a routine day (or perhaps a holiday) with you. Describe some noteworthy events of the day.

Examples of Personifying a Topic

For examples of this method worked out according to steps four and five, review the student writing on pp. 18–20. Here is another example of personification which the writer, Karen, calls "Antacid, In Case of Attacks":

> Recuperating the next morning after Saturday's Mexican feast has top priority. Meals are offered with one condition; arm yourself for oncoming upheaval. Be prepared with your best ammunition and have plenty of Alka Seltzer in case of attack.
>
> The first confrontation takes place on the border, where the Mexicans fire upon the enemy with all their artillery. The vegetable antipasto stands its ground for the first wave of attack. Nothing can stop the garbanzo beans, pitted ripe olives, tiny whole beets, hot green cherry peppers, marinated artichoke hearts or anchovy fillets. They combine forces and Alka Seltzer hasn't a chance. The large bowl of chili that is served as part of the main course continues its progressive advance. The taco hot dog with chili sauce joins the expanded forces. Alka Seltzer's main objective is to surround the antipasto and main course, capturing it when the advancement is complete.
>
> Unfortunately, when the two mugs of beer and Banana Royale gather strength, Alka Seltzer has to find another defense. More troops are called to duty and two days of battles continue. Losses and casualties occur in large numbers on both sides and the war is in its final stages. The reinforced antacid attacks the tired Mexican army with all its arms. The Mexican brigade gives strong resistance, but the battle is over. The entire Mexican militia was poorly organized for this kind of warfare. With strong forces and large-caliber guns, the attack is complete. Alka Seltzer wins with another plop, plop, fizz, fizz.

SUGGESTIONS FOR WRITING ASSIGNMENTS

1. Take notes in your journal as you work through the exercises in this chapter. Discuss with your classmates and your teacher your observations about the various methods presented here. For example, answer these questions: "Which methods do you prefer? Why do you prefer them over others? What tactics have you employed in order to make using these methods a habit?" Afterwards, write a note of advice to a high-school senior you

know who (let's pretend) has asked you for information on how to come up with ideas for writing.

2. Suppose that you are a travel agent for Odyssey International which has an agency office in your city or town. You are assigned as a client an amateur swimming club which is coming to your region for two weeks of national, finalist competition. The group consists of 12 boys and girls (ages 16–25), their 40-year-old coach, and their families, including mothers, fathers, grandparents, and assorted siblings. Your job is to compile a local recreational guide for this group.

First, develop a list of information by using one of the methods presented in this chapter. Second, arrange the information in a way that makes it clear and accessible to the reader. And, finally, write a guide for your clients to use while spending their free time in your area.

For example, students in my class wrote a guide to local beaches.

Scarborough Beach and Narragansett Beach—Largest beaches. Crowds of 10,000 common from late June on. Towel-to-towel high schoolers, stereo radios, concession-stand hangout. Showers. Good swimming. No surf.

Block Island Beach—Forty-minute ferry ride from mainland. Two-hundred-feet bluffs. Two-and-a-half miles of state-operated beach near ferry dock. Rarely crowded (Block Islanders consider 500 people a crowd; on the mainland 3,000 is a crowd.) Surf, seashells in rocky areas especially. Bird sanctuaries. Scenic walks.

Sand Hill Cove Beach—Offshore breakers protect shoreline from rough sea. Jetties run into calm waters from the shore. Undertow and seaweed are uncommon. Five hundred yards of lifeguard-patrolled "family beach." Even at high tide large amount of sand; good anytime of day or night. Around main pavilion are picnic tables and playground. Swimming lessons and exercise classes available. Concession stand. Barbecue cooking permitted in area. Rules rigidly enforced.

East Matunuck Beach—Three-quarters-of-a-mile beach front, lifeguards, occasional rough surf and undertow. Picnic lunches; no fires, no dogs permitted.

Moonstone Beach—Beach has only the basics: phone, trash barrels, portajohns, lifeguards. Fairly rapid drop off about eight feet out, but seaweed rarely washes up. Breaking surf near shore for body surfing. Nude swimming and sunbathing. Adjacent wildlife refuge—fragile sand dunes, duck and bird nesting areas. High tide reduces beachfront considerably.

Green Hill Beach—Near Moonstone. Lifeguards; body surfing; depending on weather and tide, experiences seaweed and undertow.

First Beach (Newport)—Scenic; next to Cliff Walk. Waves roar onto cliff rock continuously. Breakers farther out from shore than Moonstone. Good body surfing. Concession; showers. Lifeguards. Sometimes seaweed, undertow.

Second Beach (Newport)—One-and-a-half-mile beach set almost in cove. View of cliffs to east and west. Young, people-watching crowd. Concession (clamcakes, pizza, etc.), changing rooms. Excellent swimming. Well-kept and lifeguarded. Popular, crowded. Seldom any seaweed problem.

Third Beach (Newport)—Quarter-of-a-mile beach, lifeguards. Concession stand, changing facilities. Very light surf. Preferred by older people, families with small children. Sandcastle haven. Bird sanctuary a short drive away.

Horseneck Beach (Massachusetts)—Thirty to 55 lifeguards; huge crowds, but miles of large sand dunes lining shore provide some privacy. Body surfing is good. Main pavilion, changing room, showers, concessions.

(Beach locations from five to 55 minutes from group's Newport accommodations.)

Beachwalking and seashell hunting equipment list:

- A waterproof bag on the order of a backpack or shoulder bag that you can carry everything in and later toss in the washer.
- Sneakers are the best walking shoes, but you may prefer rubber boots if you want to wade along the shore.
- A box of self-sealing plastic sandwich bags and a roll of paper towels.
- Antiseptic spray in case you cut yourself on a sharp edge.
- A small notebook and a pen to record what you find and where you find it.

• Also, a couple of small cardboard boxes; binoculars; cloth handtowel; map; and pocketknife or penknife.[3]

Using some of the information in the class guide in addition to his own knowledge, Tom wrote the following local beach guide.

LITTLE RHODY BEACH GUIDE

Welcome to Rhode Island, the Biggest Little State in the Union. With over 400 miles of shoreline and a rich salt-water heritage it is often called America's first vacationland.

Aquidneck Island located on beautiful Narragansett Bay has three fine beaches located in the communities of Newport and Middletown.

The city of Newport has long been host to the America's Cup and the Newport-to-Bermuda yacht races. Surfing and swimming are an added attraction. Surfers have long acclaimed this area as the best surf in New England.

Newport Beach, also known as First Beach and Easton's Beach, is 1½ miles of spectacular Atlantic surf nestled close to the famous Cliff Walk. This beach offers surfing at its best. The waves are fast with razor-sharp edges and break hard from top to bottom.

Surfboard sales and rentals are available on the beach. Surfing clothing and accessories are also sold. The beach is a wonderful atmosphere for relaxation and safe swimming. There is a First Aid Room and Certified Lifeguards on duty. Pay attention to conditions; the roaring surf creates an undertow.

There are amusements for children such as a Merry-Go-Round and Kiddie bumper boats. For added enjoyment there is a snack bar, souvenir shop, arcade and a cocktail lounge.

Second Beach, also known as Sachuest Beach, is in Middletown, Rhode Island's seaside showcase. This mile-and-a-half stretch of sand and roaring surf provides vacationers with excellent bathing and surfing. Certified Lifeguards are on duty. A First Aid Station assures quick treatment of minor injuries. There are high dunes providing privacy and a windbreak for sun worshippers. Bath houses, hot showers, and rest rooms are available. Unlimited parking and a concession stand are there for your convenience.

Third Beach in Middletown is a crescent-shaped area three-fourths-of-a-mile-long, set almost in a cove. It is subdivided into three separate beaches. Third Beach Club, Peabody's Beach, and the United States Navy Beach for military personnel and their dependents.

Third Beach is situated on the Sakonnet River. The waters of the Sakonnet are calm and create safe swimming for young and old. The sand is ideal for sand-castle builders. It is a gold mine for seashell collectors when the tide is retreating. Water skiing is popular off Third Beach which has a public boat ramp. The beach is lifeguarded. Changing facilities, hot showers, rest rooms, and a snack bar add extra convenience to your fun in the sun. Parking close to the beach should be no problem if you arrive early. The Norman Bird Sanctuary and Museum is only a short drive from Third Beach. Overnight camping is not permitted.

Washington County, affectionately known as "South County" to native Rhode Islanders, boasts having the finest beaches for surfing, swimming, and seashell hunting.

Scarborough State Beach is Rhode Island's largest state beach. Young people flock here all summer from Memorial Day through Labor Day. Crowds of 10,000 people, blanket-to-blanket, are not uncommon. Unlimited parking close to a safe lifeguarded beach is an added convenience for the crowds. Scarborough Beach is known for its fine surfing and swimming. Cooking is permitted in designated areas. Over 100 picnic tables are provided for public use. No camping or overnight loitering is permitted.

Narragansett Town Beach, also called Narragansett Pier, is an ideal beach for relaxing in the sun. There is a nonresident fee and plenty of parking to accommodate all patrons. Surfing and swimming are safeguarded by Certified Lifeguards. A First Aid Station is handy to treat minor injuries. A well-managed concession stand is ready with delicious fast foods such as hot dogs, hamburgers, soda, ice cream and much more. Windsurfing and catamarans may be used in specified areas. There are no bath houses or changing facilities. Overnight camping or loitering is not allowed.

Roger Wheeler State Beach, also known as Sand Hill Cove, is another of Little Rhody's popular family beaches. It is well protected by jetties and offshore breakers. There is no under-

tow and no seaweed. It is a safe lifeguarded beach for children
to swim and play. High rolling sand dunes provide privacy
to sunbathers and adventurous youngsters. There are swimming and exercise classes for various age groups. Cooking
is permitted in certain areas. Over 80 picnic tables adorn the
site to make family gatherings more comfortable and pleasant.
Overnight camping is not permitted.

East Matunuck Beach and Green Hill Beach are well known
for having heavy surf and dangerous undertows. Certified
Lifeguards observe the safety of bathers and surfers. Picnic
tables are available for general use by beach patrons. There
are no changing facilities or hot showers. No dogs or fires
are allowed.

Moonstone Beach, now government owned, is a great spot
for body surfing and swimming. Nude bathing, once popular
at Moonstone, is now curtailed by new federal rules. The
shoreline drops off rapidly and there is an undertow. Certified
Lifeguards keep a careful watch on swimmers and surfers.
There are no bathhouses or hot showers. Portable rest rooms
and public telephones are available.

The Galilee Bird Sanctuary is located nearby. Fragile sand
dunes provide nesting for the birds and waterfowl that thrive
in this refuge.

A short ferry ride from mainland Rhode Island is Block
Island Beach. Ferries leave from several points, such as Point
Judith, Providence, Bristol and Newport. The boats are modern with snack bars and comfortable seating. Block Island
Beach offers two-and-a-half miles of surf and sand in an un-
crowded environment. Because of its location, Block Island
Beach does not get invaded with thousands of beach goers
from May until September. There are bathhouses with hot
showers, rest rooms and a concession stand where you can
purchase soft drinks and fast food. Areas are set aside for
picnicking and picnic tables are provided for beach patrons.
No camping or overnight loitering is allowed.

Horseneck Beach located in nearby Westport, Massachusetts, is state-operated and is only a 45-minute ride from Newport, Rhode Island. There is plenty of parking convenient to
accommodate the many thousands of visitors to this beautiful
beach. A main pavilion contains changing rooms, hot showers,
and rest rooms, and a concession stand. Camping areas are

available on the seashore. Plan to arrive early as these sites fill up quickly. Miles of large sand dunes provide privacy to sun bathers and a recreational area for kite flying which is popular at Horseneck Beach.

The beach is well staffed with Certified Lifeguards. Surfing is spectacular here. Enormous waves create hazardous undertows which may always be present. This beach is excellent for seashell hunting.

Seashell hunting and beachcombing are popular activities at Rhode Island beaches. Sneakers are comfortable footwear, but rubber boots may be preferred if you intend to wade along the shore. Wear a backpack or shoulder bag. It will be useful to bring along a variety of items that you may need to make your beachcombing trip successful. Bring such items as a small notebook and pen, pocketknife, a supply of plastic bags for sea shells, band-aids, and antiseptic spray for small cuts and scratches. Finally, be sure to wear sunglasses while walking along the seashore. The glare from the sun's rays off the sand and water could harm your eyes.

Notice that this guide is limited to beach activities. Of course, there are numerous other recreational activities which could be included, skiing (in winter), visits to historical sites, or spectator sports events, for example. The advantage of writing solely on one type of recreational activity is that you can provide a great deal of detail. One disadvantage is that if your readers have no interest in that type of activity, they may have little desire to read your guide. If you write about a variety of activities, you will certainly include some that will interest most of your readers; however, you will be limited in the amount of detailed information you can include about each activity. This is a typical writer's dilemma common to any number of writing situations. Discuss with your classmates ways of resolving this dilemma for your particular writing situation.

3. Let's suppose that you are a student member, along with some faculty and deans, of your college's Student Retention Steering Committee. This committee has been formed because the administration is alarmed at the freshman dropout rate, 37 percent last year; moreover, half of this loss occurs within the first six weeks of the fall semester. Your committee is charged with determining the reasons for students' dropping out, and with recommending specific measures to improve the college's

retention rate. The Dean of Students, who chairs the committee, has distributed several questions (see those following) to the committee members, asking that they bring written answers to as many of the questions as possible to the committee's next meeting. The Dean has specifically asked you to poll students and to present a written report of the poll results with recommendations. You are to organize your report according to the highest-priority items germane to the issue.

Student Retention Steering Committee
Questions

1. How can students best be recruited not just for admission but also for retention?

2. Can admissions information be useful in later retention efforts?

3. How can registration be made less frustrating?

4. Can most continuing students be advised and registered in the middle of the preceding semester?

5. Should free hours in scheduling be continued to facilitate out-of-class involvement? What hours are best?

6. Should it be easier for students to have the option of a schedule of fewer than five days a week?

7. Should the normal curriculum be designed to ensure that all students improve skills for writing term papers, for library research, reading, and studying? Will too much reliance be placed on remedial courses and services?

8. Should staffing and programs of academic counseling support services be strengthened in particular ways?

9. Should there be a required freshman seminar orientation course? What should it include? Who should teach it?

10. Should the best-qualified teachers teach at least some freshman classes?

11. Should freshmen and sophomores be encouraged to feel free to remain officially "undecided" about choice of a major if they are uncertain?

12. What functions should be performed by the Academic Advisement and Information Center?

13. How can students having upsetting concerns best be identified and assisted?

14. What are the special needs of commuters, residents, mi-

norities, nontraditional students, the handicapped, and other populations, and how can we meet those needs? Is a faculty–staff development program needed in any of these areas?

15. How can the academic advising system be improved? Should advising be compulsory?

16. How can the student body help in retention?

17. How can constructive out-of-class involvements be enhanced?

18. How can the practical and career benefits, in addition to the less tangible benefits, of liberal education be best articulated to today's student?

19. Does the student in unsatisfactory academic standing receive adequate information and guidance?

20. What should be done to ensure early feedback on academic performance in each course, especially freshman courses, and is an early warning–helping system needed regarding academic standing?

21. Is it possible to improve faculty–staff concern and caring or is this a matter of unchanging individual attitudes?

22. What additional factual data is needed to help in retention?

(Add to or modify questions as appropriate.)

Gather answers to these questions from students in several of your classes. Decide which of the methods of developing information for your report is most appropriate; write out your set of information and draft a report.

4. Let's suppose you are an architect for a bank that has just purchased a block of dilapidated downtown buildings and plans to raze them to build a $10-million office-building complex. Because the location is next to the city's historic district, the mayor, the state's director of historical preservation, and an architectural historian from the state university have grave concerns over your plans for a huge modern structure in the midst of the city's 19th-century architectural heritage. They have summoned the bank's chief executive and you to meet with them to discuss your plans. The bank executive has directed you to prepare for that meeting a defense of your post-modernist design. You and he meet to prepare a list of information for your design defense.

Problem: What major issues do you believe that group will raise? What questions should you address?

Use one of the thinking strategies presented in this chapter to develop a list of questions and answers for the building design defense. Write a draft of the defense based on your findings.

A CONCLUDING NOTE

Thinking that you can wait for the inspiration to write is an inviting notion, but it is unrealistic. There is no instant, magical way to come up with ideas for writing. Writers invent and develop ideas for papers by actively working through thinking strategies. While there are many methods which may prove successful, this chapter presents only a few methods to stimulate and focus your

THINKING STRATEGIES: A Usage Guide

Name	Complete Directions	Method Cues	Kind of Topic Best Used For
Brainstorming	p. 24	fast, random thinking	any type of topic
Particle, Wave, and Field (PWF)	p. 29	1. isolated object 2. changing, dynamic object 3. abstract or many-sided system	any type of topic— with modifications to questions asked
Cube	p. 33	describe, compare, associate, analyze, apply, argue	any type of topic, though all categories may not be applicable to all topics
Star	p. 38	What Happened? Who did it? Where and when? How? Why?	for topics involving human behavior
Metaphor	p. 42	create comparison; brainstorm ideas about the things compared	any type of topic; especially useful to make abstract idea concrete
Personify	p. 45	imagine that the topic is a person or animal	for topics that are abstract or inanimate

thinking, and to help you begin sorting through and organizing your ideas.

These methods of beginning to write on topics will be useful to you in proportion to your ability to incorporate them into your writing process. Since this involves changing your writing habits, you will have to make a special effort—practicing daily, experimenting with various methods, and modifying them to suit your purposes.

Finally, these methods of inquiry have great practical use to you in a number of problem-solving situations, not only in your writing course. As the suggestions for writing assignments indicate, you can use these strategies to develop useful information on problems in other courses and in the world beyond the walls of college classrooms. Refer to the usage guide as necessary when developing ideas for writing.

NOTES

1. For the invention strategies in this chapter I am indebted to Elizabeth and Gregory Cowan, *Writing* (New York: John Wiley & Sons, 1980); Richard E. Young, Alton L. Becker, and Kenneth L. Pike, *Rhetoric: Discovery and Change* (New York: Harcourt Brace Jovanovich, 1970); Kenneth Burke, *A Grammar of Motives* (Berkeley: University of California Press, 1969); William F. Irmscher, *The Holt Guide to English*, 3rd ed. (New York: Holt, Rinehart and Winston, 1981); and James C. Raymond *Writing* (*Is an Unnatural Act*) (New York: Harper & Row, 1980).

2. T. Obenkaram Echewa, "A Nigerian Looks at America," *Newsweek*, 5 July 1982, p. 13.

3. Some of this information came from Ann Peters, "Summer's a breeze at the seashore," *The Providence Sunday Journal*, 4 July 1982, Section E, pp. 1,3; and Martha Smith, "Take home a piece of the beach," *The Providence Sunday Journal*, 4 July 1982, Section E, pp. 1–2.

3

DRAFTING AND ORGANIZING IDEAS

Draft: writer : : Sketch : painter

(A draft is to the writer as a sketch is to the painter.)

To prepare for painting a portrait, artists sketch their subject first. Sketching is their method of studying their topic, of roughing out its general form. They are not trying to get it right nor get it all down the first time, but rather are testing their perspective on the topic, trying out techniques, working out effects, and connecting contiguous parts of the subject.

For writers, drafting is similar to the artists' sketching; it is a process of trial and error, a search for an essay's form and meaning. Using ideas they have developed by a thinking method, writers begin selecting, connecting, and expanding some ideas, while discarding others. Since the process of drafting sentences and paragraphs is the writer's first opportunity to develop ideas fully in language, the writer is essentially explaining to himself or herself what he or she knows about the topic. During and after the initial drafting process for an essay, the writer appraises the writing by addressing questions that relate to the particular writing situation:

What do I really want to say about this topic?
What is my major or central point (main idea)?
To whom am I writing (audience)?

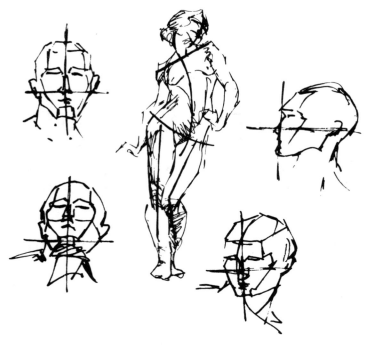

Figure 3.1

What specific effect do I want to have on my audience?

What end result do I intend the essay to effect (purpose)?

How can I arrange my ideas most effectively to achieve my purpose for this audience (order)?

What details have I supplied to support my ideas (supporting details)?

How am I connecting one idea to another (transitions)?

As I write, am I beginning to see a different idea emerging as the major or central point (revised main idea)?

These questions are not asked in any particular sequence; rather, the writer asks them again and again at various stages in the drafting process while trying to develop ideas, and while seeing where the writing takes him or her.

DRAFTING IDEAS FROM A LIST

Example One

Let's assume that you are a tropical-fish enthusiast and you have decided to write directions for 10-year-olds to set up a beginner's marine aquarium. Suppose, also, that you have brainstormed this list of information.

a marine aquarium
set-up procedures and maintenance
equipment
tank
fluorescent-light hood
gravel
coral, shells, plants
filters
seawater
bicarbonate of soda (baking soda)
hydrometer
fish
steps
sterilize tank, make seawater, test salinity, put in gravel, filters, shells, plants, and fish

Since this writing assignment involves designing a fairly straightforward process, your primary task is to arrange the use of the equipment in a step-by-step procedure which beginners can follow successfully. You might begin developing and diagramming the order and relationships of the items of information this way:

Process	Equipment	Steps involved
1. Sterilize the tank.	aquarium tank	Wash tank thoroughly with soap and water. Rinse well.

Process	*Equipment*	*Steps involved*
2. Make seawater.	seawater powder tap water	Mix.
3. Test for saltiness.	hydrometer baking soda	Run test. Add soda as needed for alkalinity (PPH) level.
4. Prepare tank.	filters, gravel, seawater, shells, plants	Set up filters; add gravel, shells, plants, and water.
5. Place fish in tank.	tropical fish	Purchase fish. Place in running marine aquarium.

Having arranged various items in an order with connections implied, you may now draft the information in sentence and paragraph form. Kathleen, a tropical-fish enthusiast who was in my class, drafted the information this way:

SETTING UP A MARINE AQUARIUM

Audience: Children, Ages 10–12

Purpose: To give children an awareness of a unique hobby and some basic facts about marine aquarium set-up procedures.

Pets are becoming an increasingly important addition to many American households. Nearly everyone enjoys animals; many people keep a pet or would like to do so. While cats and dogs are the more traditional form of pets, there are others—guinea pigs, birds, and tropical fish—which also enjoy tremendous popularity. However, if you wish to bring into your home truly the most exotic of pets, consider populating a saltwater aquarium.

Everyday, you will watch with fascination the remarkable world beneath the ocean. In a saltwater aquarium you can recreate the natural environment of marine life. Looking into your fish tank, you will peer at live sponges, corals and fish in a variety of colors impossible to imagine. With a relatively easy set-up procedure and regular maintenance, you will be able to study the mysteries of the sea.

The two largest pieces of equipment involved in setting up your aquarium will be the all-glass tank and the lighted fluorescent hood. The light in your tank will help simulate the hours of darkness and daylight that fish are accustomed to in their natural environment. A successful marine aquarium attempts to duplicate nature as closely as possible to insure the health of its fish. You should buy the largest size tank you can afford because the greater volume of water in a large tank provides a more comfortable environment for your pets.

The following steps in setting up your marine aquarium explain each piece of equipment needed and what it does. You must begin by sterilizing your new tank. The process, very simply, is to wash and fill the tank with a solution of salty water. *tap*

like running

Because saltwater fish have high oxygen requirements, two filters are needed to aerate your aquarium. The first filter, called an undergravel filter, is a sturdy plastic sheet punctured with evenly spaced holes. This filter lies under a two-inch layer of crushed coral gravel. The second filter is located outside the tank and has plastic tubes running into the water. Operating together, these two filters provide water movement, oxygen, and also, very importantly, removal of uneaten food and waste products.

Preparing your "ocean" is accomplished by mixing with ordinary tap water a special man-made seawater powder which contains all the essential trace elements and minerals found in natural seawater. After the water has been mixed, you must test it for salinity, which will indicate whether your ocean has too much, too little or just the right amount of salt for your pets to live. The test is not a difficult one and is made by utilizing a simple instrument known as a hydrometer.

During   antichlorine

tank

acid or base

PH indicator

When the salinity of your water is correct, you will add a few drops of a specialized solution designed to remove any unwanted chemical substance from the water. The addition of several tablespoonsful of bicarbonate of soda insures that the PH level of your synthetic saltwater is equal in alkalinity to natural ocean water.

Your aquarium is now ready to support life, but it won't

truly recreate the ocean floor until you've built a coral reef.⌉
The coral and shells you would like to see in your tank can
be found in most aquarium-supply stores. To make certain
that they do not contain potentially dangerous decaying plants
or animals, be sure to rinse shells and coral thoroughly before
putting them into your tank.

While the coral reef you build in your aquarium will indeed
be pretty, it serves a far more important function.⌊The saltwa-   *13*
ter pets you will place in your tank come from an environment
where coral is always present; it provides them with a home
and protection from predators. In the aquarium, as in nature,
your fish depend on the coral reef for privacy and safety.⌋

⌊Finally, you can take that long-awaited trip to the aquarium
store where you will find some of the most incredible creatures
of this earth. You can choose a pet from any color of the
rainbow—bright yellows, vibrant blues and violets, greens,
polka dots and stripes.⌋⌊You'll see fish so oddly shaped that
they don't look like fish at all and animals resembling flowers   *and*
that have tiny orange clown-fish living inside them.⌋ Real
seahorses will float gracefully through the water past living
corals.⌋ You'll feast your eyes on these awesome sights and
marvel that these animals can become your pets. If you are
willing to provide these delicate saltwater creatures with nourishment and a clean, healthy environment, they will open up
to you all the secrets of their world beneath the sea.

Examine Kathleen's arrangement and development of the
information. Is the process clearly ordered and explained?
Would you suggest any changes in her arrangement? Does she
move smoothly and clearly from one idea to another? If there
are confusing places or missing information, suggest ways in
which Kathleen could resolve the problems in a revision of the
draft. Refer to the questions on pp. 57–58 for a basis on which
to assess Kathleen's draft.

Example Two

Let's consider a different sort of writing assignment, one a bit
more complex than explaining a process: comparing and contrasting information. Dr. Wilson, an ophthalmologist (a specialist in
eye structure, function, and disease), has made a thorough exami-

nation of a 40-year-old patient who has worn hard contact lenses for 20 years; here are Wilson's notes:

> Patient complains that over past several weeks wearing time must be reduced to 5–7 hrs. daily because of eye irritation. Could be a warning of trouble ahead.
>
> No lens damage.
>
> No diagnosable eye damage.
>
> Possibility of corneal abrasion or corneal "bubbles" developing if patient continues to wear hard lenses for many more years.
>
> Hard lenses provide best vision correction: 20–20; however, seem not as effective for reading and writing as for distance.
>
> On soft-lens trial patient remarked: 1. significantly greater eye comfort; 2. sensitivity to light much less
>
> Vision correction with soft lens much less effective. Patient has 2.50 diopters of astigmatism. Soft lenses correct only about $\frac{1}{2}$ to $\frac{3}{4}$ of that. Hard lenses and glasses correct all of the astigmatism. Patient's subjective response indicates that while he enjoys the comfort of soft lenses, his sense of loss of visual acuity is significant and worrisome. Especially concerned about vision during nighttime driving.
>
> Patient wearing glasses more frequently and for longer duration in recent weeks. Doesn't mind wearing glasses now as did years ago. Only minor complaints: needs new prescription and lacks peripheral vision contacts provide.
>
> New lens prescription for glasses:

		Spherical	Cylindrical	Axis
D.V.	O.D. − 3.75	−1.25	X165
	O.S. − 3.25	−1.50	X10

> Patient has seen new lightweight plastic eyeglass frames and lenses which he likes. Thinks wearing glasses may go with his graying hair and mature look.

As he reads over his notes in preparation for making recommendations to the patient, Dr. Wilson adds some more information:

Remember to tell patient that soft-contact-lens maintenance is more time consuming than hard-lens maintenance.

Continuing to wear either hard or soft contact lenses increases this patient's likelihood of needing bifocal-lens eyeglasses for reading and writing.

Mention that none of my patients at or about 45 years old continue to wear hard lenses, because of the presence or the probability that such long-term wear into middle age may precipitate corneal damage and, thus, vision impairment.

Assist Dr. Wilson in preparing his recommendations to the patient. Organize the items of information for easy comparison and contrast. To do so, follow these guidelines:

1. Sort out all of the items of information into three separate lists under these headings: Hard Contact Lenses, Soft Contact Lenses, and Eyeglasses;

2. Read over the information in each list and select the main, most important, or broadest idea in each list;

3. Reorganize each set of information by placing the main, most important, or broadest idea at the top and arranging the other items under it. Indicate some order of relationship between the ideas of each set.

For example, the first list of information under "Hard Contact Lenses" could look like this:

1. Over past several weeks wearing time reduced to 5–7 hrs. daily because of eye irritation. This could be a warning signal of trouble ahead.

2. No lens damage.

3. No eye damage.

4. Could cause this patient corneal abrasion or corneal "bubbles" if he continues wearing them for many more years.

5. Provide best vision correction (20–20), including astigmatism correction.

6. Seem less effective for reading and writing than for distance vision.

7. Continued lens wear increases likelihood of needing bifocal lenses for reading and writing.

8. At about 45 years old my patients discontinue hard-lens wear because of the presence or the probability of eye (corneal) damage.

Item 4 is the most important or main idea in this list; all others seem to support it or to be less central to the patient's needs at this point in his life. The schema in Figure 3.2 represent one way of reorganizing this set of information with Item 4 at the top.

Main Idea

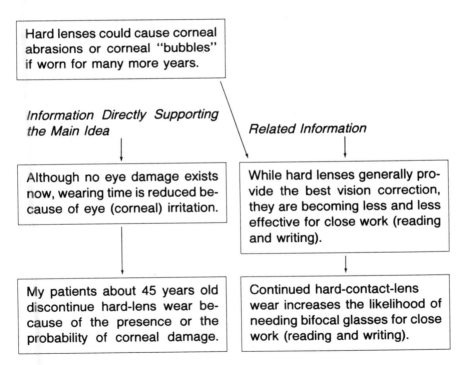

Figure 3.2

In Figure 3.2 the information is organized and related in three ways: first, it is arranged in three new categories (main idea, information directly supporting the main idea, and related information); secondly, the information is ranked in order of importance within each category with the most important items at the top; and, finally, information from separate items has been connected to other items or combined into fewer items, using words and sentence structure to indicate relationships. (See, for example, the sentences beginning with "Although" and "While.")

If you have reorganized and developed the items listed under the other two headings, then Dr. Wilson's notes should be prepared for drafting.

Complete Wilson's task by making a recommendation to the patient and drafting a statement supporting your recommendation. Compare your arrangement and development of ideas with others, by reading each other's statements. Exchange reasons for your choices and share suggestions for rearranging if the statements were to be revised. Refer to the questions on pp. 57–58 for a basis of assessing the various statements.

Example Three

Let's look at still another kind of writing task often assigned in college courses: the reasoning or argument paper. In a sociology class which is debating a series of issues, Kyle has been selected to present an argument on premarital sexual intercourse. He first sketches this design skeleton for information. (See Figure 3.3.) Figure 3.4 shows another typical pattern for the pro–con argument.

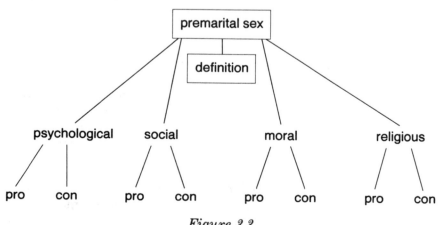

Figure 3.3

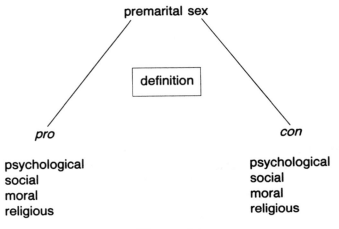

Figure 3.4

During a visit to the library, Kyle develops the following sets of information. See Figures 3.5, 3.6, 3.7, and 3.8.

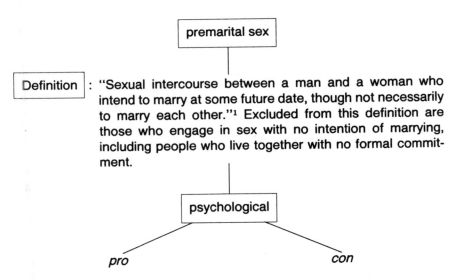

Figure 3.5

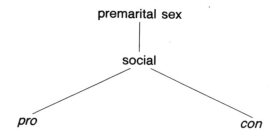

Figure 3.6

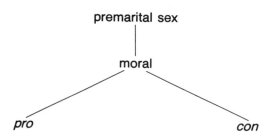

Figure 3.7

Kyle's next step is to state his central point or main ideas. He drafts this straightforward introductory statement:

We are supposedly living in a sexually liberated society. Yet sexuality continues to be a major problem which requires study by social scientists. In my remarks today I will address a part of this problem, the issue of premarital sexual intercourse. Specifically, *I will define premarital sex and present*

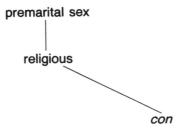

premarital sex

religious

con

Most traditional organized religions
confine sexual activity to within the
bounds of marriage; discourage
pre- and extramarital sex.

Figure 3.8

*arguments for and against it from the perspectives of psy-
chology, society, morality and religion; finally I will conclude with a statement of my personal stance based on my
research for this presentation.*

To present his argument on premarital sex Kyle could, of course,
simply write out a more fully developed version of the information
as it appears in Figures 3.5–3.8. But wise writers would present
the material in a way that—while being fair-minded—is most
persuasive and favorable to their point of view. Therefore, Kyle
has many options for arranging and developing the information,
and connecting or combining ideas.

*Try out some options, using your classmates as the audi-
ence who assesses their relative effectiveness.* For example, first
assume that Kyle's personal stance is against premarital sex
and that his primary reasons are listed under "social." In what
order would you arrange the information? Would you add any
information? Next, assume that Kyle favors premarital sex; for
his reasoning assume that he presents an integration of ideas
listed under "psychological" and "social." What information
would you select as the major idea from the four listed under
"pro" in those two headings? How would you develop a cohesive
argument using all four items? Would you have to add or delete
information or could you accomplish your purpose by effective
arrangement, development, and combinations of the information
listed? Suggestion: One way of developing information in order

to make it more substantial, concrete, and credible is to cite specific examples. Notice that Kyle's information includes no specific examples of individual situations to illustrate his general statements. Again, you may want to refer to the questions on pp. 57–58 for a basis on which to assess the available options.

CHECKLIST ON A PROCESS AND PRINCIPLES FOR DRAFTING

On the basis of the three preceding examples and the exercises you completed for them, a general process for drafting should be evident. (See Figure 3.9.)

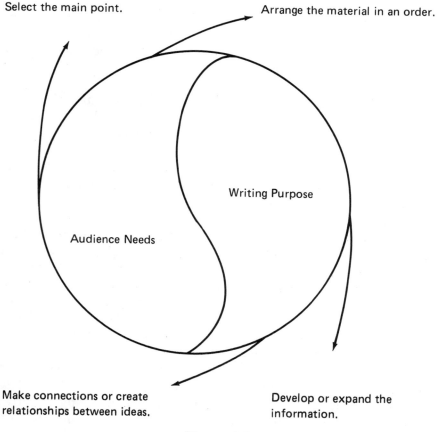

Figure 3.9

While you may perform these activities sequentially, much like steps in a recipe, you may also vary the order of activities, combine more than one activity in a single operation, and repeat some activities several times before you achieve the end you want. Your methods of thinking and your unique composing habits will govern the way you enact this process. No matter how you work through the process you will find it helpful to allow yourself to be guided by the dual principles of writing purpose and audience.

Discussion and Illustration of Drafting Process and Principles

Read through your notes several times, *selecting the main points* you want to make. To identify which ideas are main points and which ideas are supporting, writers often look for key words in their notes. When a writer is looking for a main or central concept in a list of information, the key words are the broadest, most general, or all-encompassing words. Quite often key words are repeated in a passage or list. Scan the list of information below and circle the words you believe are key words. (Remember: broadest, most general, all-encompassing.)

- Since the Civil War, the government has employed compulsory means to draft citizens for military service.
- At the outbreak of World War I a selective draft system was developed for active service.
- Deferment of college men from the military draft gave assurance that men could continue to complete a college education.
- During peace time the draft has been inactive.
- People should look at the recent reactivation of draft registration through historical perspective.

I trust you circled such words as "draft registration," "draft system," "military draft," and "draft." "Draft" is the key word in this list of information. Once a writer has identified the key word, the next task is to find the statement which is the major, central, or main one in the group. The statement containing the broadest, most general, or all-encompassing information is the main or chief idea in the group.

Before going on, reread the preceding list of sentences and select the one that contains the main idea.

The first four sentences in the list each present a bit of specific historical information about the draft. The last sentence calls for people to see a relatively recent event (reactivation of draft registration) in "historical perspective." Thus, if you selected the last sentence, you picked a winner because it contains the main or major point. All of the other sentences serve to illustrate or support the general concept of a historical view of the draft system.

Make judgments about the relationships among various pieces of information and arrange the material in an order accordingly. When you are writing a paragraph telling someone how to do something or telling about the events of a day, an order or a sequence of ideas often becomes apparent. Reread Mura's freewriting exercise, p. 11, to review her system of marking time. However, even when you are not showing time or writing about a process, you can arrange your ideas in a number of effective orders. Often, writers place their major idea at the beginning or at the end of a paragraph. The writer in Chapter 2 who compared students to circus performers (p. 44) opened with his major idea and followed with several sentences of specific examples.

In the following draft paragraph, the writer wants to build up to her major point, so she leads us along with her to recreate the special feeling which is the point of her paragraph. Therefore, she withholds stating her general point until the end.

The screen door opens wide and creaks just before it slams shut behind me. As I step out into the beautiful spring day I breathe the light, crisp air easily. I am on my way from my house with a shovel and plastic bag in one hand, to a small stream a half a mile away. I am walking quickly now because I know the treasures that await me. In the distance I hear the rhythmic dribbling of a neighborhood basketball game; within a few steps this game is overpowered by the approaching sounds of the upcoming stream. The stream is by no means big nor deep but to the ears of this seven-year-old it is indeed both as big and as deep as an ocean. Once within a few feet of the stream I immediately go to the spot which ended my treasure hunting the day before. Looking around to insure my privacy and the safety of my hunt, I realize that I am far from the distant sounds of my bustling neighborhood and I am grateful for this special place of solitude.

When the structure of ideas is not chronological or sequential, however, the writer must design an order based on some principle of idea association or logical reasoning. A sound method for designing such an order for a set of ideas is trial and error. Sometimes writers find it useful to draw a diagram or a figure, depicting the meaning they intend, that is, noting the centrality of the key words and showing the relation of supporting ideas. Any number of diagrams or figures could serve this purpose. For examples, look at the diagrams in this chapter. You can create other graphic designs to represent the way you see ideas and how they relate to each other: overlapping circles, pie slices, interlocking chain links, an umbrella, even a sectional sofa. Let yourself be limited only by the structure suggested by logic or by the ideas themselves and by your own visual perception.

Using the set of information listed below, try your hand at creating a graphic design to illustrate the main idea and the relationship of the other information to it.

- Brisk walking, jogging, swimming, and bicycling are all aerobic exercises.
- Aerobic exercises push your cardiorespiratory system (heart, lungs, and blood vessels) to work at a faster rate.
- Exercising aerobically offers various benefits, improving your physical fitness and your sense of well-being.
- Through aerobic exercise you can tone up your muscles and rid yourself of the demon flab.
- Aerobic exercise increases your endurance, defeating the foe fatigue.

Now, following the order illustrated in your graphic design, write out the sentence in a paragraph which states the main idea and develops and supports it. You may add or eliminate words if you wish. Compare your graphic design and paragraph to those of your classmates. Share your understanding of the information, discuss how you chose a design to represent it, and explain your purpose in writing it out as you did.

Develop or expand the information. While you have been working through the exercises in the section on finding a main point and on arranging the material in an order, you have also been developing or expanding the ideas.

Practicing writers experiment with a number of ways of developing the same material in order to increase their writing effectiveness. For example, the information on the military draft could be developed in several ways, including these two:

Draft: Version One

Why the uproar over the President's reactivating draft registration? For the last 200 years the draft has been a fact of life for American men. During the Civil War communities had quotas to fill for military service. Ever since then, the government has had legal means to compel male citizens to serve in the armed forces. In 1917, when World War I broke out, and the draft had to be employed on a large scale again for the first time since the 1860s, the system was refined to be selective of who was drafted, permitting men in certain professions and those attending college to obtain deferments. During the Vietnam war, men protested the draft more out of disagreement over the morality of that particular war than over any disagreement with the principle of the draft itself. If people look at the recent reactivation of the draft in a historical perspective, few—except for true conscientious objectors—should protest. After all, any country worth living in has to maintain a standing armed force. In this case, our national history is on the President's side.

Draft: Version Two

The recent reactivation of draft registration provides an opportunity for people to look at the selective-service system from a historical perspective. Its history is filled with abuses and prejudice. During the Civil War when the government first used compulsory means to draft men for military service, people could bribe corrupt local politicians in order to avoid service. The rich were favored; the poor were abused. At the outbreak of World War I a *selective* draft system was introduced. This process of selection continued through World War II, the Korean War, and the Vietnam War. Under the selective draft "college men" were deferred from active service. At this time in our glorious national history "college men" was another term for white and rich (not always intelligent, though). So, throughout its history America's draft system has been abusive of and prejudicial against the poor and the minorities. For one, brief period about 10 years ago, the government experimented with drafting men by drawing lots. During this peacetime while the draft system is inactive we should enact a law to make this truly democratic system, the lottery draft, permanent.

Practice developing such versatility yourself. Read over the lists of information in Figure 3.10[5] and develop or expand the information and draft in three different statements for computer novices entitled 1. "You and Computer Programming," 2. "Here's How to Program Your TI-99/4A Computer," and 3. "Let's Talk BASIC." The particular title (or writing purpose) of each statement obviously affects the choices you will make in completing this exercise. Share your statements with other classmates and discuss your various means of developing the material.

Make connections between ideas. Of course, you have already been making connections between ideas. That is, you have been showing the relationship of ideas to the main idea and to each other in the exercises you have been doing in this section of the chapter. You may have observed that many connections between ideas, combinations of ideas, or transitions from one idea to another are determined largely by other choices a writer makes: selecting a main idea, deciding on a principle of arrangement or order. However, as you have probably also noticed, when one writes an initial draft, many possible options for relating ideas still exist. Experienced writers practice making connections between ideas, remaking connections, and testing them to see which ones work most effectively for certain purposes and audiences.

Study, for example, how the various ways of connecting and combining ideas in the passages below effect subtle changes in meaning and effect.

Original version

Altogether, despite a relatively unadorned simplicity, boys and girls, as I recall, were happy and contented in those days

BASIC is

- a computer language
- short for *Beginner's All-purpose Symbolic Instruction Code*
- the invention of John Kemeny and Thomas Kurtz of Dartmouth College
- only one of many computer languages
- popular
- easy to learn
- powerful
- like English in some "commands": PRINT, GO TO, RUN, END

TI BASIC is

- a dialect of BASIC
- the language of the TI-99/4A Computer

COMPUTER is

- used for personal, business, hobby, education

PROGRAMMING a computer is

- telling it what to do
- when to do it

TO PROGRAM TI-99/4A need to know

- the language of the computer (TI BASIC)
- the way you talk to the computer (typewriter keyboard)

CAN PROGRAM

- graphics
- sounds
- music
- number games
- word games

Figure 3.10

before the so-called "Roaring Twenties". Automobiles were few, and the radio was unknown before KDKA began to broadcast in the initial year of that storied decade. Television, of course, was a quarter-century in the future, and the only juke box in town for many years was that in the New Mason lobby—a mechanical violin that produced surprisingly beautiful music. Youth had yet to experience the more accelerated, more hectic, tensions of the years after the confident, hopeful postwar decade. And depression was not even believed to be possible—nor another war.[6]

Second version

Boys and girls were happy and contented, I can assure you, in those days before the so-called "Roaring Twenties," despite a relatively unadorned simplicity. Automobiles were few, the radio was unknown before KDKA began to broadcast in the initial year of that storied decade, and, as you know, television was a quarter-century in the future. The only juke box in town for many years was that in the New Mason lobby—a mechanical violin that produced surprisingly beautiful music. Thus, youth had yet to experience the more accelerated, more hectic, tensions of the years after the confident, hopeful postwar decade. Furthermore, neither a depression nor another war was even believed to be possible.

Third version

As I recall, boys and girls were happy and contented in those days before the so-called "Roaring Twenties," perhaps because of a relatively unadorned simplicity. For example, for many years the only juke box in town was a mechanical violin in the New Mason lobby that produced surprisingly beautiful music. Before KDKA began to broadcast in the initial year of that storied decade, the radio was unknown. And, of course, television was a quarter-century in the future. Furthermore, automobiles were few. Therefore, youth had yet to experience the more accelerated, more hectic, tensions of the years after the confident, hopeful postwar decade. So a depression was not even believed possible—not to mention another war.

You may notice that I have selected a passage of distinct style and, other than connecting or combining ideas differently, I have made no other changes; yet, the differences between the versions are significant. Such is the power of the way ideas are connected or combined. In fact, in the third version the meaning of the ideas themselves change as the structure in which they appear changes. Discuss with your classmates the differences in meaning and effect in the three versions.

Experiment with various ways of connecting and combining information. Using information from Tables 3.1, 3.2, and 3.3,[7] draft a statement on the health risks of smoking, on reasons other than health risk for quitting, or on how to stop smoking. Once you have drafted a statement, underline words that function as connectors or transitions. Then *draft a second version of the statement, employing other means of connecting ideas or creating relationships between ideas.* Discuss with your classmates the various changes in meaning and effect in your two versions.

Table 3.1
SOME EFFECTS OF SMOKING

A two-to-three times greater chance of dying from a heart attack. Since heart disease is our leading killer (675,000 Americans will die of a heart attack this year), smoking actually causes more deaths through heart disease than through lung cancer.

Twenty-five times the chance of developing lung cancer. If you can manage exposure to asbestos as well, you can increase your chances of getting cancer to about 70 times that of a nonsmoker. And don't forget an increased chance at cancer of the larynx (voicebox), lip, mouth, pancreas, and bladder.

Emphysema is a sure thing. Destruction of lung tissue is a direct effect of smoking, so every smoker develops emphysema to some degree. How much depends on how much you have smoked. If you live long enough, your emphysema will get to the point where just getting up to go to the bathroom will leave you out of breath and exhausted. If you tend to underestimate the latter, try breathing through a straw sometime. Get one that has a small enough diameter that it makes you work to breathe while sitting down. Now get up and try to move around and do something, still breathing through the straw. Get the picture? This is called suffocation.

Dead and sick babies. Miscarriages are at least twice as common when the mother smokes heavily. Smoking mothers have 55 percent more congenitally deformed babies. Low weight at birth is associated with increased chances of death and disease in a baby and babies born to smoking mothers weigh about 200 grams less than the average. Infants whose mothers smoke are more likely to be admitted

Table 3.1 *(continued)*

to the hospital during the first year of life for pneumonia or bronchitis. Lead accumulates in the blood of unborn children whose mothers smoke.

A deadly interaction with oral contraceptives. The death rate for smokers on the Pill is about six times the rate for nonsmokers, according to studies by the Population Council. This is a far higher rate than if the risk of smoking were simply added to the risk of oral contraceptives.

The menopause occurs earlier. While studying the relationship between heart attacks and the menopause, investigators unexpectedly discovered that smokers experience the menopause at significantly younger ages than nonsmokers do.

The country loses over 27.5 billion dollars each year. This is the price a UCLA study puts on the death and disability due to smoking. It amounts to over $450 for each of the 60 million smokers in America. And that doesn't count the money it costs for the cigarettes themselves.

Table 3.2
OTHER EFFECTS OF SMOKING

You stink. So do your clothes, car, office, home. To the extent that you expose them to your smoke, so do your spouse and kids. If they smoke, tell them that they stink all by themselves.

You are ugly. Dermatologists report that women who smoke develop more facial wrinkles and do so sooner than those who don't.

You are tough to love. Kissing a smoker may not be exactly like kissing a dirty ashtray, but it's close enough.

You have little sense of taste or smell. Smoking decreases these senses. You don't know what you've been missing.

You spend the vacation money. A two-pack-a-day habit costs over $400 per year for the cigarettes alone. That's plenty for a week at a resort, several new suits, round-trip air-fare to London, or numerous other treats.

You are a fire hazard. According to the National Fire Protection Association, smoking is the major cause of fatal residential fires.

Table 3.3
A PROCEDURE TO QUIT SMOKING

Pick a day to stop. Get definite as to when you are actually going to do something. Make it about one month in the future.

Start cutting down before your day to stop. Addiction to nicotine cigarettes is *real*—so make it a little easier to stop by reducing the

Table 3.3 (*continued*)

dosage of nicotine. One good way to reduce is to pick "nonsmoking hours" and then extend these hours gradually.

Make it more difficult to get at your cigarettes. Wrap them in paper, put them in a box or a locked desk drawer, in an inconvenient pocket of a coat, and so on.

Switch to cigarettes low in tar and nicotine. This will help only if you don't change your method of smoking. Many smokers who switch to low tar and nicotine cigarettes smoke more of them, smoke them further down toward the butt, and/or take more puffs in an effort to satisfy their nicotine addiction. This is probably more unhealthy than their previous habit. Switch cigarettes only as part of a conscious plan to decrease nicotine, and make sure the switch does that.

Smoke only half the cigarette.

Chart your progress. Know how much, when, and where you smoke.

Use substitutes. Mints, gum, and so forth replace the oral activity provided by smoking.

On your day to stop, treat yourself to something. Have a big dinner, go to a movie or a play. Get rid of the ashtrays and other smoking equipment. Exercise—a long walk is especially good. Brush your teeth immediately after eating. Allow yourself something you want—even a cocktail or extra cup of coffee.

Don't worry about gaining weight. After you have kicked the habit, you can work on this. And the odds are overwhelmingly in favor of returning to your original weight.

Expect to feel down for a few days. This is part of becoming unaddicted. If you need the help of your physician, don't hesitate to get it.

Drafting Process Demonstrated on a Full Essay

So far, we have been studying drafting procedures and principles for small units of writing. These procedures and principles are essentially the same for longer units. However, increasing the amount and complexity of information requires a writer to expend more energy and be alert to handling greater idea activity, just as a juggler must when throwing more balls in the air or when trying to juggle long knives instead of balls. To demonstrate the procedures and principles on a longer work, I will discuss how I drafted the essay "Lake O' the Woods" from the set of information I developed through the particle, wave, and field method. Of course, it is impossible to show the process as it actually occurred—the starts and stops, the mental wanderings, the sorting, the connecting, the moving on, and the returning again to original points. However, I will describe as dynamically as possible my thinking and writing activities and show what the draft looks like at each step of development. While my process is only one of a number of effective ways of drafting, it may serve as a useful model in discussions of process with your classmates.

As I mentioned in the previous chapter, when I reworked my ideas according to the particle, wave, and field method, I discovered a new purpose: to take a historical look at our time at the cabin. However, I could not fully articulate that new purpose until I had written out my ideas in complete sentences and paragraph drafts. So, I just began sorting through the list (see pp. 31–33), selecting main points as best I could according to my rough concept of purpose, and expanding the material by writing out a first draft. Here's what I wrote: (Sentences with main ideas appear in italics.)

1. *My uncle's cabin at the Lake of the Woods, West Virginia was a two-story, white-frame lodge we called "the cabin."* It had a completely knotty-pine-panelled interior. The floors were finished hardwood. At one end of the first floor (the livingroom) was a stone fireplace. It was a very large livingroom with three sofas and a large picture window. Next to it was the dining area where we ate at a long picnic table. Off the dining area was a small, well-equipped kitchen. Glass-paned French doors led outside. There was a master bedroom and bathroom off the livingroom. Upstairs there were three bedrooms; there were bunkbeds for us in one of them. The whole place was filled with antique furniture and appointments.

2. *The lake stood 150 yards down a sloping hillside from the cabin.* Midway between the cabin and the lake was a large dinner bell on a post; there was a loveseat around it. A six-foot-wide dock was built from the shore into the water. We kept our rowboat tied to a stake near the dock. The water was crystal clear, of greenish tint. About 20 feet off the end of the dock we had a 10-foot-square float (made of planks on 55-gallon drums).

3. *On the first day there was a lot of cleanup work to do.* We kids went to work helping paint the dock. This was the first time we had painted anything and we were pretty sloppy. We painted with an oil-base paint all morning. Since the

weather was warm, we didn't wear any shirts, just shorts. Well, we got a sunburn and paint all over us, especially on our hands, arms, and legs. My aunt used turpentine to clean the paint off us. Boy! did we scream at the sting of her rubbing turpentine on our sunburns!

4. *This particular year was one of the seven-year cycles when locusts swarm.* We couldn't believe the deafening noise and the number of them swooping down from the sky onto the trees. For a long time after they died my brother and I found empty, shell-like carcasses stuck onto the tree bark of the locust trees. The shells look like light-brown plastic molds with eyes and everything.

5. *We were always warned to watch for snakes.* Mother had read us the instructions from a Red Cross booklet, "what to do when you see a snake." I don't remember seeing many, but one time mother and we kids came upon a blacksnake sunning itself on the lawn. It was as startled as we were and it slithered off into higher grass. We ran, skipping and screaming to the house with our eyes glued to the grass, expecting to see more snakes. Not one of us, not even mother, remembered the booklet's instructions to freeze and not panic.

6. *My brother and I took charge of the boat, it seemed.* I don't remember when they started allowing us to go out in it alone; we probably had lifejackets, though I can't remember. Anyway, we were always asking permission to go out in the boat and were always being warned not to go too far and not to stand up in it. He and I were always competing, seeing who could row farthest, who could get from one point to the next fastest. And we always wanted to row when adults went out in the boat. *I remember our taking Dr. Wells (my aunt's father) fishing.* We always loved it when he came to visit. He was country-raised, and he seemed to really like us kids, and he had funny country-wise sayings for things. I remember he always brought very long night crawlers to fish with. He always asked one of us to get one out of the can. He'd say, "Get me one of those snakes, Petey." So we started calling worms "snakes" after that. We learned how to bait a hook and how to take bluegills (also called sunfish) off the hook without getting stuck by their fins.

7. *I remember that we kids took swimming lessons at the YMCA so that we would know how to swim well at the lake.*

We never wanted to leave the water even when it was cold. My mother would say, "Come here this minute; your lips are blue!" We swam around the dock; we always played games underneath it, holding onto the pilings and climbing over the wood structure underneath it. *I distinctly remember our uncle teaching us how to dive.* Always encouraging us with directions ("point your arms over your head, palms together; bend over and point your hands at the water; now jump!"), he would hold our ankles and give us a flip when we jumped to get our legs up and prevent a bellyflop. Somehow we learned how to dive. I wonder how many times our uncle had to flip our legs up until we got the knack. (the hang of it?)

8. We had large family meals (about 15 of us). Sometimes in hot weather meals would be served out on the back patio or in front, looking down at the lake. But mostly I remember sitting at the long picnic table, elbow-to-elbow, eating fresh sweet corn, tomatoes and summer squash some local farmer had raised. It was a good feeling of security being in a large family and mealtimes always seemed the happiest times. *In the evenings we'd all sit outside, often with weekend visitors, and the grown-ups would talk politics or tell stories of the old days.* I can remember them telling some stories over and over, and each time a story was enjoyed as if it were being told for the first time. When darkness fell and the mosquito attacks began, we'd adjourn to the large livingroom. Except for the dead heat of mid-July, the mountain nights were cool and breezy. Usually, there'd be a log fire in the fireplace and the adults would talk some more, long after we'd been tucked in for the night. Sometimes a loud laugh would wake one of us and we'd all sneak out to the hallway or the top of the stairs and eavesdrop, hoping to hear something "juicy."

9. *My mother had three brothers.* The two younger ones went to war against Hitler as did my father. When they returned from the war in which my father was killed, the middle brother, a new-car dealer, bought this lakefront property in the mountains of northwest West Virginia, bordering the southwest Pennsylvania line. The three brothers pitched in to build the cabin. Some carpenters, plumbers, and a stonemason were hired and others helped. Friends would lend a hand. My grandfather worked and supervised every day's work. They erected the cabin in one summer. *I don't remember*

how old I was when we first started going to the lake, but around the summer of 1950, when I was going on seven, my mother took my brother, my twin sister, and me to the lake for the entire summer. A poliomyelitis epidemic had scared our family. One distant cousin, who lived across the state from us, and one of my brother's playmates, who lived on the next block, had both contracted the disease. We were taken to the mountains in hopes of escaping this dread crippler.

10. *One day, after some weeks in our mountain retreat, my mother said we got "cabin fever" (boredom).* She took all of us kids for a drive, seven miles down the mountain road (part of which was just a dirt and gravel surface) to the nearest civilization, a village called "White House," on the Pennsylvania–West Virginia state line. It had a general store, with a gas pump out front, some small churches, assorted houses. We got gas, groceries, sodas and popsicles and headed farther into civilization to the next town and a moviehouse where we saw a movie and ate popcorn. When my uncle came up to visit for the weekend, he was furious, fearing that we kids had been exposed to polio germs. He felt my mother had undermined the whole escape scheme because she got cabin fever. I guess they had quite an argument. I don't recall hearing it, but years later I remember it being told in a family story. None of us got polio on that day on the town, though there may have been a stomach ache or two in the crowd.

11. After having the cabin for about eight years, my uncle sold it for cash to move from an apartment into a house of his own. I don't remember missing it right away. By now we were spending three weeks each summer in Boy Scout and church camps. It would be many years before we'd understand what that lake lodge meant in our lives. We had taken its luxury and beauty for granted. *Now that such a property value and such a time as that summer—of carefree play, learning responsibilities of living in nature—are beyond and behind us, we realize its value. And we realize the value of growing up in a large, loving family that looked after us well.*

As you can see, this is unfinished writing. Some sentences within paragraphs do not fit too well with others and several paragraphs are merely independent units of thought, not connected parts of a larger whole. But this writing, unfinished as it is, has served the purpose of helping me know better my ideas about the topic. With this new understanding of ideas, I can begin focusing more clearly on my purpose and begin to consider audience needs.

During my drafting session I found it helpful to take 10- or 15-minute breaks between writing out each set of sentences. Also, before going on to reconsider my writing purpose, I took an overnight break. Not only did this give a rest from the physical and mental exertion of writing, but it also allowed relaxed thinking time. (Good writing ideas often occur during such rest periods between writing sessions—in the shower, during a trip to the supermarket, or while scanning the newspaper; so, I keep pencil and paper at hand to jot down any insights I get during leisure time.) When I resumed drafting after the overnight break, I saw the material from a different perspective, one that helped me realize more clearly different relationships between ideas. At this point I had to remind myself to remain open to adding to, deleting, or modifying my draft. During this stage the writing should remain messy, tentative, and in flux, although I have a natural reflex to clean it up and be done with it.

The new writing purpose that was incubating during my drafting session and rest period came into focus: I wanted to take a look back at a time of family growth and closeness during a historical period of uncertainty and fear (post-World War II and polio epidemic); I wanted to reminisce about the value that time held for me personally. So I returned to my drafting work to design an arrangement of the material to fulfill that purpose. To search for an appropriate sequence of ideas I copied each paragraph onto a large note card, placing a number at the top of each card to indicate the paragraph's position in the original draft. Then I experimented with creating new sequences of ideas by moving the cards around and reading through the various arrangements. As I settled on a new sequence of ideas, I renumbered the cards to indicate their new positions.

Here's the original and the new order of paragraphs:

Original order	New Order
1. description of cabin	1. the building of the cabin
2. the lake, dock, boat, float	2. description of cabin

3. first day's activities
4. swarm of locusts
5. snakes
6. rowboating and fishing
7. swimming and diving
8. time with family: meals, stories, and so on
9. the building of the cabin and why we went for the whole summer: polio epidemic
10. cabin fever
11. looking back on what it all meant

3. the lake, dock, boat, float
4. first day's activities
5. swimming and diving
6. rowboating and fishing
7. why we went for the whole summer: polio epidemic
8. cabin fever
9. time with family: meals, stories, and so on
10. looking back on what it all meant

The next step was to return to drafting, because, although it is easy to move the cards around on a desk top, the ideas on the various cards cannot simply be shuffled into a new context. In order to continue the process of rearranging ideas in an order that better fulfills my writing purpose, I began changing paragraphs to "fit" them into their new context.

Revised or newly added information is placed in italics below to show where I attempted to make better connections between ideas after rearranging the paragraphs.

When I was young, my family spent our summers at a mountain lodge on a lake.

My mother had three brothers. The two younger ones went to war against Hitler as did my father. When they returned from the war in which my father was killed, the middle brother, a new-car dealer, bought this lakefront property in the mountains of northwest West Virginia, bordering the southwest Pennsylvania line. The three brothers pitched in to build a lodge. Some carpenters, plumbers, and a stonemason were hired and others helped. Friends would lend a hand. My grandfather worked and supervised every day's work. They erected the cabin in one summer.

This summerplace at the Lake of the Woods, West Virginia was a two-story, white-frame lodge, we called "the cabin." It had a completely knotty-pine-panelled interior. The floors were finished hardwood. At one end of the first floor (the livingroom) was a stone fireplace. It was a very large livingroom with three sofas and a large picture window. Next to it was the dining area where we ate at a long picnic table. Off the dining area was a small, well-equipped kitchen. Glass-paned French doors led outside. There was a master bedroom and bathroom off the livingroom. Upstairs there were three bedrooms; there were bunkbeds for us in one of them. The whole place was filled with antique furniture and appointments.

The lake stood 150 yards down a sloping hillside from the cabin. Midway between the cabin and the lake was a large dinner bell on a post; there was a loveseat around it. A six-foot-wide dock was built from the shore into the water. We kept our rowboat tied to a stake near the dock. The water was crystal clear, of greenish tint. About 20 feet off the end of the dock we had a 10-foot-square float (made of planks on 55-gallon drums).

On our first day there each summer we had a lot of cleanup work to do. Once we kids went to work helping paint the dock. This was the first time we had painted anything and we were pretty sloppy. We painted with an oil-base paint all morning. Since the weather was warm, we didn't wear any shirts, just shorts. Well, we got a sunburn and paint all over us, especially on our hands, arms, and legs. My aunt used turpentine to clean the paint off us. Boy! did we scream at the sting of her rubbing turpentine on our sunburns!

However, most of our memories are of pleasant things, like swimming, boating, and fishing. I remember that we kids took swimming lessons at the YMCA so that we would know how to swim well at the lake. We never wanted to leave the water even when it was cold. My mother would say, "Come here this minute; your lips are blue!" We swam around the dock; we always played games underneath it, holding onto the pilings and climbing over the wooden structure underneath it. I distinctly remember our uncle teaching us how to dive. Always encouraging us with directions ("point your arms over your head, palms together; bend over and point your hands at the water; now jump!"), he would hold our ankles and give us a flip when we jumped to get our legs up and prevent a bellyflop. Somehow we learned to dive. I wonder how many times our uncle had to flip our legs up until we got the knack.

My brother and I took charge of the boat, it seemed. I don't remember when they started allowing us to go out in it alone; we probably had lifejackets, though I can't remember. Anyway, we were always asking permission to go out in the boat and were always being warned not to go too far and not to stand up in it. He and I were always competing, seeing who could row farthest, who could get from one point to the next fastest. And we always wanted to row when adults went out in the boat. I remember our taking Dr. Wells (my aunt's father) fishing. We always loved it when he came to visit. He was country-raised, and he seemed to really like us kids, and he had funny country-wise sayings for things. I remember he always brought very long night crawlers to fish with. He always asked one of us to get one out of the can. He'd say, "Get me one of those snakes, Petey." So we started calling worms "snakes" after that. We learned how to bait a hook and how to take bluegills (also called sunfish) off the hook without getting stuck by their fins.

I don't remember how old I was when we first started going to the lake, but around the summer of 1950, when I was going on seven, my mother took my brother, my twin sister and me, along with our two cousins, to the lake for the entire summer. A poliomyelitis epidemic had scared our family. One distant cousin, who lived across the state from us, and one of my brother's playmates, who lived on the next block, had both contracted the disease. We were taken to the mountains in hopes of escaping this dread crippler.

One day, after some weeks in our mountain retreat, my mother said we got "cabin fever" (boredom). She took all of us kids for a drive, seven miles down the mountain road (part of which was just a dirt and gravel surface) to the nearest civilization, a village called "White House," on the Pennsylvania–West Virginia state line. It had a general store, with a gas pump out front, some small churches, assorted houses. We got gas, groceries, sodas and popsicles and headed farther into civilization to the next town and a moviehouse where we saw a movie and ate popcorn. When my uncle came up to visit for the weekend, he was furious, fearing that we kids had been exposed to polio germs. He felt my mother had undermined the whole escape scheme because she got cabin fever. I guess they had quite an argument. I don't recall hearing it, but years later I remember it being told in a family story. None of us got polio on that day on the town, though there may have been a stomach ache or two in the crowd.

Storytelling was a tradition in our family. Sunday dinners, birthdays, and holidays were always occasions for large family meals followed by storytelling. The cabin provided another scene for storytelling. Sometimes in hot weather evening meals would be served out on the back patio or in front, looking down at the lake. But mostly, I remember sitting at the long picnic table, elbow to elbow, eating fresh sweet corn, tomatoes, and summer squash some local farmer had raised. It was a good feeling of security being in a large family and mealtimes always seemed the happiest times. In the evenings we'd all sit outside, often with weekend visitors, and the grown-ups would talk politics or tell stories of the old days. I can remember them telling some stories over and over, and each time a story was enjoyed as if it were being told for the first time. When darkness fell and the mosquito attacks began, we'd adjourn to the large livingroom. Except for the dead heat of mid-July, the mountain nights were cool and breezy. Usually, there'd be a log fire in the fireplace and the adults would talk some more, long after we'd been tucked in for the night. Sometimes a loud laugh would wake one of us and we'd all sneak out to the hallway or the top of the stairs and eavesdrop, hoping to hear something "juicy." *At such times we never had a care about the future beyond tomorrow's fishing or going berrypicking so Grandma could bake more pies. We didn't know this was a temporary thing.*

However, after having the cabin for about eight years, my uncle sold it for cash to move from an apartment into a house of his own. I don't remember missing it right away. By now we were spending three weeks each summer in Boy Scout and church camps. It would be many years before we'd understand what that lake lodge meant in our lives. We had taken its luxury and beauty for granted. Now that such a property value and such a time as that summer—of carefree play, learning responsibilities of living in nature—are beyond and behind us, we realize its value. And we realize the value of growing up in a large, loving family that looked after us well.

You may notice that the new order of the paragraphs is arranged on the principle of chronology or time. Therefore, I moved the earliest information on the cabin, the building of it (originally part of paragraph nine), to the essay's opening. By placing the paragraph on the cabin's initial history first, I was emphasizing historical information over other types of information. Therefore, some information about daily events, such as the description of the locusts and snakes (originally paragraphs four and five) become much less significant for the new writing purpose. So I deleted paragraphs four and five.

There are other ways of organizing this essay: had I wanted to emphasize the outdoor activities we kids participated in at the lake, I could have chosen a different paragraph sequence and a subsequently different development of ideas. For example, to focus on our fun in the natural environment, I could open the essay with paragraph two to set the scene and then follow with paragraphs six and seven, presented as "story narration." In this type of essay I would develop more details on outdoor activities. I would expand, for example, the information from paragraphs four and five (locusts and snakes) and I might delete paragraphs eight and nine. And I would probably rewrite paragraph 10 (on cabin fever) to focus more on the activities of the day and less on the family conflict over my mother's decision to take us to town.

Still another way of organizing this essay draft would be by comparison and contrast. I could write about the good and bad things at the Lake 0' the Woods. To set up this pattern or arrangement I would make two lists, labeled "Good Things" and "Bad Things." To develop a comparison–contrast essay I would sort all of my information into the two groups; as a result I might have to write out new draft paragraphs, especially to make my writing intention clear to my readers.

However, I chose a chronological order for the essay idea because I wanted to give a historical, or reminiscent, look at a particular time in my life. In addition to placing the events in a particular period of time (post-World War II, polio epidemic), I wanted to emphasize the sense of family history or tradition, the stability and order we sensed from being in our family. Therefore, I "shaped" the ideas to fit that intention. For example, my original draft paragraph eight presented the ideas of large family gatherings at mealtimes and the storytelling that followed. (See p. 83.) To make this paragraph fit better into my evolving idea of family history I began with a new main idea, "Storytelling was a tradition in our family." The germ of this new main idea was buried in the middle of the original paragraph.

There still remains a lot of work before this material can be called an essay, but it is beginning to take shape. I will put it away for a time and return to revise it. You will see the results in the next chapter.

EXERCISES IN DRAFTING

The following exercises are designed to give you practice in the individual drafting procedures just presented.

PART ONE. 1. a. Select a paragraph you have drafted (perhaps one from the exercises at the end of Chapter 2). b. Underline the main idea, circling key words. c. Then number or mark the supporting details. d. Draw a diagram or a figure illustrating the main idea and supporting points. e. Using your diagram or figure only, explain your paragraph idea to a friend or a small group of classmates. f. Finally, immediately after explaining your paragraph idea to someone else, write it out again "from scratch," not referring to your previous draft, diagram, or figure. Discuss the differences between the two drafts with your classmates or write about them in your journal.

2. Circle key words, underline the main ideas, and number or mark the supporting details or ideas in the following paragraphs. Explain to your class, or a small group of your classmates, your reasoning in the decisions you made.

a. Someone asked me why a surgeon would write. Why, when the shelves are already too full? They sag under the deadweight of books. To add a single adverb is to risk exceeding the strength of the boards. A surgeon should abstain. A surgeon, whose fingers are more at home in the steamy gullies of the body than they are tapping the dry keys of a typewriter. A surgeon, who feels the slow slide of intestines against the back of his hand and is no more alarmed than were a family of snakes taking their comfort from such an indolent rubbing. A surgeon, who palms the human heart as though it were some captured bird. Why should he write? Is it vanity that urges him? There is glory enough in the knife. Is it for money? One can make too much money. No. It is to search for some meaning in the ritual of surgery, which is at once murderous, painful, healing, and full of love.[8]

b. Home is not the town, nor the neighborhood, nor even the house in which you were brought up. It is the people. Not just Mom and Dad and brother and sister, it is the kindergarten teacher; the town librarian with the pince-nez glasses; the lady across the street who only gave out apples at Halloween; the best friend who made you feel so obsolete at times; the old maid aunt who substituted for the grandmother whom you never knew; the boy who taught you how to kiss, and then, how to cry. These things are home. It is the knowledge and joy that is gained from these people. When this warmth is taken away there is nothing. Yet, it will never be taken away, for it is stored in a secret compartment in the mind and when memory revives this warmth, this familiarity, the heart swells.

PART TWO. 1. Using the set of information provided below and that from Chapter 2 on pp. 33–34, follow these directions:

- Read over the writing notes.
- Select a main idea from one of the areas: particle, wave, or field; or describe, compare, associate, and so on. Write your main idea on a sheet of paper.
- Write out several points to support the main idea you have selected.
- Draw a diagram or figure illustrating the paragraph idea you have designed.
- Explain your paragraph idea to a friend or to a small group of classmates. Write down any modifications you may see needed as a result of your explanation.
- Write out a draft of the paragraph.

2. Again, using appropriate information from the set provided below, draft an essay for *one* of the following situations.
Note: You may develop new information as well.

a. You have asked your academic adviser (or academic dean) for a letter of recommendation to an employer who is considering you for a part-time job. You are explaining to the adviser (or dean) that taking this job is important, because it may lead to a full-time job offer after you graduate.

b. You are explaining to your academic adviser (or dean) that you must drop a course this semester and take on a part-time job in order to support yourself partially.

Topic: Holding a part-time job
Method: Particle, wave, and field (PWF)

Particle
- specific area of interest
- jobs available: newspaper ads
- amount of time available to work
- reason why job needed
- hourly wage rate
- transportation and other costs involved with job

Wave
- relation of this job to types of work you have done in the past: building experience and developing skills
- working with others
- how long you plan on holding this job
- wage raises at regular intervals
- changing duties with more experience on the job
- possibilities for advancement in this line of work

Field
- how working changes you as a student (e.g. your study habits, social relationships, participation in organized sports, and so on)
- how this job fits in with your long-range career goals

3. Suppose that you are in *one* of the situations below.

a. You are a member of a student government committee that has been asked to draft a report to the student union programming board on the effects of having video games on campus.

b. You are a member of a student government committee negotiating with a video-game corporation for holding a regional competition at your campus next semester. Of course, your committee is attempting to get the corporation to assume all of the costs associated with the event. You write a draft of the proposal.

c. You are a city council member working on a program to restore abandoned buildings in your community. You are to draft an argument to a federal funding agency to provide money for mortgages and building improvements.

Note: You may use relevant information from Chapter 2, if you wish. (See pp. 36–38 and 40–41.) Or, develop your own information according to one of the methods presented in the last chapter.

A CONCLUDING NOTE

I want to repeat something from the opening of the chapter: look at drafting as a painter looks at sketching, as an initial search for form and meaning, as trial and error. A writer's job is not complete even though his or her first draft appears to be an essay. While a writer may be addressing the questions listed on pages 57 and 58 while drafting an essay from writing notes, essentially the writer is explaining a topic to himself or herself during the initial drafting. As the writer learns more about the topic, the drafting is reassessed and the questions readdressed.

Depending on the topic and the writing situation writers' experiences with drafting can be pleasurable or painful. Here's how William Howarth describes author John McPhee's process of drafting:

Writing a first draft is painful work for any writer, whether it moves like lightning or like glue. McPhee spends twelve-hour stints at his office, not writing constantly, but "concentrating" and distilling his research into prose. Some authors overwrite and later boil down; he culls before ever typing a phrase. He likens this method to the sport of curling, where great effort is spent sweeping the ice clean to advance each shot. With writing comes the need for endless decisions, mostly on what *not* to say, what to eliminate. The process is nerve-racking and lonely. His family sees less of him, he also cuts off most visitors and phone calls. Sometimes he talks to editors or friends about problems, but then generally follows his own counsel. Facing the typewriter for long stretches, he generates excess energy like a breeder reactor. A fly buzzing at sun-struck windows is not more manic, and often hard physical exercise is a welcome distraction. Tennis, squash, and basketball are favorite outlets; he professes to play at a level that "attracts ample company and no attention." In fact, he is capable of great intensity on the court, but he dislikes opponents who are arrogant or childish. Arthur Ashe plays in McPhee's preferred style, unpredictably full of contours and strata. Writing is the same sort of game: he has spent a long time learning to move *against* a habitual thought or phrase, which is always the easiest, oldest rut to follow.[9]

No matter how pleasurable or painful drafting is for you, now that you finally have written out your ideas in sentences and paragraphs, they may look good to you upon first glance. On the other hand, you may have had a difficult struggle getting to this point: looking quickly over your draft, you may think the ideas are not worth much. Do not trust your judgment at this point. You need a rest period (as long as time permits) in order to forget your recent writing history with this particular draft. So, take a break before going on to revise according to the guidelines set forth in the next chapter.

NOTES

1. Eustace Chesser, *Is Chastity Outmoded?* (London: The Windmill Press, 1960), p. 81.
2. Ibid., p. 86.
3. Ibid., p. 87.
4. "The New Morality," *Time*, 21 November 1977, p. 111.

5. Information in these lists was modified from *Beginner's BASIC* (Lubbock, Texas: Texas Instruments Inc., 1981), pp. 5–6.

6. Robert C. McClelland, *Masontown, Pennsylvania, And Its Environs: A Contribution to Their History* (Norfolk, Virginia: The Norfolk College of William and Mary, 1962), p. 126.

7. Information in Tables 3.1, 3.2, and 3.3 comes from Donald M. Vickery, *Life Plan For Your Health* (Reading, Massachusetts: Addison-Wesley Publishing Company, 1978), pp. 136–137, 139–140, 141–142.

8. Richard Selzer, *Mortal Lessons: Notes on the Art of Surgery* (New York: Simon and Schuster, 1976), p. 15.

9. William L. Howarth, ed., *The John McPhee Reader* (New York: Random House, 1977), p. xvii.

4

REVISING

Writing develops like a seed,
not like a line.[1]

Completing an essay draft often exhilarates a writer, just as reaching the 10-mile mark often gives a marathon runner an emotional high. However, the runner has 16 more miles to go to complete the marathon, a test of skill and endurance. The writer, too, has quite a way to go before finishing the writing assignment, but one big difference is that writers retrace their steps again and again, that is, go over again and again their putting of ideas into words to compose meaning. Rather than stretching out neatly in a straight line one after another, as the runner's feet progress on course, the writer's ideas spread out in many directions at once. To do a thorough job of developing and focusing their ideas, writers search back and forth over the entire course of their zigzag and circuitous thinking. This is difficult and time-consuming work; it is also a test of skill and endurance.

Roland Barthes uses a different comparison to illustrate this point; he says that rather than developing by placing word after word in a line, writing sprouts like a seed, sending out stem, taproot and lateral roots to support the plant. Both comparisons are meant to convey the idea that writing is a complex activity; a writer's thoughts go out in many directions at once and it takes diligence to pursue them and write them down in a meaningful form.

Revising the writing that evolves from such a complex process cannot be done effectively in one sitting, nor at one stage in the writing process. Thus, writers develop the habit of continually reviewing their writing. Throughout the composing process, they revise, in other words, re-see, look at their writing intention anew and compare it to the form they are giving it in the text being drafted. Conversely, writers continually look at the written text for what it can teach them, for what they can discover from it. Whether the writing purpose or the meaning which is evolving from the text is more dominant in shaping the final essay form is often a matter of the particular writing situation. The key is that writers always examine their writing in relation to the intended meaning as well as being open to discovering new possibilities from their newly written words.

Like drafting, revising is a dynamic process; while the steps in the process are identifiable, they are not reducible to separate and sequential, recipe-like steps. However, in this chapter as in the last, I present revising activities in a step-by-step fashion in order to demonstrate them. Follow the guidelines as long as they serve you helpfully, but be flexible, modifying, combining, and repeating activities as you define your own revising process. After some weeks of focused writing practice—experimenting with discovery methods, practicing drafting procedures, and working with revising strategies—you will begin to move easily from one operation to the other and back again.

REVISING PROCEDURES

To help you develop the writer's practice of revising here are some strategies which may be illustrated this way:

Look for the Pattern

Let's suppose you have just drafted a paper. After a respite from your drafting activities, at least an interval of a day or so, reread the draft. Read carefully, but do not pause to ponder minor details. At this point do not fuss over editing details: spelling, punctuation, and so on. Rather, focus your attention on the overall pattern of the piece. Ask yourself, "What is the piece's pattern?" In other words, what is the main idea? How is it stated? Or, How is it implied? In what way is the main idea developed and supported? Ask yourself if you've gone about developing your ideas in the best way.

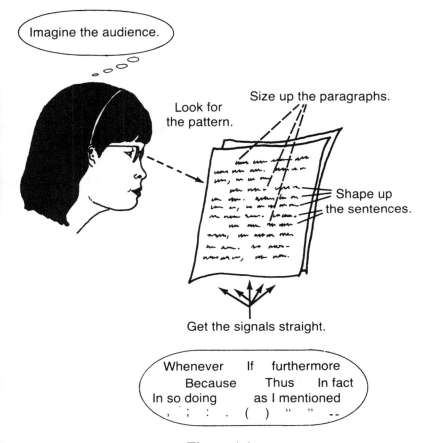

Figure 4.1

To identify the main idea, read through your draft a paragraph at a time. Circle key words and underline what you believe to be the central, or major, point of the paragraph. Test your identification of the main idea by drawing a diagram or a figure to represent it and the supporting details of the paragraph. Using your diagram or figure, explain your writing idea to someone else. Jot down other ideas that occur to you during this testing procedure and incorporate them into the paragraph as appropriate.

To test the effectiveness of your supporting details, ask several questions about them: Do they illustrate, explain, or justify my main idea? Do they seem sufficient or are more details re-

quired to make the point clear and convincing? Are the connections between my main idea and the supporting details clear?

It is likely that you may come to see a new or expanded main
idea. Reorganize and rewrite on the basis of your new understanding of the topic. Do not be tied down to your original idea, sentence, and paragraph arrangements. It may be very difficult for
you to throw away whole sentences and paragraphs from your
first draft, but do so if they stand in the way of expanding or
creating a new organizing principle for your writing.

For example, when Ellen began writing about her experiences
as a swimmer, she drafted an essay organized chronologically,
beginning with her experiences as an infant; here are the opening
lines:

I have always liked water. Even as a baby, I never minded
taking a bath. Like most babies, my sisters dreaded this activity and particularly hated having their hair washed. While
they screamed at the top of their lungs, I would sit placidly
as my mother poured the water over my head. However, when
I began swimming lessons at age four, I quickly found that
my favorite place was under water. As part of our lessons,
we often played Ring-Around-the-Rosy. Upon chanting,
"Husha, Husha, we all fall down!" we all ducked our heads
down into the water. At this point I used to like to stay down
and would only come up when my teacher pulled me up.

Consequently I spent many of my summers' hours at the
nearby pool. Though I occasionally swam laps, my favorite
activity remained swimming underwater. I dreamed of the
time when "they" would include this skill as an Olympic event.
Muffled cheers rang in my ears as I practiced gliding from
one end of the pool to the other, trying not to come up for
air.

This activity also gave me a pleasant sense of aloneness.
Loud noises became hushed, movements slowed, and the gentle touch of the water cooled my skin. The water lifting my
hair accentuated my feeling of weightlessness as I floated
peacefully through this liquid environment.

At age 12, my penchant for submerging myself led to a
very few suspenseful moments for those with their feet firmly
planted on the soil.

As she reread the draft paragraphs Ellen discovered that her original main idea ("I have always liked water") was not as compelling to her as another one which emerged from one of her originally subordinate points ("This activity also gave me a pleasant sense of aloneness.") Using this new idea of seeking solitude in the pool as her organizing principle, Ellen rewrote the opening this way:

> As a 12-year-old child, I spent many of my summer's hours at the nearby pool. Though most of my friends saw it only as a place to "cool off," I looked on the pool as my personal haven. Suffering from the effects of puberty, I personified Jekyll and Hyde. My moods rapidly shifted from very high to very low. The pool offered me temporary escape from my disconcerting and frenzied existence. I worked off some of my nervous energy swimming laps. However, I preferred swimming most of these laps underwater.
>
> Underwater swimming gave me a pleasant sense of solitude. Diving into seven feet of water, I would hover, a sea horse, near the floor of the pool. Loud noises hushed and my movements slowed. Almost imperceptibly, the water lifted my hair as I drifted weightless through this liquid environment. From above, the sunlight cast a hazy glow on churning brown arms and legs. I loved this feeling of numb detachment. Water dulled my senses, a welcome respite for my frazzled nerve endings which new hormones racing through my system had set jangling.

You can see that Ellen's new main idea is represented in these two sentences: "I looked at the pool as my personal haven," and "Underwater swimming gave me a pleasant sense of solitude." Using this idea to reorganize her thinking about her swimming experiences, Ellen generated ideas that had not occurred to her before. She also found much of her earlier information irrelevant and therefore discarded it. Such dramatic changes in one's writing goals are common to writers who look anew at the ideas in their drafts.

Imagine the Audience

When you began developing ideas for writing, and when you first sketched out those thoughts in sentences, you were explaining to yourself what you knew about the topic. Now that you have done so and have had time to reflect and to begin reshaping those sentences out of a better understanding of the topic, you are free to consider the needs of your readers.

We call those readers the audience, even though they don't hear us speak our words as an audience hears a musician play a concerto. The principle is the same: like a musician, you are performing in order to communicate to others.

To imagine the audience answer these questions as fully as you can: Who will read your essay? What do you know about their age level, interests, educational, social, and economic background? What can you assume that they will know about your topic? What must you explain? If your intention is to entertain them, what is the best method to use? If you want to persuade them, how can you be convincing and not offensive? If you plan to educate them, how can you teach them something without sounding dull and boring, or without "talking down" to them? In order to meet these concerns about audience, pretend that you are reading each sentence to a small group of people seated around a table with you. Imagine what the audience's response will be to each one and revise on the basis of your estimate. (See Chapter 5 for a further discussion of audience.)

Size Up the Paragraphs

There are no rigid rules for building paragraphs; paragraphs are dynamic units of thought which can be developed in several ways. As you revise, ask yourself whether all the sentences in a paragraph relate to a common idea, whether the sentences fit together like jigsaw-puzzle pieces, and whether the sentences develop the common idea sufficiently.

In turn, also ask yourself about the relationships of paragraphs: Do all the paragraphs relate to the main idea or organizing principle of the essay? Are the ideas clearly connected? In other words, do the paragraph ideas move from one to the other in an interlocking pattern? Or are there gaps where one paragraph idea leaves off and the following one picks up the discourse?

For an example let us look again at Ellen's *first* draft, beginning where we left off last time:

It happened one night. One of my junior lifesaving instructors asked me if I would like to walk on the bottom of the pool.

Eagerly I replied that I did. He handed me an eight-pound weight belt. Normally we used this belt to simulate a dead body lying on the bottom of the pool. Excitedly I put it on and then stepped off the side into 10 feet of water.

Walking along the floor of the pool reminded me of an astronaut walking on the surface of the moon. I expended a huge amount of energy to travel a minimal distance. However, my efforts succeeded in bringing me some distance away from the side of the pool. Needing air, I started to surface with some difficulty. The weight belt held me back quite a bit. Finally I burst into the waning sunlight. Unfortunately, my maternalistically inclined sister had decided that I was drowning. As I came up, she latched on to one of my wrists so that she could drag me to safety. Having accustomed myself to below-sea-level activity, I in no way agreed with her hypothesis. Annoyed, I shook loose crying, "Get out of here!!"

Among the observations you may make about these paragraph drafts is the fact that they are very loosely constructed; they have little coherence other than the mere energy of the narrative flow holding them together: first this happened and then that. Also, most statements carry general information rather than specific detail. This may well become much more evident when you read Ellen's revision. The one bit of specific detail in this draft which is engaging is her fantasizing while underwater ("astronaut walking on the surface of the moon"). In revising, Ellen seizes upon this specific detail to redesign the paragraphs into an engaging story:

I played alone, an adventurer on a quest for exciting and heroic action. A pool tag clenched between my teeth became a hunting knife and suddenly I assumed the identity of Tarzania, Queen of the Jungle. Snaking through murky waters, I pushed aside hungry piranha, knowing that fierce and cannibalistic warriors hunted for me on the surface. The word "danger" meant nothing to me . . .

Other times I was Mata Hari sent to infiltrate enemy lines on a secret nighttime mission. By squinting my eyes, the light blue water of the pool was transformed into the dark gray waters of the English Channel. Though the current tried to pull me back, my stroke remained strong and graceful. In record time, I traversed the Channel underwater, a feat never performed by any other human being . . .

One time, my penchant for submerging myself almost led to an early demise. On this particular night, one of my junior lifesaving instructors asked me if I would like to walk on the floor of the pool. Eagerly I replied that I did. He handed me an eight-pound weight belt, normally used in simulating a dead body on the bottom. Excitedly I buckled it on and jumped into 10 feet of water. As I descended, I underwent yet another of my metamorphoses.

"Her feet touched bottom. E. F. Finch, deep sea diver and underwater scientist, began exploring the ocean floor, searching for the flora whose distillate would prove the cure for cancer. She expended a huge amount of energy to travel a short distance, but the effort was worth it if she could save the world from the horrors of that dread disease . . ."

Not having Dr. Finch's oxygen tanks, I interrupted my reveries to come up for air. The weight belt held me down, making my ascent very difficult and, also, tiring. When I reached the surface, I found my sister waiting for me. Sure that I was drowning, she latched on to one of my wrists to drag me to safety. I shook loose like a person who does not wish to be awakened from a pleasant dream.

Thus, finding a new writing purpose for this essay enabled Ellen to write paragraphs which contain concrete supporting details, relate closely to the main point, and develop the ideas sufficiently.

Shape Up the Sentences

Grammatically speaking, a sentence is a set of words, usually a subject and a predicate (a verb and its complement) which conveys a complete thought. If you have difficulty writing grammatical sentences consistently, consult a handbook of English grammar and ask your instructor to give you some exercises to practice until you develop the ability to write grammatical sentences in all of your finished work. (Also, consult Chapter 6.) But merely writing grammatical or correct sentences is not good enough to satisfy most readers' demands for interesting sentences. Not only should you size up your sentences for a style that will interest readers, but also you should look for ways of expressing your ideas more clearly in fewer words, of connecting ideas more fully within sentences, and of varying the sentence patterns and lengths.

One method of sizing up your sentences is to read them aloud separately, beginning with the last sentence in your paper and moving forward to the first. When you read a sentence in which the meaning or sound doesn't seem quite right, copy it on a separate sheet of paper and write out two different versions of it: first, write out the idea of the original sentence in the simplest, shortest sentence possible; second, write out the idea of the original sentence using more style and word texture. See if either version sounds better in context with the sentences preceding and following it. Perhaps neither of the two new versions is quite right, but an amalgam of them, a third version, makes the best sentence sound and sense.

For example, here is a sentence from Ellen's original draft and two revisions of it:

Original Version

My need for air now desperate, my fingers tore away the clasp of the belt.

Shorter, Clearer Version

Now desperate for air, I tore away the belt clasp.

More Stylish Version

Like a fish out of water, I was desperate for air and clawed viciously at the clasp of the heavy belt.

Set the Tone

By sizing up the paragraphs and shaping up the sentences, you may already have set an appropriate, consistent tone in your writing. In speaking, tone, or the varying sounds of your voice, carries your meaning just as much as the words do. In writing, the words carry tone and meaning simultaneously. The tone of your language arises out of the form of the language or the way it reads and appears on the page. So you must spend some time deciding what tone is appropriate for your writing purpose and for the audience. Certainly you want to develop a versatile, varying tone, while staying within your range of voice, one that is natural to you. (No good soprano would try to sing second bass, although she might be capable of singing mezzo soprano.)

Practice writing within your voice until you feel you have created an appropriate tone. To see if you set an appropriate tone and maintain it throughout the piece, read the piece aloud or tape it and play it back while imagining audience response. Let someone else read the piece and listen to the tone as it comes through another's voice. (See Chapter 5 for further discussion of voice.)

Ellen concluded her first draft in an inappropriate, flippant tone:

> Well, I didn't drown but I sure as hell killed off an awful lot of brain cells. This might explain why I asked to walk on the bottom of the pool again the very next night. Anyway, though I still enjoy an occasional underwater lap through the pool, it no longer fascinates me as it did when I was a child.

Perhaps her problem with tone resulted from her uncertainty about what point she really wanted to make in writing the essay, because in her revision—when she discovered a new writing purpose—her concluding remarks and the tone in which she wrote them took on new seriousness:

> I had been under for almost four minutes when I pushed through into the waning sunlight. Two lifeguards stood poised on the edge, readying themselves to retrieve my dead body. Though I *did* almost drown, I look back favorably on this experience. It taught me several things about myself. I found that I could act rationally in a situation where many other people would have panicked. Suddenly I felt more intelligent, braver, and more mature than ever before. This experience brought me to the realization that no matter what problem or crisis I face, like Odysseus, I will survive.

Get the Signals Straight

In the last chapter while discussing connecting and combining ideas, I illustrated the use of transition words and phrases. As you revise a draft, it is again time to look at idea transitions. But this time look at them from a slightly different perspective: Consider the reader's need for assistance in moving from one idea to the next. Your reader is not familiar with your material as you are. It's all news to him or her. So, whenever possible, prepare the reader for idea transitions. For an example, let's reread two versions of one of Ellen's short paragraphs. Here's the original version:

> It happened one night. One of my junior lifesaving instructors asked me if I would like to walk on the bottom of the pool. Eagerly I replied that I did. He handed me an eight-pound weight belt. Normally we used this belt to simulate a dead body lying on the bottom of the pool. Excitedly I put it on and then stepped off the side into 10 feet of water.

And here's her revision which contains new ideas in addition to new connections and transition markers. I have circled transition words and italicized newly connected or combined ideas.

> (One time,) my penchant for submerging myself almost led to an early demise. (On this particular night,) one of my junior lifesaving instructors asked me if I would like to walk on the floor of the pool. Eagerly I replied that I did. *He handed me an eight-pound weight belt, normally used in simulating a dead body on the bottom. Excitedly I buckled it on and jumped into 10 feet of water.* (As I descended,) I underwent yet another of my metamorphoses.

Writers also use punctuation marks to aid readers. Like traffic signals and road signs, punctuation marks tell readers whether to continue reading full speed ahead, to slow down for curves of meaning, to pause at an intersection between two ideas, or to stop at the end of a thought. For your reader's sake make certain that you use appropriate punctuation marks. Just as faulty traffic signals can cause traffic jams or accidents, so faulty punctuation can confuse readers or cause them to mistake your meaning.

By your use of punctuation, you also determine how your writing will be read. Changing certain punctuation marks can make significant changes in meaning. For example, read the two versions of the passages below. How is meaning affected by the punctuation changes?

Version 1

The most profitable kind of computer crime is program adjustment, while this may be the most technologically advanced white-collar crime. Increased knowledge of computer programming has made it quite widespread. Programs can be adjusted to accomplish just about anything if one can figure out how to use them. There is virtually no chance of being caught.

Version 2

The most profitable kind of computer crime is program adjustment. While this may be the most technologically advanced white-collar crime, increased knowledge of computer programming has made it quite widespread. Programs can be adjusted to accomplish just about anything. If one can figure out how to use them, there is virtually no chance of being caught.

Version 1

Mark suffered from several symptoms he exhibited: arm waving, compulsive handwashing, obsessive smelling of objects, and severe temper tantrums. Most of these behaviors began at two years old when they were excessive enough to be considered abnormal. Mark was hospitalized for treatment.

Version 2

Mark suffered from several symptoms. He exhibited arm waving, compulsive handwashing, obsessive smelling of objects, and severe temper tantrums. Most of these behaviors began at two years old. When they were excessive enough to be considered abnormal, Mark was hospitalized for treatment.

While punctuation is usually considered a matter for editing, I present it here as a concern for revising as well as editing. When writers edit their writing, they make certain that the punctuation marks are *correct* and when they revise their writing, they make certain that their punctuation marks are *appropriate* for their writing's meaning.

Note: Consult the punctuation guide in your college dictionary or a handbook of grammar and punctuation to check the signals you send to the reader. Watch especially for misuse of the comma; since we use the comma frequently for so many different types of pauses, it is easy to use it unnecessarily or when we should use another punctuation mark, for example, a semicolon or a period.

Since you have seen portions of Ellen's essay in the process of revision, perhaps you would like to see the entire piece revised. There is still some reworking and editing left to be done on it, but the new writing idea has been pretty well shaped up.

As a twelve-year-old child, I spent many of my summer's hours at the nearby pool. Though most of my friends saw it only as a place to "cool off," I looked on the pool as my personal haven. Suffering from the effects of puberty, I personified Jekyll and Hyde. My moods rapidly shifted from very high to very low. The pool offered me temporary escape from my disconcerting and frenzied existence. I worked off some of my nervous energy swimming laps. However, I preferred swimming most of these laps underwater.

Underwater swimming gave me a pleasant sense of solitude. Diving into seven feet of water, I would hover, a sea horse, near the floor of the pool. Loud noises hushed and my movements slowed. Almost imperceptibly, the water lifted my hair as I drifted weightless through this liquid environment. From above, the sunlight cast a hazy glow on churning brown arms and legs. I loved this feeling of numb detachment. Water dulled my senses, a welcome respite for my frazzled nerve endings which new hormones racing through my system had set jangling.

I played alone, an adventurer on a quest for exciting and heroic action. A pool tag clenched between my teeth became a hunting knife and suddenly I assumed the identity of Tarzania, Queen of the Jungle. Snaking through murky waters, I pushed aside hungry piranha, knowing that fierce and cannibalistic warriors hunted for me on the surface. The word "danger" meant nothing to me . . .

Other times I was Mata Hari sent to infiltrate enemy lines on a secret nighttime mission. By squinting my eyes, the light blue water of the pool was transformed into the dark gray waters of the English Channel. Though the current tried to pull me back, my stroke remained strong and graceful. In record time, I traversed the Channel underwater, a feat never performed by any other human being . . .

One time my penchant for submerging myself almost led to an early demise. On this particular night, one of my junior lifesaving instructors asked me if I would like to walk on the floor of the pool. Eagerly I replied that I did. He handed me an eight-pound weight belt, normally used in simulating a dead body on the bottom. Excitedly I buckled it on and jumped into 10 feet of water. As I descended I underwent yet another of my metamorphoses.

"Her feet touched bottom. E. F. Finch, deep sea diver and underwater scientist, began exploring the ocean floor, searching for the flora whose distillate would prove the cure for cancer. She expended a huge amount of energy to travel a short distance, but the effort was worth it if she could save the world from the horrors of that dread disease . . ."

Not having Dr. Finch's oxygen tanks, I interrupted my reveries to come up for air. The weight belt held me down, making my ascent very difficult and, also, tiring. When I reached the surface, I found my sister waiting for me. Sure that I was drowning, she latched on to one of my wrists to drag me to safety. I shook loose like a person who does not wish to be awakened from a pleasant dream.

Quickly I dropped back down through 10 feet of water. Unhappily I noticed I had inhaled little of the air I needed in fighting off my would-be-rescuer. My first ascent having sapped my strength, I knew I must get rid of the weight hugging my waist. Pulling up on the buckle, I discovered the catch had jammed.

Suddenly my sister appeared. Again she seized my wrist. Irritated by this intrusion, I tried to wrest my arm from her vise-like grip. I knew she could never carry me to the surface with the belt around my middle. Furthermore, I needed both hands to undo the belt. Precious seconds flew by as we struggled. At last, she left me alone.

Now desperate for air, I tore away the belt clasp. As the belt slid to the floor, I kicked towards the surface, clawing my way to the top, neck outstretched so that my nose would strike air first. My heart pounded in my ears and the impulse to inhale almost overwhelmed me.

I had been under for almost four minutes when I pushed through into the waning sunlight. Two lifeguards stood poised on the edge, readying themselves to retrieve my dead body. Though I *did* almost drown, I look back favorably on this experience. It taught me several things about myself. I found that I could act rationally in a situation where many other people would have panicked. Suddenly I felt more intelligent, braver, and more mature than ever before. This experience brought me to the realization that no matter what problem or crisis I face, like Odysseus, I will survive.

Revising Activities Demonstrated: Part One

Let me discuss each of the six revising activities I employed while reworking the "Lake O' the Woods" draft. (See pp. 86–90.) As I stated about drafting procedures, revising activities are dynamic and interrelated. Thus, I did not follow them rigidly from first to last. Rather, I moved back and forth over various drafting and revising activities. Sometimes I also worked on two activities in the same operation. However, for demonstration purposes, I discuss the activities separately, although you can see that they are often interdependent. As you read through this section, you may wish to refer to the completed revision which appears on pp. 115–119.

Look for the Pattern

Rereading the draft of "Lake O' the Woods" several days after writing it, I see that the draft contains primarily a description of the cabin and an accounting of some of my family's activities there. You may recall my discussion in the last chapter (p. 78) about reshaping the original major point of the essay. As I stated, the more I thought about it, the more I saw the possibility of expanding my purpose to show that the activities carried a sense of family tradition and warmth during a time when the larger scene was threatening (post-World War II, polio epidemic). Using this expanded focus on the topic, I reexamine each paragraph, adding and deleting significant portions of information to redesign the overall pattern of the essay. For example, the essay's emphasis had to be shifted from the cabin as an object (particle) to the cabin as a place of family life during one period of time (wave); furthermore, revised concluding remarks could place this essay or "story" of the cabin in context with other stories in the family's oral tradition which were used to bind it together (wave and field).

Imagine the Audience

I retitle the essay "A Cabin of Family Stories" to inform the reader directly and initially of the general topic. Still, I hope the title leaves enough unsaid to stimulate the reader to read on, looking for a fuller understanding of the title's meaning.

I open the essay as a story because storytelling is an effective way to engage an audience's attention and because I want to illustrate one of my family's traditions, namely, storytelling itself. Since I was originally writing this essay for my writing class, few of whom were born until a decade after the time of the events, I had to sketch enough social history to set a historical context for the personal drama. Rather than writing an expository paragraph on the postwar era, I weave ideas about the current events into the story and I rely on the use of special words to set the scene. (I say more about this in the section "Set the Tone" below.)

In revising the portions of the essay that present the cabin and the kids' activities, I devise ways of inviting the audience to make connections between the place or activity and the meaning it held for my family. To accomplish this I sometimes make an explicit statement, about sibling rivalry for instance, or I refer to my family using the incident as a tie that binds by recalling it in a story years later.

Size Up the Paragraphs

Enlarging the organizing principle of the draft requires performing major surgery on the paragraph organization. Comparing the draft to the revised version, you can see several additions, deletions, and rearrangements of material. For example, I select key activities out of paragraphs three through six, reorganizing them and adding summary or interpretive comments on them. Furthermore, I discard certain less significant details or relegate them to single sentences; for example, compare the original paragraphs seven and eight (pp. 88–89) with their rearranged and revised versions (pp. 117–118). In addition to reshaping paragraphs in the body of the paper, I make significant additions to the introductory and concluding paragraphs in order to establish and summarize the essay's main points.

Shape Up the Sentences

Numerous sentence revisions appear in the final version. Here are a few examples and comments on them:

Original (from paragraph three)

A six-foot-wide dock was built from the shore into the water.

Revision (begins paragraph five)

A six-foot-wide dock protruded 25 feet into the water.

The revision changes the sentence from passive to active verb voice, adds detail (25 feet), and eliminates an unnecessary prepositional phrase.

Original (second sentence in paragraph five)

I remember that we kids took swimming lessons at the YMCA so that we would know how to swim well at the lake.

Revision (begins paragraph six)

Mother had enrolled us kids in YMCA swimming lessons to be assured that we could swim safely at the lake.

This revision focuses on the fact that we children took swimming lessons to relieve Mother's concern about safety.

Original (begins paragraph nine)

I don't remember how old I was when we first started going to the lake, but around the summer of 1950, when I was going on seven, my mother took my brother, my twin sister, and me to the lake for the entire summer. A poliomyelitis epidemic had scared our family.

Revision (begins paragraph 10)

One summer around 1950, when I was about seven, we were quarantined at the lake. My mother took us three kids to the lake for the entire summer because a poliomyelitis epidemic had scared our family.

Besides reducing the length of the passage by eliminating unnecessary words, the revision sharpens the main idea by adding "quarantined" and by linking the action to its cause with the subordinate conjunction "because."

Set the Tone

I rely on a number of elements to set the tone, the primary one of which is the opening narrative paragraph. To evoke the postwar era I use special words, such as "bittersweet," "matériel," "barracks," and "round of enemy artillery fire." I attempt to recreate the sense of the cabin being built: "digging and pouring footers," "measured boards precisely," "mitered their ends true," "hammer's echo." Other words set the tone of a poignant, nostalgic backward glance in which the grandfather and his sons are enveloped in an aura of hard work and devotion to family: "it rose out of the skill, strength and dogged persistence of an aging father and his three sons," a "sense of family pride and unity."

Get the Signals Straight

In the last chapter I pointed out the connecting and combining I did while drafting the essay. Throughout the revising process, as I continue to reformulate the essay, it is necessary to make new idea connections, combinations, and transitions. For example, look at paragraphs six and seven in the draft (p. 88). You may notice that the last sentence of paragraph six is not well connected to the rest of the paragraph idea, nor does it lead into the idea in the next paragraph. In the revision (p. 117) I remove that sentence to another paragraph; this leaves paragraph six with better sentence unity. Then in the new paragraph I create the transition idea of family storytelling as a lead into the following paragraph about our quarantine.

Although I use standard punctuation, I frequently use the semicolon to show close relationship between ideas in separate sentences, the colon to introduce a series of items, and quotation marks on occasion to indicate special emphasis.

Here is the completed revision. After you read it you may refer to the original draft to examine the results of revising. Remember that while there are changes at all levels (word, sentence, and paragraph), the changes all resulted from my reseeing my purpose in writing on the topic.

A CABIN OF FAMILY STORIES

They built it in a single summer during the days following World War II, bittersweet days for Mother: her brothers returned from the war against Hitler, but her husband did not. The second oldest brother, who had taken over the family business, bought the lakefront property in northern West Virginia for a mountain retreat. He procured wood from army surplus matériel; as barracks were dismantled, the beams, boards, and windows were sold to build homes, businesses, and in this case, a summer cabin.

Although it belonged to Uncle Tom, from beginning to end it was a family affair. With Grandfather planning and supervising each day's work, the brothers threw themselves into digging and pouring footers, erecting the frame, and nailing on the sides and roof. They would hire a plumber and a stonemason, and others would pitch in from time to time. But it rose out of the skill, strength, and dogged persistence of an aging father and his three sons. For the father it was the familiar challenge of creating something useful and beautiful. In his prime he had supervised the building of imposing, multipurpose structures, for his private business and for his community government. But this was an opportunity to work with his sons as grown men, reunited after a long separation during the war years, years of uncertainty and worry he could now forget as he measured boards precisely, mitered their ends true, and shouted at his sons to nail them just so to make the joint. For the sons it was the chance to pound away frightful memories, knowing that the clap of sound was the hammer's echo off the lake, not a round of enemy artillery fire. To be sure there were disputes; these four men's lifelong divergent views and personal differences survived the war intact, but they stuck with the project to its completion. It may have been the building itself which held them together, but I like to think it was their sense of family pride and unity.

Too young to witness any of the cabin's beginnings, I would learn of it piecemeal some years later as the men told the family history after Sunday dinners at the cabin, and retold it years later following Sunday dinners at home long after the cabin had been sold.

What we always called the cabin, others referred to as a lodge: a two-story, white frame structure with knotty-pine interior walls, hardwood floors, a small, well-equipped kitchen, a dining area with a long, picnic-style table (this, too, from army surplus), a spacious livingroom with a stone fireplace, exposed 20 feet from floor to ceiling. A large wagon-wheel light fixture of chimneyed lights hung over the livingroom. Three bedrooms were tucked away in the second-story loft where my brother, my sister, and I slept in bunkbeds. A master bedroom and bath led off the livingroom. Antique rugs, lamps, and furnishings appointed the rooms.

The green crystal lake stood 150 yards down a sloping hillside from the cabin. We viewed it from the large picture window in the livingroom or through the French doors which led outside from the dining area. Midway between the cabin and the lake a large dinner bell hung on a post, encircled by a loveseat. I never saw any lovers on the seat, but we kids would run around the seat ringing the bell until an adult made us stop. The bell was reserved for announcing mealtime or calling for help.

A six-foot-wide dock protruded 25 feet into the water. One of those first summers they drained the lake to allow the residents to build docks. My father's younger brother dug the footholes and sunk the pilings; my other uncles constructed the frame and laid the plank flooring. A few summers later when the dock needed repainting Mother put us kids to work, stripped down to our shorts so we wouldn't ruin our clothes with the oil-based paint. The morning of painting went rapidly; by noon we had coated the dock as well as our hands, arms, legs, and feet. The strong summer sun had also burned us, so where our skin wasn't painted white, it was bright pink. My aunt rubbed turpentine onto our sunburned skin to remove the paint. When they retold the story some time later, they said we screamed and jumped as if we had St. Vitus's dance.

Mother had enrolled us kids in YMCA swimming lessons to be assured that we could swim safely at the lake. We swam around the dock and played tag games underneath it, holding onto the pilings and climbing over the wooden structure underneath it. We never wanted to leave the water even when it was cold. My mother would say, "Come here this minute;

your lips are blue!" Uncle Tom taught us to dive off the dock, encouraging us with directions, "Point your arms over your head, palms together. Bend over and point your hands at the water. Now jump!" Holding us by our ankles, he would give us a flip when we jumped to get our legs up and prevent a bellyflop. Somehow we learned to dive. When we told the story later, we wondered how many times our uncle had to flip our legs up until we got the knack.

About 20 yards off the dock's end they had anchored a 10-foot square float made of planks bolted to a base of 55-gallon drums. My brother and I raced to the float and back to the dock countless times. Finally, we built up enough endurance and courage to swim the width of the lake and back. I know I wouldn't have attempted it had it not been for his encouragement. Encouragement? More like the older brother's dare. I swam to save face.

My brother and I competed at boat rowing, too. He and I were always seeing who could row farthest. And we always wanted to row for adults who went out fishing in the boat. I remember our taking my aunt's father, Dr. Wells, fishing when he visited. He really liked us kids and he had funny country-wise sayings for things. For example, he always brought very long night crawlers which he called "snakes." So we started calling worms "snakes," too, and laughed and thought of Dr. Wells everytime.

Although I don't remember fishing much, we apparently did quite a lot, according to family history. Of course somehow I learned how to bait a hook (as well as my squeamish sister's) and how to take fish off the hook without getting stuck by the fins. But fishing isn't as uppermost in my memory as picking berries, being frightened by a blacksnake, collecting locust shells, and playing with the shy boy next door, whom mother said was filthy rich. These are the things I recall most vividly.

Of course, we warmed so many winter evenings with cabin tales that sometimes now I can't distinguish between my actual memories of an event and my memory of it through family storytelling. Take the summer we were quarantined, for example. Around 1950, when I was about seven, we were quarantined at the lake for the entire summer because a poliomyelitis epidemic had scared our family. One distant cousin, who lived across the state from us, and one of my brother's playmates, who lived on the next block, both had contracted the disease. We were taken to the mountains in hopes of escaping this dreaded crippler.

One day, so the story goes, after some weeks in our mountain retreat, my mother claimed we kids got "cabin fever." She took us for a drive, seven miles down the mountain road (part of which was just a dirt and gravel surface) to the nearest civilization, a village called White House, which straddled the state line. It had a general store, with a gas pump out front, some small churches, and assorted houses. After getting gas, groceries, sodas, and popsicles, we crossed into Pennsylvania, farther into civilization to the next town which had a movie-house where we watched a musical and munched on popcorn. When my uncle came up for a weekend visit, they say he was furious, fearing that we kids had been exposed to polio germs. He felt Mother had undermined the whole quarantine scheme, because she got bored. I guess they had quite an argument. As usual, they kept us out of earshot, but I heard it reargued years later when it was embellished this way or that depending on who retold it.

Yes, storytelling was a family tradition at our large family gatherings for Sunday dinners, birthdays, and holidays. Evening mealtime at the cabin provided another scene for our family raconteurs. Sometimes in hot weather, meals would be served out on the back patio or on the front lawn, looking down at the lake. But mostly I remember sitting inside elbow-to-elbow at the long picnic table, eating fresh sweet corn, tomatoes, and summer squash some local farmer had raised. Belonging to a large family gave me a feeling of security and mealtime with its stories always heightened that sense.

Time, of course, has a way of changing things. Older family members die; younger ones move away. New family patterns evolve. Evening TV plays most nights now and we hear fewer stories of the old days. But at the cabin on those cool, breezy, mountain evenings there'd be a crackling log fire in the fireplace and the adults would talk long after we kids had been tucked in for the night. Sometimes a loud laugh would wake us and we would sneak out to the top of the stairs to eavesdrop.

After having the cabin for about eight years, my uncle sold it for cash to move from an apartment in his father's home into a house of his own. I don't remember missing it right away. As teenagers we were spending three weeks each summer in Boy Scout and church camps. Something called dating also complicated our lives considerably. It would be many years before I would understand what our time at that cabin on the lake meant. I had taken for granted its luxury and beauty as well as what it had afforded us: a time of carefree play, while learning about nature and being nurtured in the values of growing up in a large, loving family. The building may be gone, but that cabin of memories is everpresent. In fact, I have recreated those goneby moments, endowing them with my personal meaning by writing this essay as my family did by storytelling.

Revising Activities Demonstrated: Part Two

You have already read one of Ellen's essay drafts and its revision. During the same semester she wrote a more complex and intriguing essay comparing composing a piece of writing to preparing for a costume party. About a year later when she was participating in a second writing course, Ellen revised that essay and then wrote an analysis of it. Here is her revision analysis which I believe may be useful in giving you a look at how another writer assesses her work. As you read her analysis, you may find it helpful to refer to the essay she is discussing which is printed beginning on page 130. After you have perused it, record in your journal the ideas you find most noteworthy in Ellen's work. Discuss with your classmates and address these questions: What is your response to her view of writing and herself as a writer? In what ways are you like Ellen as a writer? How do you differ from her? What ideas on revision have you learned that are most helpful to you?

Revision Analysis of "Costume Party" Essay

On every writer's horizon looms that difficult task of revision. Nothing causes greater anguish than the struggle to make writing say exactly what one wants it to say. Yet nothing gives a writer more satisfaction than a successful revision of her work. A successful revision is evidence of great skill, fortitude, and perseverance. It is a process whereby one critically studies and analyzes a draft, reshaping and refining the prose. An experienced writer substitutes, deletes, adds to, and reorders her material to achieve new meaning. Using these four major principles, I will discuss my own process of revision.

I have chosen to revise an essay I wrote a year ago. The essay compares writing to being invited to, and then preparing a disguise for, a costume party. This was not a first draft. I had not planned to make any major organizational or thematic changes. With some minor changes on the sentence level, I would be finished. So I thought. Once I began the actual process of revision, I soon discovered that I had not always said what I meant to say, at all. To begin, I separate and look at each paragraph individually.

An opening paragraph should set the stage for the rest of the paper. While the main idea of my first paragraph is fairly clear, I have a tendency toward verbosity. Out of three sentences, two are equally long. In this paragraph, my objective is to vary sentence length, thereby improving my style.

My first step involves separating each sentence into its simplest kernel sentences. From there, I delete words that add little meaning to the sentence. For example, my opening sentence loses little by cutting "upon receiving an invitation." I only imply that I have received an invitation in my revised sentence. However, now the audience realizes that deciding whether to accept the invitation is far more important than receiving it. A subtle change in stress sometimes clarifies meaning. The substitution of "hesitate" for "thinking carefully" in this sentence better connotes the feeling of indecision I want to show.

Likewise, the second and third sentences easily survive the loss of unnecessary words. In sentence two, I substitute "promises an enjoyable evening" for "will take part in an enjoyable activity." It now sounds less stuffy, less formal. More importantly, "promises" seems less absolute; I would have no trouble deciding to attend a party if I were so certain of a good time, even if incapable of creating a dazzling costume. My audience understands the purpose of an R.S.V.P. No need to beat them over the head with it. Therefore I also delete from sentence two "that goes far beyond a simple agreement to attend." Not yet sure of my meaning, I had skirted around the theme I wished to project in my original draft, using an overabundance of words. Nevertheless, verbosity cannot hide uncertainty; it can only annoy the reader by forcing him or her to guess what the writer really meant to say. By taking responsibility for my words, my voice as narrator becomes stronger. I reduce the risk of tiring out my audience by deleting unnecessary words from sentence three. Finally, I add a fourth sentence to tie this paragraph to the next, but, overall, the organization remains the same.

I began to think about seeing the costume party as a challenge only as I became immersed in revising the body of the essay. Having only implicitly hinted that it was a challenge in my draft, I found it helped to say it explicitly. It gave me a pattern to follow, a sense of direction in my revising process. Finding a way to express this idea in my first paragraph was another challenge in itself. This was the last, as well as the hardest, paragraph for me to revise. One reason might have been my reluctance to relinquish any of what I felt was the controlling paragraph of the paper. A writer is often schizophrenic, having two personalities like Dr. Jekyll and Mr. Hyde. The Artist is the imaginative, creative part of the writer; the Critic is that side of the writer that analyzes, criticizes and edits her work. While I struggled to revise paragraph one, the Artist in me impeded the Critic, afraid the Critic would harm the creative ideas themselves. This Artist still wanted to say what she had said. Anything else was an invasion of my paper's privacy. It was only when I let these two sides of myself work together that I began to creatively revise, injecting new life into my words. Stubbornness is the bane of all writers.

Unlike my first paragraph, my second changes drastically in both organization and content. I introduce the idea of an approaching deadline here instead of later, explaining why anxiety "tinges" my excitement. Note, too, that the position of this physically descriptive sentence changes. As a rule, the last sentence of a paragraph ought to relate to the one preceding it. In my original version, the first and last sentences of paragraph two read:

> The decision made, I accept the invitation. . . . At the same time, I will have the opportunity to be one of those who stand out in a crowd.

Notice that these two sentences cannot exist as a paragraph. They have no cohesiveness, no meaning. Now look at the first and last sentences of the revised version.

> The challenge to be one of those who stand out in a crowd proves too enticing to me. . . . Excitement courses through my veins, tinged with the anxiety of an onrushing deadline.

Though expansion of the idea of "challenge" would help the reader, one sentence forms a bridge, easily traversed, to the other.

A short, terse statement often carries force that a long, rambling sentence cannot. With its abruptness, I try to let sentence two in paragraph two show a strong commitment to the project. Determination now seems to ooze from the words, also. I further illustrate my sense of purpose by putting sentence three into an active verb voice. "Relishes" is a stronger word than "appeals," making my excitement a more believable emotion. Again I add a new sentence to my narrative in the form of a question that allows the reader to see that the decision-making process must continue.

Paragraph three of the original essay seems flat and monotonous; it does not say what I want to say in the way I want to say it. I have on my hands a paragraph fraught with anxiety. Its style and tone are plodding, indicating that I, as narrator, am afraid to make a mistake lest anyone think me dull, unimaginative, and uninspired. As narrator, I need to project a more positive image. After combining the sentences in a variety of ways, playing with word order, diction, and sentence arrangement, I use half of my original sentence two to open the paragraph. Unable to fit the original opening sentence into my new schema, I finally discard it completely. Likewise, I discard most of sentence four, incorporating the remaining fragment into sentence three of the original draft. My final revision involves substitution. In sentence four, "will be unique" replaces "should commingle skill with originality." In redefining and clarifying what I meant to say, I express myself more clearly. Self-confidence improves my style; the sentences now vary in length and are, I think, clearer to the reader. With this display of newly found self-confidence, I control my anxiety and not vice versa. My audience should now feel that I will accomplish all I set out to accomplish as I create my disguise.

I choose not to revise paragraph four as it works fairly well already. Using varied sentences, I show that imagination alone cannot create a successful costume. Order must grow out of chaos. I must have a critical sense of my work, a discriminating eye when putting this costume together. Often, when revising, one discovers that deciding what should stay is as important as deciding what should go. As a writer becomes more experienced, her judgment in evaluating her writing also improves. She learns when to leave well enough alone.

In paragraph five, I work on simplifying and reorganizing ideas. Eliminating some of the wordiness, I substitute "begin ordering" for "commence trying to order" in sentence one. I drop the conjunction "and," insert "because," and reorganize sentence two, achieving clarity in this process. It becomes sentence three in my revision because it makes more sense to have a person respond to a difficult task with frustration than to have that person frustrated before she starts. Sewing seems a more creative activity than incorporation. Therefore I revise sentence two according to this philosophy, dropping the businesslike quality of the previous version. Little changes in the last sentences of the paragraph.

Paragraph six remains pretty much the same. I make one exception; I remove the semicolon, splitting the second sentence in two. Somehow, the sentences seem to come into their own when I do this. With two short statements, I make my words more absolute, more certain, more final. They lose some of their impact when joined.

I combine several equally short sentences in a variety of ways in the next paragraph. Combining sentence three with "I do not want to be exposed too soon" changes the idea of exposure. In the original version, the mask only reduces one's exposure from her audience. The revision makes clear that a mask can only delay that exposure for a while. At every costume party there comes a time when all participants must unmask, whether they want to or not. In reworking sentence two, then, I discover what I really meant to say. So that there are not three short sentences in a row, I combine sentences five and six. Not wanting to depress my audience, I remove the personal put-down in sentence 11. However, I also remove it because my perception of myself has changed in the last year, as well. I no longer feel as fallible as I did when first writing this essay. Inserting "sighs fill the air" into sentence 10 more clearly explains my reason for sighing, the frustration mentioned in the last paragraph. Previously, my audience might have misunderstood it to be insecurity and low self-esteem. A writer must be careful not to unintentionally mislead her audience. Though the paragraph is now two sentences shorter, varied sentence length makes for easier reading. I have also succeeded in making it more concise.

As I study my original draft, I find sentence three of paragraph eight extremely weak. My tone is flippant and I confuse the emotion "fright" with the emotion "anxiety." When writing a comparison paper, the comparisons made should parallel each other. My revision strengthens the comparison between writing a paper and preparing a costume. I must choose my topic carefully *because* I want to write an original paper. Ergo, "for" replaces "and" because it is more closely synonymous with the word "because." Though simply a matter of word choice, it better fits the meaning I wish to project.

Something totally unexpected happens when I begin revising my next paragraph. I discover that, in one short year, I have evolved as a writer. I no longer believe in half of what this paragraph says. True, a thesis statement serves as a starting point, but for the reader not the writer. A writer sometimes finds her thesis statement only after hours of work on her thesis. Ideas hatch and formulate in the process of writing and rewriting. One cannot know what she is going to say until she says it. With this in mind, I attack this paragraph with fervor. The revision gives more attention to writing as a process of trial and error. In this way it resembles the process of creating a successful disguise. Since I have changed the function of the mask in a previous paragraph, I must express my reasons for being disturbed by an imperfect piece of prose in another way. I now bring up a point that I have not touched upon before: how writing is a part of me. New ideas will surprise a writer as she searches for new meaning.

Perhaps because I was not totally sure of my theme in the original draft, I am again flippant in my final paragraph. In putting myself down, I can say, "I told you so" when people say they are not sure what I meant either. I shirk the responsibility of my words. This must change. So, I keep the first two sentences, scrub the rest, and invent a new ending for my essay. Along with my first paragraph, this ranks as a most difficult passage to revise. I would not do well to end my paper with a whimper. As a student I have not yet reached my potential as a writer, so I include this idea in my revised final paragraph. This paragraph is now more polished than my previous attempt, fuelling my hypothesis that I have not achieved my potential. Yet.

Now these paragraphs must be recombined to form a finished essay. I check to see that my transitions between paragraphs are coherent and logical. At this point, I also check for grammar and punctuation errors. With a few more changes, including further additions, deletions, substitutions, and reorganization, I am at last ready to abandon this revision.

With this paper, I have tried to show revision as a process of discovery. In substituting, reordering, adding to, and deleting from my work, I have achieved new meaning. It is now up to you as my audience to judge how well I have done so.

Note: You may also be interested to reread Ellen's journal entries written while she worked on this revision; see p. 17.

Here is the essay Ellen has been discussing. First the original and revised versions of each paragraph are printed so you may make comparisons. Then the full text of the essay revision is printed.

Original Version: Paragraph 1

Upon receiving an invitation to a costume party, I always think carefully before accepting. Although it means I will take part in an enjoyable activity, I realize that it requires an R.S.V.P. that goes far beyond a simple agreement to attend. I must first decide whether I have the time, skill and imagination needed to create something that I will be presenting to an audience for approval.

Revised Version: Paragraph 1

I always hesitate before accepting an invitation to a costume party. Though it promises an enjoyable evening, this invitation requires much more of me than a simple R.S.V.P. I must first decide whether I have the time, skill, and imagination to produce a disguise worthy of an audience's approval. Only then can I accept this challenge to be creative and original.

Original Version: Paragraph 2

The decision made, I accept the invitation. Excitement tinged with anxiety courses through my veins. The prospect of legitimately assuming another identity appeals to the schizophrenic side(s) of my personality. At the same time, I will have the opportunity to be one of those who stand out in a crowd.

Revised Version: Paragraph 2

The challenge to be one of those who stand out in a crowd proves too enticing to me. I accept the invitation. My schizophrenic personality relishes this opportunity to assume another identity. But whose identity should I assume? Excitement courses through my veins, tinged with the anxiety of an onrushing deadline.

Original Version: Paragraph 3

I worry because I have only a limited amount of time to prepare my costume. The deadline causes most of this anxiety, but I need a clear head in order to produce results. I spend days considering how I want to portray or reveal myself to my potential audience. In order for me, and my costume, to be judged a success, I must choose my disguise carefully. My attire's design should commingle skill with originality lest my critics remain unimpressed by my handiwork.

Revised Version: Paragraph 3

One needs a clear head to produce desired results. Excessive worry must not hamper my progress. I choose my disguise carefully, spending days deciding how I want to portray myself to my potential audience. My attire's design will be unique lest my critics remain unimpressed.

Original Version: Paragraph 4

Now comes the real chore. I assemble all the materials I need to begin. A soft, red, billowy cloth suits me but one color alone will not do. Assorted odds and ends of different shapes, sizes, and colors will help distinguish this dress from others. I outline my material carefully. Without a pattern or form my creation will be undefined and incomprehensible to those judging it. However, being insecure and indecisive, I change this outline several times. At first, the outline looks too constricting. Another time, I fear I have drawn it lopsided. And so it goes.

NO REVISION OF PARAGRAPH 4

Original Version: Paragraph 5

Once I settle on the pattern I want to use, I commence trying to order the mass of material laid down before me. It takes so long and I feel so frustrated. Blues, greens, and yellows must somehow be incorporated into the red cloth without taking away or destroying its elegance. I find I must leave my project for awhile in order to gain an objective perspective.

Revised Version: Paragraph 5

Once I settle on the pattern I want to use, I begin ordering the mass of material laid before me. Scraps of blue, green and yellow material must be sewn into the red cloth without destroying its elegance. I am frustrated because it takes so long. After awhile, I abandon my project in order to gain an objective perspective.

Original Version: Paragraph 6

When I return, hours later, I feel the need to take the whole thing apart and put it back together in a totally different way, though I keep the chosen outline. I pay close attention to detail; this costume must be perfect all the way down to the last stitch.

Revised Version: Paragraph 6

On returning, hours later, I find the need to take the whole thing apart and put it back together in a totally different way, though I keep the chosen outline. I pay close attention to detail. This costume must be perfect all the way down to the last stitch.

Original Version: Paragraph 7

My mask takes shape from papier maché. I choose full coverage of my face as I want to reduce my exposure when I arrive at the party. I am insecure about the role I have chosen. Still, without the mask, the disguise virtually does not exist. Great care will go into its decoration. Painstakingly, I paint my character's face. Not one drop of paint should be out of place. Everything must be perfect. I struggle not to make the eyes too wide or close-set. The brush slips and one nostril becomes bigger than the other. Sighs fill the air as my fallibility continually hits me across the side of the head. Finally, I complete the entire project and stand back to admire it. Oh well, it's the best I can do.

Revised Version: Paragraph 7

My mask takes shape from papier maché. When I arrive at the party, my face should be entirely concealed. Still insecure with the role I have chosen, I do not want to be exposed too soon. Moreover, without the mask, the disguise virtually does not exist. Great care goes into its decoration. Painstakingly, I paint my character's face so that not one drop of paint is out of place. Everything must be perfect. I struggle not to make the eyes too wide or close-set. Sighs fill the air when my brush slips and one nostril becomes bigger than the other. Finally, I complete the entire project and stand back to admire it. Oh well, it's the best I can do.

Original Version: Paragraph 8

I go through a similar process when I receive an "invitation" to write. Here too, I must decide whether I have the time, the skill and the imagination needed to create something worthy of my audience. Deadlines continue to frighten me although I have laughed (however weakly) in the face of many of them. My incubation period for any writing I do lasts several days, analogous to the length of time spent in deciding on a costume. I must choose my topic carefully, and like a costume, my paper will have an identity of its own.

Revised Version: Paragraph 8

I go through a similar process when I receive an invitation to write. Here too, I must decide whether I have the time, the skill, and the imagination needed to create something worthy of my audience. Deadlines still cause me considerable anxiety. The incubation period for any writing I do lasts several days, analogous to the amount of time I spend choosing my disguise. I must choose my topic carefully, for like a costume, my paper will have an identity of its own.

Original Version: Paragraph 9

Assembling and sorting all I need to commence writing constitutes the real chore. Selecting a thesis statement or an opening sentence takes a great deal of time. My thesis statement serves as a starting point; it allows me to shape my thoughts much like the outline allows me to shape my costume. As in the multicolored costume I like to see variety in my writing. It often takes me several revisions and reworkings before I am fully satisfied. Writing can be a very frustrating activity, more so than making a costume. I feel more disturbed if I produce an imperfect piece of prose than I do if I produce an imperfect disguise. At least the mask protects the wearer from being recognized, from being exposed if that exposure is unwanted. The writer finds herself totally exposed to an audience's criticism. Writing can be an agonizing process. I sometimes stay in my pajamas all day, as if I were ill, if I am working on some form of writing.

Revised Version: Paragraph 9

Assembling and sorting all I need to begin writing constitutes the real chore. Playing with the overall structure of whatever I write takes a long time. However, this process of writing and rewriting allows me to shape my thoughts, much like the outline allows me to shape my costume. As in the multicolored costume, I like to see variety in my writing. It often takes me several revisions before I am fully satisfied. Writing can be more frustrating than making a costume. I feel more disturbed if I produce an imperfect piece of prose than I do if I produce an imperfect disguise. My writing is more a part of me. I cannot divorce myself from it as easily as I can shed, and then throw away, my costume. Moreover, a writer finds herself totally exposed to an audience's criticism. Writing can be an agonizing process. I sometimes stay in my pajamas all day, as if I were ill, if I am working on some form of writing.

Original Version: Paragraph 10

When I go to the costume party, deep down I know my disguise has a hint of that polished, well-balanced, flowing style I sought all along. With my writing I am never quite sure. My heart pounds when it comes time to "unmask." I pray I will hear someone saying, "Wow, how gorgeous! What an imagination, what creativity . . ." Having had my fallibility hitting me on the side of the head the entire time I have struggled with this paper, I have no such fantasies of ever hearing that said about this work.

Revised Version: Paragraph 10

When I go to the costume party, deep down I know my disguise has a hint of that well-balanced, polished style I sought all along. With my writing I am never quite sure. I can only guess by gauging my audience's response. But I must continue to accept the challenge to write so that I will see my writing become more polished. When it does, only then will I applaud myself.

Revised Text: Comparison of Writing and Costume Party

I always hesitate before accepting an invitation to a costume party. Though it promises an enjoyable evening, this invitation requires much more of me than a simple R.S.V.P. I must first decide whether I have the time, skill, and imagination to produce a disguise worthy of an audience's approval. Only then can I dare to be creative and original.

The challenge to be one of those who stands out in a crowd proves too enticing to me. I accept the invitation. My schizophrenic personality relishes this opportunity to assume another identity. But whose identity should I assume? Excitement courses through my veins, tinged with the anxiety of an oncoming deadline.

Excessive worry must not hamper my progress. I need a clear head to produce desired results. I choose my disguise carefully, spending days deciding how I want to portray myself to my potential audience. My attire's design must be unique lest my critics remain unimpressed.

Now comes the real chore. I assemble all the materials I need to begin. A soft, red, billowy cloth suits me but one color alone will not do. Assorted odds and ends of different shapes, sizes, and colors will help distinguish this dress from others. I outline my material carefully. Without a pattern or form my creation will be undefined and incomprehensible to those judging it. However, being a little insecure and indecisive, I change this outline several times. At first the outline looks too constricting. Another time, I fear I have drawn it lopsided. And so it goes.

Once I settle on the pattern I want to use, I begin ordering the mass of material laid before me. Scraps of blue, green, and yellow material must be sewn onto the red cloth without destroying its elegance. I am frustrated because it takes so long. After a while, I abandon my project in order to gain an objective perspective.

On returning, hours later, I feel the need to take the whole thing apart and put it back together in a totally different way, though I keep the original outline. I pay close attention to detail. This outfit must be perfect all the way down to the last stitch.

My mask takes shape from papier maché. When I arrive at the party, I want my face entirely concealed. Still insecure with the role I have chosen, I do not want to be exposed too soon. Moreover, without the mask, the disguise virtually does not exist. Painstakingly, I paint my character's face, taking care that not one drop of paint is out of place. Everything must be perfect. I struggle not to make the eyes too wide or close-set. My sighs fill the air when my brush slips and one nostril becomes bigger than the other. Finally, I complete the entire project and stand back to admire it.

I go through a similar process when I receive an invitation to write. Here too, I must decide whether I have the time, the skill, and the imagination to create something worthy of my audience. Deadlines still cause me considerable anxiety. The incubation period for any writing I do lasts several days, analogous to the amount of time I spend choosing my disguise. I must choose my topic carefully, for like a costume, my paper will have an identity of its own.

Assembling and sorting all I need to begin writing constitutes the real chore. Playing with the overall structure of whatever I write takes a long time. However, this process of writing and rewriting allows me to shape my thoughts, much like the outline allows me to shape my costume. As in the multicolored costume, I like to see variety in my writing. It often takes me several revisions before I am fully satisfied. Writing can be more frustrating than making a costume. I feel more dissatisfied if I produce an imperfect piece of prose than I do if I produce an imperfect disguise. My writing is more a part of me. I cannot divorce myself from it as easily as I can shed, and then throw away, my costume. Moreover, a writer finds herself totally exposed to an audience's criticism.

Writing can be an agonizing process. I sometimes stay in my pajamas all day, as if I were ill, when I am working on some form of writing.

When I go to the costume party, deep down I know my disguise has a hint of that well-balanced, polished style I sought all along. With my writing, I am never quite sure. I can only guess by gauging my audience's response. Still, I must continue to accept the challenge to write so that I will see my writing become more polished. When it does, only then will I applaud myself.

EXERCISES IN REVISING

1. Turn to page 14 and read "Memories of Childhood Recalled" from John's journal. The paragraph seems to begin with the main idea in the first sentence; however, the details of the paragraph support another main idea. What is it? Revise the paragraph, placing the main idea first and composing shorter, clearer versions of John's sentences.

2. For each audience listed write two or three paragraphs on the topics. What expectations about certain audiences require changes in tone and development of your ideas?

    a. Jogging shoes
       audience 1: 10-year-old schoolchildren
       audience 2: college cross-country runners
    b. The fraternity and sorority system
       audience 1: potential pledges
       audience 2: members of your school's Pan-Hellenic Council (leaders of the fraternity and sorority system)
    c. Comic-book collecting
       audience 1: fellow collectors
       audience 2: 10-year-old schoolchildren

3. Suppose that you are the author of "Lake O' the Woods" and you decide to revise it so as to compare and contrast the good and bad things about your experience there. Review the material given (pp. 86–90). Then state your main idea and make notes on how you would reorganize the information in each paragraph, including what you would delete and what you would

add. Of course, you may also want to rearrange the order of
the paragraphs. Give reasons for the changes you make.

Note: For an example of such notes on revising intentions,
see pp. 111 and 114. Before doing this exercise, you may find it
helpful to read the section on comparing and contrasting on pp.
231ff.

4. Make appropriate revisions in the following student paragraphs, concentrating on organization, clarity of ideas, and economy of words.

a. This report is to evaluate the need for a public park at
982 West Street. This report appraises the needs of the children, residents, and the motorists in the area. The parcel of
land in question is at 982 West Street. The lot is 135 feet
wide by 142 feet deep. The total amount of land at this location
is .44 acre. At this time the land is owned by the city. The
city has no plans for future development at present. A park
to serve the entire community could be constructed on this
parcel.

b. My personal exercise program is a combination of strongly
tuned mental drills. My program is based on the idea that
no exercise is good exercise; therefore, the key word to this
program is rest. After my waking rest period I usually run
a sprint from my bedroom to the kitchen. Upon waking from
a good night's sleep, I usually like to rest about an hour before
getting out of bed. Once in the kitchen I begin an early morning weight program, by adding weight on in the form of breakfast. It is during the post-meal relaxation period that I begin
my mental drills. Eating is quite tiresome so I advise another
rest period after breakfast.

c. Brian Stuart is 16 years old. He strolls in from school at
about 2:30 P.M. each weekday afternoon. He absorbs three
hours of "Star Trek" and television game shows before dinner.
He might open a book between seven and eight o'clock, before
prime time. Questioned about his day, Brian grunts a few
stock answers, "O.K. same as yesterday. No homework, so
don't worry." When the jeans and torn sweatshirt finally reach
the clothes hamper, they reek of beer and smoke. As this
routine becomes habitual, Brian's parents wonder if the money

they spent on the new swimming pool might have been put to better use enrolling their son in a private school.

d. The devastating inflation which swept through our nation's economy in the 1970s ushered in a new economic era dominated by cost-of-living adjustments built into labor contracts. Both the private and public sectors have witnessed the widespread use of this contract clause. Nowhere is the use more rampant than in the government and pension plans. An army colonel may retire at 42 and receive over $1,000 a month retirement pay. The colonel may also hold down another job. Some of my readers might disagree with my position that this is an exorbitant cost to taxpayers. Some might say, "It's worth paying this great sum of money to retired service people to keep our national defense strong." To these readers, I reply "Hogwash!"

5. Select an essay you composed some time ago. (One written a few weeks ago will serve for this exercise, although one from a year or so ago might serve better.) Reread the essay, circling key words and underlining the essay's main idea. Study the overall pattern to see if you can envision an expanded main idea. Write out as many alternate main ideas as you can. To aid you in this you may wish to draw separate diagrams or figures illustrating the various new main ideas and details you could use to support each of them. Or you may wish to draw up (if you have not previously) a list of information from the essay according to one of the methods in Chapter 2. Select one and revise the essay according to the guidelines outlined in this chapter.

6. The paragraph below, written by the English novelist, D. H. Lawrence, contains an extended metaphor of the thinking or decision-making process. Read the paragraph carefully.

The mind makes curious swoops and circles. It touches the point of pain or interest, then sweeps away again in a cycle, coils round and approaches again the point of pain or interest. There is a curious spiral rhythm, and the mind approaches again and again the point of concern, repeats itself, goes back, destroys the time-sequence entirely, so that time ceases to exist, as the mind stoops to the quarry, then leaves it without striking, soars, hovers, turns, sweeps, stoops again, still does not strike, yet is nearer, nearer, reels away again, wheels off into the air, even forgets, quite forgets, yet again turns, bends, circles slowly swoops and stoops again, until at last there is the closing-in, and the clutch of a decision or a resolve.[2]

No doubt you recognize the metaphor of the thinking process as a bird of prey. Using your own experience of thinking out writing ideas and making revision decisions, write a journal entry discussing the appropriateness of this metaphor and create your own extended metaphor for the mind as it works.

A CONCLUDING NOTE

As I stated at the beginning of the chapter, completing an essay draft often exhilarates a writer because he or she has put ideas into words, has created order out of the chaos of random thoughts. A major difficulty in revising, if properly done, is opening oneself up to new discoveries, facing again the chaos of new thinking. Professor Ann Berthoff says,

> Now, chaos is scary: the meanings that can emerge from it, which can be discerned taking shape within it, can be discovered only if students who are learning to write can learn to tolerate ambiguity.[3]

Thus, I close with the request that you try earnestly to tolerate ambiguity throughout the revising process, that you play with meaning making, that you experiment with various versions before settling finally on one that you are willing to share with an audience.

NOTES

1. Roland Barthes, *Writing Degree Zero*, trans. Annette Lavers and Colin Smith (New York: Hill and Wang, 1968), p. 20. I read this line first when Nancy Sommers quoted Barthes in an article entitled, "Revision Strategies of Student Writers and Experienced Adult Writers," *College Composition and Communication*, 31 December, 1980, pp. 378–388. My indebtedness to Sommers' work is evident in my approach to revision in this chapter; I am also indebted to Linda Flowers' work on problem solving and reader- and writer-based prose: "Writer-

Based Prose: A Cognitive Basis for Problems in Writing," *College English* 41 (September 1979) pp. 19–37, and *Problem-Solving Strategies for Writing* (New York: Harcourt Brace Jovanovich, 1981).

2. Warren Roberts and Harry J. Moore, eds., *Phoenix II: Uncollected, Unpublished, and Other Prose Works by D. H. Lawrence* (New York: The Viking Press, 1959).

3. *The Making of Meaning* (Montclair, New Jersey: Boynton/Cook Publishers, 1981), p. 70.

5
VOICE, AUDIENCE, AND PURPOSE

Think of your reader as a partner in communication.

The first chapter presented writing exercises and the following three chapters described and demonstrated the writing process. Beginning with this chapter, I will focus on particular aspects of the process, on the nature of language, and on the relationship of the writer to the topic and the audience.

This chapter is devoted to voice. When you speak, you give an interpretation or an emphasis to your words by your voice tone. When you want to vary the interpretation or emphasis to convey a particular meaning or to relate to a specific audience, you simply shift your tone of voice. For example, think of the simple command, "Shut the door, please." Read that command out loud as you would to each of these audiences: a younger brother who, unannounced and unwelcome, has opened your bedroom door; a guest of your parents who has just entered the front door of your home; your best friend who has just entered the campus radio-station studio room where you are illegally tape recording music from the radio station's library; a student you tutor in mathematics who has just joined you in the residence-hall study lounge.

Your written words also convey voice tone. However, voice tone in written language does not come from vocalization as in spoken language. It comes from your prose style, from the rhythm and form of your written language. As a reader reads your writing to discover your meaning, he or she also "hears" your voice. In other words, the reader infers your attitude toward the topic and him or her from the way you have written your ideas. Although the reader may do it unconsciously, he or she is taking cues from your words in order to answer such questions as: Is this writer being logical, fanciful, humorous, romantic, or forthright about the topic? Is this writer angry, puzzled, sarcastic, resigned, or pompous? Are any of those feelings being directed at me, the reader? While there is much to be said about style, I will confine my remarks here to that aspect of it we call voice, particularly as it reveals the writer's attitude toward the audience and toward the writer's purpose for writing.

Nearly 200 years ago when the scholar James Beattie defined communication, he expressed the essence of the relationship between writer and reader: "Communication takes place when a speaker or writer assumes his hearer or reader as a partner in his sentiments and discourse, saying *We*, instead of *I* or *Ye.*"[1] Writers originally compose for themselves, trying to formulate ideas on a topic; ultimately, however, writers want to communicate these ideas to someone else, a friend, classmates, or a teacher (unless, of course, the writing is in a private diary). To communicate ideas effectively to a reader, writers must invite the reader into a partnership; they must ask the reader to share in their ideas, to join in a writing adventure, to participate in a triangle of communication. Not to do so, writers fail to create such a triangle of communication. There are a number of ways to fail to do so and some of them relate to the writer's voice.

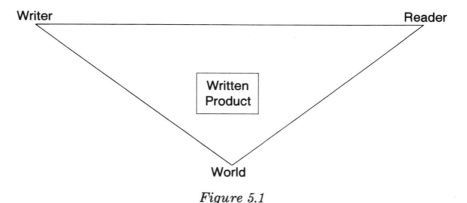

Figure 5.1

One way a writer may commit this error is by speaking only to his or her own interests and needs, failing to take into consideration the reader whose interests and needs are different. The reader senses by the writer's tone of voice that he or she is left on the outside of the communication triangle trying to look in.

A second way the writer may fail to invite the reader into a partnership is by separating himself or herself from the reader through condescension or accusation. In this case, the reader may sense that he or she is being talked down to or having a finger pointed at him or her.

Often, beginning writers don't realize their failure to invite the reader into a partnership; in other words, they are unaware that the tone of their writing voice is somehow off-putting to the reader. Therefore, in this chapter I present examples of inappropriate voice tones, and exercises in hearing the voices in the writer's words; I also ask you to practice pitching your own voice appropriately to invite the reader to join you in a communication partnership.

Before going on, you may find it helpful to review the section on audience in the last chapter (pp. 101–102), especially the questions on audience a writer should address when composing.

FORGETTING THE AUDIENCE

Since writers begin writing by sketching out their ideas in words for their own understanding and by asking and answering questions for themselves, it is understandable that they may forget to "translate" their original language for readers. In the first example following, the writer, who was just learning how to use a still-picture camera, opened an essay on photography with this paragraph.

PHOTOGRAPHY: HOW TO BEGIN

Learning about photography, the art of reproducing figures onto pictures, has touched every aspect of my life. I can depict just about anything in pictures. I may put my emotions into visual expression. Photographs preserve memories of my friends, events at home, or scenes from my past. I have never had so much fun with something since I played with toys as a child.

In each sentence the writer's voice is exclaiming the wonders of photography or simply expressing enthusiastic feelings about photographs. This writer is so intently involved with her topic that she has forgotten to address some essential questions: "How can I draw the reader into this exciting activity? How can I enable him or her to understand photography as I do?" The voice in this paragraph might be appropriate for beginning an essay entitled "Shutterbug Excitement," but not to open a "How To" essay. Perhaps one of these two voices would more effectively engage a reader:

First Revision

Learning about photography can touch every aspect of a person's life. An amateur photographer can depict just about anything in pictures, such as putting his emotions into visual expression. Photographs can preserve memories of his friends, events at home, or scenes from his past. An amateur photographer can have more fun with a camera than he has had with anything since he played with toys as a child.

Second Revision

How would you like to preserve memories of your friends, events from home, or scenes from your past? You can depict just about anything in pictures, such as putting your emotions into visual expression. In fact, learning about photography can touch every aspect of your life. You can have as much fun with a camera as you did with toys as a child.

Here is someone who is also very engaged in his topic; however, his problem of voice is a bit different:

EXERCISES FOR WEAK BACKS

Backache, a day-to-day problem, causes many people to take time off from work or school each year. As many as 25-million Americans seek medical care for backache. I exercise regularly for a bad back, since I am one of the several people to complain to their doctors each year.

While this second writer has seen beyond his own involvement with the topic to other people's relation to it, he has not found a natural voice in which to address them as potential readers; rather, they are lumped into amorphous groupings: "many people," "25-million Americans," and "several people." Write a revision which you feel has a more appropriate tone of voice for readers who may also have weak backs. Compare your version with your classmates' and discuss the changes you made.

TALKING AT THE AUDIENCE INSTEAD OF TO IT

The other extreme from failing to invite the readers to join in learning about a topic, is to address them too boldly or to speak somehow unpleasantly to them. Does this writer's voice make you feel uncomfortable?

ECTOTHERMY *VS.* ENDOTHERMY DINOSAURS

Much of the information I present here has been introduced to me in biology classes. My knowledge, however, was not as extensive then as it is now. Since it becomes necessary to deal with experimental data, I will have to tone down the biological jargon or explain it to you novices. It's like playing the simplest chess game possible without eliminating the most paramount strategic moves. Get ready for a lesson in natural history.

This voice sounds too didactic, what my students call "teachy-preachy." Certainly we all have a lot to learn about dinosaurs and other topics, but a writer should not make us feel inadequate for not yet knowing something of these special topics. This writer is over-serious about his topic. Perhaps he forgets what it was like to be a novice. Or, perhaps he is simply unaware that his tone conveys an attitude of superiority through using the passive verb voice ("has been introduced to me"), long, impersonal clauses ("Since it becomes necessary to deal with experimental data"), and direct address ("you novices" and "get ready for a lesson").

Another writer opened an essay on ecology with this paragraph:

Municipalities dump barges of trash and garbage in the ocean daily. Factory workers are exposed everyday to poisonous fumes and gas. Each spring farmers pour tons of chemicals into the soil without thinking what harm they'll do when they end up on the ocean floor. For years strip miners have gouged deep ruts into the earth's bosom, leaving them to erode the soil. In Vietnam soldiers defoliated rain forests without worrying about the animals they left homeless or how many decades it will take for vegetation to grow again. When are you people going to wake up and live ecologically?

Motivated by outrage at our society's behavior, this writer strikes out at his readers for the misdeeds of many. Most readers deplore the conditions the writer cites, but none will feel much like cooperating with someone who attacks them recklessly. The writer of the next passage also misplaces her anger. Instead of inviting the readers to join her in protesting certain kinds of advertising, she shakes her finger at them.

ADVERTISING OR BRAINWASHING

I refuse to be one of the ridiculous little people who believe that Coke adds life, or that some perfume will help me have an Aviance evening. I wouldn't buy a certain product simply because the skipper of a boat in my toilet water told me to. And don't you go on dreaming about how some dumb toothpaste will give you sex appeal. Don't let advertisers brainwash you.

PARTNERS IN COMMUNICATION

In order to give their effort at communication the best chance of being received, experienced writers address their readers in a friendly, respectful tone of voice. The voices in the following introductory sentences are quite different, but they all have one thing in common: they sound like the voices of people seated across a table talking to acquaintances. Don't you agree?

I COULD JUST DIE!

I'm just your average, everyday overachiever. By the time I'm 30 I'll be a member of the elitist ulcer club, and hate every minute of it. I have been molded into a hard-working, reward-expecting woman. Why, I'll be the next Marilyn Monroe, or the first woman in space or in the White House. Frankly, I can't tell what I need more, the challenge of a goal or the praise after reaching it. Maybe you can help me think through this dilemma.

This writer is nearly as wrapped up in her topic as the author of "Photography," the first writing sample. However, she uses modifiers and transition words to sound as if she is speaking informally to the reader: "*your* average, *everyday* over-achiever," "Why," and "Frankly"; in addition, she uses contractions "I'm," and "I'll," and direct address, "Maybe you can help me." Of course, this direct address is not the finger-pointing kind, but the assistance-asking kind.

The next four writers also use direct address and two of them ask rhetorical questions, in other words, questions asked only to emphasize their points, no answer being expected.

COME, VISIT ME

Go through the hole in the courtyard fence, you know, by the hopscotch court; turn left at the corner where the old guy sells knishes, and walk down two blocks to 105th street. Cross at the corners of 105th and K. Go past Leslie's house, to the street with the blue house on the corner and two poodle statues on the front lawn. Mine is the first yellow house on the left: 105–37 Flatlands 8th Street, Brooklyn, N.Y.

LIFE-TICKET OUT OF THE DOLDRUMS

Do you find yourself feeling tired, and sluggish? Do you become depressed easily or have difficulty dealing with stress? Has your life become monotonous and sedentary? If you suffer from any of these symptoms, you may simply need a vigorous exercise program to shake loose from those humdrum chains.

A WALK IN THE WILDERNESS

Let's pretend we turned the clock back to a beautiful July morning in the middle of the 1930s. As we walk down a country road, sipping nickel pop, purchased at Cornell's Gas Station, we feel the call of the wild and decide to visit nearby Skeleton Valley.

THE ABC'S AND THE ME-GENERATION

"A-B-C-D-E-F-G, H-I-J-K-LMNOP, Q-R-S, T-U-V, W-X, Y and Z. Now I know my ABC's, _____ _____ _____ _____ _____ _____ _____."

Remember the tune? Recall the words? Chances are you filled in the blanks with: "Tell me what you think of me." Or was it: "Next time won't you sing with me?" Let's think about that for a moment.

In one writing assignment students in my class pretended to write to schoolchildren (nine to 12 years old). Here are opening paragraphs from three of their essays:

BE GOOD TO YOUR HEART

Let me introduce myself. I am the hardest working muscle in your body. I began working before you were born and will continue working until you die. I am your heart.

SETTING UP A MARINE AQUARIUM

If you wish to bring into your home truly the most exotic of pets, consider a saltwater aquarium. Everyday, you will watch with fascination the remarkable world beneath the ocean. In a saltwater aquarium you can recreate the natural environment of marine life. Looking into your fish tank, you will peer at live sponges, corals and fish in a variety of colors impossible to imagine. With a relatively easy set-up procedure and regular maintenance, you will be able to study the mysteries of the sea.

WORKING FOR FUN AND PROFIT

Let's talk money! Everyone needs it and all of us enjoy spending it. Finding cash creates a problem for people your age. With the video games costing a quarter or more, many of you quickly run out of money. So, how can you fill your pockets with cold cash?

Do you think these writers engaged their readers' attention by using voice effectively? What would you change if the audience were adults? Why would you make such changes?

Of course, a writer can engage a reader's interest and gain his or her trust without using direct address. The tone of informal discussion plus the descriptive and narrative language in the following selections work effectively to attract the reader to the writer's ideas.

FLEETING YOUTH

I remember a long time ago (it must be 15 years now) how at the old house we sat under the old cherry tree early on August evenings, Mom and Dad and us kids. Its limbs stretched cooling shadows over us. Crickets serenaded when we were quiet, but, usually, we boys rough-and-tumbled with Dad. Mary Elizabeth and Mom smoothed the grass and watched us or talked together, looking toward the western horizon.

MAY PROCESSION

April has a few days like this: a teasing taste of summer warmth and it's back to winter-like chill. The school playground is busy with games like marbles, hopscotch, and jump rope. But I sit apart, longing to be picked for the May procession. I would walk at the head of the line, mouse-brown hair swirling about my shoulders, my white satin dress billowing out from starched petticoats, my white, patent-leather shoes setting a regal cadence from school to the church. Two ushers would help me mount the ladder to place the wreath on the Blessed Virgin's head. The bell ringing the end of recess startles me and I realize I'll never be chosen. Still the longing doesn't go away.

FITNESS SEEKERS

Throughout the country people are jogging, swimming, lifting weights, and playing racquetball, striving to get back into shape or to remain physically fit. An exercise craze is sweeping the nation as more and more people begin to realize the mental and physical health benefits of exercising regularly. Suites of roommates dance aerobic exercises; office workers swim at lunchtime. Business people stop at a gym on the way home for a workout. Americans young and old are joining the ranks of fitness seekers.

Figure 5.2 illustrates the qualities of appropriate voice tone present in the previous selections.

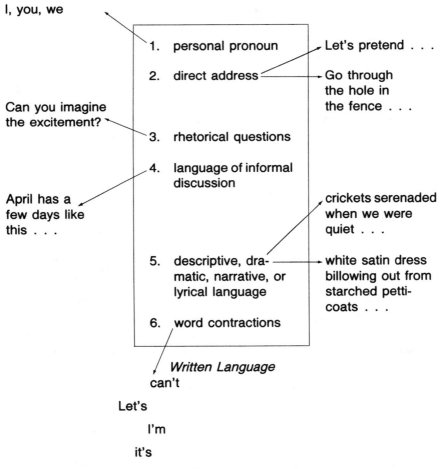

I, you, we

1. personal pronoun — Let's pretend . . .

2. direct address — Go through the hole in the fence . . .

Can you imagine the excitement?

3. rhetorical questions

4. language of informal discussion

April has a few days like this . . .

crickets serenaded when we were quiet . . .

5. descriptive, dramatic, narrative, or lyrical language — white satin dress billowing out from starched petticoats . . .

6. word contractions

Written Language

can't

Let's

I'm

it's

Figure 5.2

Use *personal pronouns*, especially "I" instead of "this writer" and "you" instead of "the reader." This simulates a face-to-face discussion between you and the reader. Direct address is an even more informal approach to the reader which can draw him or her into your writing adventure as long as the reader senses a respectful tone in it, rather than a condescending or accusatory one. *Rhetorical questions* can function somewhat as direct address does; they too are directly addressed to the reader. However, according to the convention the reader is not literally being asked to respond to the question. Sometimes the function of a rhetorical question is to make the reader feel as though he or she has heard the writer thinking aloud in a question. Other times, the rhetorical question is used merely as a means of emphasizing a point. It is possible to use rhetorical questions inappropriately, that is, by sounding impertinent, cute, or too playful for your audience. So, use care in formulating rhetorical questions.

Special forms of language and special word uses can also convey appropriate voice tone. Generally speaking, the *language of informal discussion* puts a reader at ease and engenders the feeling of respectful but comfortable discussion between acquaintances. One form of writing informally is to use *word contractions;* these connote informal language because they are almost always used in informal speech. Some composition teachers·may feel that writers should not use contractions in polished essays. You may notice, for example, that I have not used contractions in writing most sections of this book. I did, however, use them in writing "Cabin of Family Stories." Using precise *descriptive, narrative, dramatic,* or *lyrical* language is often very effective in engaging the reader's attention. Furthermore, using precise, detailed language often shows the reader that you are well versed or knowledgeable in the topic.

A Further Note on Voice and Writing Purpose

As we have seen, having a too-excited or an over-serious engagement with a topic can cause a writer to speak in an inappropriate tone of voice. However, given a reasonable engagement with a topic, a writer still has many appropriate options of voice tone from which to choose, among which are humorous, playful, concerned, helpful, scholarly, witty, instructive, entertaining, routine, dramatic, even blank, or devoid of emotion.

Of course, in many cases, you may find an appropriate tone easily, even unconsciously. However, as a check, you may find it helpful to ask yourself pointedly to describe your attitude toward your topic: "What is my writing purpose? How do I feel about this topic? Do my feelings *color* my tone of voice?"

Also, the qualities of voice set forth here are presented to help you develop a natural, informal voice in your prose style. This type of style is most appropriate for informal essay writing. It may not be appropriate for certain kinds of academic discourse you may be asked to write in college courses. For example, a convention—in other words, a customary practice—in some professional or academic writing is that the information be presented in a direct, objective format, uncolored by the writer's personal style. Adhering to this convention, the writer may adopt a stance of impersonality or invisibility. The following selections illustrate two ways in which writers fulfill the expectations of their audiences for a formal, impersonal tone:

> The Basic Premise of this paper is that household sector net capital gains are an important omitted variable in most consumption and saving studies. Its major contribution is the empirical finding of the significant effects of capital gains on personal saving that have eluded previous investigators. These striking results can be attributed to three innovations incorporated in this study: (1) the use of a new detailed net capital gains data base carefully constructed by Robert Eisner; (2) the separation of total net capital gains into components by groups of assets; and (3) the division of each of those components into expected and unexpected elements.
>
> Four components of total net capital gains are found to play an extremely important role in accounting for the recent fluctuations in personal saving: (1) expected net capital gains on owner-occupied housing, land, nonprofit fixed capital, and noncorporate equity; (2) expected net capital gains on consumer durable goods; (3) expected net capital gains on the net financial assets of the household sector; and (4) unexpected net capital gains on net financial assets.[2]

This paper reviews the literature in an area of research that has been developing quite dramatically within the past few years, namely, the analysis of children's reactions to dental situations. The research in this field is extensive solely in terms of the number of articles published, involves analyses of children from different ages and different social strata, and encompasses a broad spectrum of measures and variables. This research becomes particularly meaningful when it is viewed from the perspective of those who have criticized psychological studies for not having ecological validity (see Bronfenbrenner 1977). Studies on dental fears certainly do not deal with contrived settings and can safely be presumed to deal with real anxieties.

This review has three purposes. First, there is the intent of merely informing psychologists of a series of findings of which they seem to be unaware, at least as witnessed by the failure of many authors to mention studies of dental fears in their textbooks as well as by informal reactions of surprise by many of this writer's colleagues when they were informed of the scope of dental research. Second is the purpose of presenting generalizations of behavior and of relating the research to issues of concern to the developmentalist, such as to origins of fears and factors influencing their appearance. Third, it is hoped that criticisms and interpretations will serve as a stimulus for additional study.[3]

If you have questions about the appropriateness of voice for any of your college writing assignments, consult with your instructor before you begin writing.

EXERCISES IN PITCHING VOICES

A key to using a suitable voice, of course, is hearing it. Just as some people are better than others at singing and hearing correct pitch and rhythm in musical notes, so it is with the tone and rhythm of prose. If you have difficulty "hearing" voice in your writing and in others', here are some exercises to improve your hearing:

1. Listen to the way you talk and the kind of words you use with different people: family or roommates, teachers or bosses, dates or new acquaintances, young children, and telephone callers. Record notes on the various "voices" you use in different situations.

2. Read aloud from your journal, essays, textbooks, and lei-

sure reading material. Practice changing your vocal expression by reading dramatically: overdramatize a passage, then underplay it. Read in a mournful tone, then a jubilant one. Read a sentence literally, then ironically, that is, intending a meaning different from the literal one.

3. Read the information and directions on labels of foods, shampoos, book jackets, and other goods. Write words and phrases to describe the voices you hear in the language.

4. Select two passages from the student writing on pp. 139–142. Rewrite them, using appropriate tone.

5. Reread "Come, visit me," p. 143; rewrite it using an appropriate but more formal tone.

6. Select a passage from your journal or an essay and rewrite it three times, using a different tone of voice each time. Discuss with your classmates how the changes in voice affect the content of the passage.

7. In an essay entitled "Why Montaigne Is Not a Bore," Lewis Thomas discusses what interests him in the French author's writing. Here is one of Thomas' remarks:

> Montaigne makes friends in the first few pages of the book, and he becomes the best and closest of all your friends as the essay moves along. To be sure, he does go on and on about himself, but that self turns out to be the reader's self as well. Moreover, he does not pose, ever. He likes himself, to be sure, but is never swept off his feet after the fashion of bores.[4]

As a writer, Montaigne certainly invites one discriminating reader, Lewis Thomas, to join a communication partnership; although they were very different men who lived 400 years apart, Thomas could identify with Montaigne's voice ("that self turns out to be the reader's self"). Take a cue from Lewis and write a journal entry on how your sense of self—confidence, immodesty, insecurity—affects the voice in your writing. You might also write another journal entry on "the fashion of bores" in which you list characteristics in writing which you find boring to read.

8. Reread the selections which illustrate the impersonal, formal tone of some kinds of academic discourse (pp. 148ff.).

a. Specifically, how do these selections differ from earlier selections such as "May Procession" (p. 145) or "Fitness Seekers" (p. 145)? Why is an impersonal style useful and desirable for certain types of writing?

b. Select a passage of your own writing which exhibits a personal, informal tone; rewrite it in the impersonal, formal tone of academic discourse.

c. Familiarize yourself with other varieties of style in academic discourse by studying the prose of your textbooks and by requesting from each of your instructors a representative or model reading selection in his or her particular academic discipline. Write entries in your course log describing the various tones of voice presented in these selections.

NOTES

1. *Elements of Moral Science*, II (Philadelphia: Matthew Carey, 1794), section 865, p. 230. I am indebted to Jacques Barzun for this reference.

2. Joe Peek, "Capital Gains and Personal Saving Behavior," *Journal of Money, Credit, and Banking*, 15 February, 1983, p. 1.

3. Gerald Winer, "A Review Analysis of Children's Fearful Behavior in Dental Settings," *Child Development* 53 (October, 1982), p. 1111.

4. *The Medusa and the Snail: More Notes of a Biology Watcher*, (New York: The Viking Press, 1974), pp. 147–148.

AN
INTERCHAPTER NOTE

Midseason Pep Talk

When people begin a new activity—playing a musical instrument, learning chess or tennis, or beginning to write computer programs of their own design—they perform enthusiastically. They eagerly read instructions, complete warm-up exercises, practice serving and charging the net, or test command after command in hours of trial and error. No task is too menial for novices who are eager to learn. Because they are anxious to do well, they pay attention to minute details; because their expectations are high, they work tirelessly to get it right.

During the next several weeks many of the beginners excel at the activity and continue working vigorously, spurred on by early success. However, success does not come so easily for others and they falter. Practicing is a hit-or-miss proposition. Boredom glazes over their once-bright eagerness. Their expectations lowered, these people view new challenges as threats. These folks need a sip of the picker-upper soft drink; they need to rediscover reasons to commit themselves to the hard work of learning new skills.

Students in my writing classes behave in these ways. So, like a good coach, I gather them 'round me in the locker room (after a hard workout on the parallelism bars, let's say) and I give them my midseason pep talk. It goes something like this:

"I see some long faces here and there. Murphy, where's the old zip? Pezatti, we need more of your one-liners to give us some juice for the late innings."

"But there's too much work in this class," someone blurts out.

"Yeah, we have other classes, too, ya know," another pipes up.

"Besides, mid-terms are coming up and you want two revisions in the same week," a third chimes in.

"Okay, okay," I assert in my most authoritative voice, holding up my hands, palms out, traffic-cop style. Really, I am praying someone doesn't shout, "Off with his head!" It doesn't take much to bestir college freshmen to riot. In the cafeteria the playful flight of a square of lime jello with half a Bartlett pear as navigator can transform even a peace-loving philosophy major into a butter-pat terrorist. I go on the offensive to regain the momentum.

"Let's look at this class in perspective. Sure, you have other classes. And nobody came here to major in English composition. And, furthermore, I realize that some of you have to spend more time doing work for this class than any other. But . . ."

"But, nothin'. Everyday I work for this class. And look at the grade you gave me on the last paper!" This petulant remark comes from a good athlete whose meaning-making abilities are not yet as well-developed as his skills at starting a fastbreak or his strategies for going to the hoop under pressure.

"Okay, Curtis. Hold on a minute. I write everyday, too. But I don't expect to get a big payoff, like a grade, every time I put pen to paper. Do you have any idea how many times I've written and rewritten this textbook? And I'm still not finished with it. Besides, if you had been practicing revision strategies as long as you've been running picks off the post, you could write circles around George Plimpton.

"But, as I was saying before I was so rudely interrupted by the Disgruntled One here. . . ." Curtis and I exchange good-natured smiles ". . . . the work in this course is fundamental to the work you will do in all courses requiring critical thinking and writing. Isn't that just about everything?

"So, I don't ask you to write your pens dry just to please me. I ask you to work for goals that transcend the requirements of this course. I call on you to become Writers, with a capital

"W." Become Writers because they think about the world around them. Writers don't follow the crowd blindly. They are skeptics. They question what they read. And, yes, they even question the wisdom of some schoolwork. But Writers question out of a desire to discover, to learn root causes, to hear a sound rationale."

Some bemused looks call me down from the heights of my rhetoric.

"Okay, I know. Enough of this eloquence crapola. Well, you have to realize that I get all pumped up about this. After all, teaching comp is my life." They chuckle and I'm glad the irony isn't lost on them.

"So, let's talk pragmatics. I don't underestimate the time it takes you to put together a draft every week. But for you to make anything we can call progress, you have to work at break-neck pace. And working on these assignments *will* help you develop thinking and writing skills you'll need in other courses and on the job. When you're out there working in a corporation or in a social-service agency or freelancing, you are going to face writing situations all the time. Sure, your reasons for writing will be more meaningful and real then: you'll be responding to a memo from your boss or composing a report for a committee or drafting a grant proposal. But, basically, you'll be employing the same process that we're practicing now. And if you think you're hassled to meet deadlines now, just wait till your paycheck depends on it, not just a grade in some freshman comp course.

"So, let's get with the program. We've got half a semester to go till the scales fall from your eyes and you become geniuses. Seriously, take a deep breath and a big snort of self-discipline. Remember, we're writing for the little writer's community we've got going here. Let's act like writers composing for and responding to each other.

"Next meeting we begin sentence combining. Put your game hat on and 'play' through the assigned exercises. Next time, we'll work in groups and then begin discussing what sentence combining does for writers. I'll be in the rest of the day; if anyone wants a conference, drop in."

That pep talk does the trick. Well, usually. By the way, if you need a morale boost at this point in the work of your course, try some of these suggestions:

• Write out some journal entries, explaining in detail why you may be "sagging at midterm."

• Share your concerns with a group of classmates and develop some strategies for supporting each other.

• Reread the first chapter and renew your commitment to the fundamental regimen of daily practice.

• Discuss your situation with your instructor or your academic adviser.

We all hit slumps. Yes, even Writers. Slumps are a normal part of the warp and woof of life. How one deals with slumps is what separates Writers from mere scribblers. Be a Writer. They grab the gusto.

6
SENTENCE STRUCTURE AND SENSE

A perfectly healthy sentence,
it is true, is extremely rare.

Henry David Thoreau

The sentence is the basic unit of complete thought in prose writing. It is the writer's building block. With it he or she can create a variety of useful and beautiful compositions. Because the sentence is so fundamental to designing effective forms for his or her ideas, the writer needs to develop the ability to create various sentence structures. In fact, quite often the difference between mediocre form and effect in a draft and superior form and effect in a revision of the draft lies in the development of ideas and their presentation in effective sentence structures. The sentence examples and exercises in this chapter are designed to familiarize you with various sentence patterns and to give you practice imitating and creating them.

Note: If you have difficulty writing grammatically correct sentences consistently, you may find it helpful to complete the review exercise before going on. Turn to p. 189.

MAKING SENTENCE STRUCTURE AND SENSE: PART ONE

As I have been suggesting, a writer's ability to show precisely the complex relations of ideas depends on his or her ability to create various, specific sentence structures. A writer's ability to devise a variety of sentence patterns is also central to the composing of an engaging, unique style. Thus, building effective sentence structures is the key to making good sentence sounds and sense, to both fulfilling your writing purpose and satisfying your readers' needs. Let me illustrate the point; read this information about the writer Robert Penn Warren:

> Warren is honored. His humility is remarkable. He is genial, generous, and candid. He strives in his conversation and in his works for the exact phrase. He often tests several phrases aloud for one that conveys his exact meaning.

Now read the same information combined in two sentences:

> For a man so honored, Warren is remarkably humble, genial, generous, and candid. Striving in his conversation as in his works for the exact phrase, he often tests several aloud for the one that conveys his exact meaning.[1]

The first version requires that the reader scan five simple sentences for the same information the second version presents in two complex sentences. Furthermore, in the first version the separate units of information all appear equally significant, bearing no particular relation to one another since they are all written in independent clauses. What can the main point be? How do the ideas relate to one another? In the second version, however, only two ideas are presented in main or independent clauses:

1. Warren is remarkably humble, genial, generous and candid, and
2. he often tests several (phrases) aloud for the one that conveys his exact meaning.

These are the two main ideas of the passage. The other two ideas are presented in a phrase or a dependent clause, showing that the writer sees them as subordinate to the main ideas. Developing subordinate and coordinate relationships between ideas in this way makes reading less work for the reader because it clarifies the relationships of ideas within passages. A writer needs a flexible turn of mind and a variety of sentence structures at his or her fingertips to accomplish this effectively.

The following exercises present lessons and practice in combining, embedding, or rearranging sentence elements to create various patterns and meaning. Since changing a sentence's structure alters its meaning (even if only slightly), a writer needs to try out a number of versions from which to select the one version most appropriate to the writing situation. He or she needs to determine which idea should be the main or dominant one presented, which idea should be subordinate or supportive to the main one, and how this main–subordinate relationship should be expressed. For example, notice the emphasis shift in the following versions of essentially the same information.

Version 1

Although the Boston Red Sox finished first in their regional division, they did not win the American League Pennant race.

Version 2

Although the Boston Red Sox did not win the American League Pennant race, they did finish first in their regional division.

The sample sentence is made up of two clauses; by moving the subordinating conjunction ("although") from one clause to the other and by changing the clause order, the writer emphasizes either the Red Sox' success within their division or their failure in the pennant race. Try your hand at manipulating meaning and structure by combining the following sets of simple sentences into various single-sentence versions.

Exercise 1

Directions: Using subordinating conjunctions, combine the following sentences into as many different versions as you can. Study the shifts in sound and meaning from one version to another.

Note: Some common subordinating conjunctions are *although, as, because, if, since, unless, until, when, whenever, whereas, wherever, while, why.*

Example

Mr. Downer regularly reads the newspaper from front page to comic strips.

Mr. Downer rarely reads a book, fiction or nonfiction.

Although Mr. Downer regularly reads the newspaper from front page to comic strips, he rarely reads a book, fiction or nonfiction.

Or,

Mr. Downer regularly reads the newspaper from front page to comic strips, *whereas* he rarely reads a book, fiction or nonfiction.

1. Marcia played tennis very well.
   Marcia rarely practiced serving, basic strokes, or tennis strategy.
2. Antonia's mother makes 60 dollars a day.
   Antonia's mother works on a coal-stripping machine.
3. The average American business person spurns high culture.
   American corporate funding of the arts increased dramatically over the past five years.
4. Nathan whistled while he worked.
   Nathan whistled only to keep his mind off his boring job.

Exercise 2

Directions: 1. Write out four sets of simple sentences as above. 2. Using subordinating conjunctions, combine each set in as many different versions as you can, studying the shifts in structure and meaning from one version to the next.

In addition to combining sentence elements to illustrate the main–subordinate relationship of ideas, experienced writers use other structural means to clarify complex relationships among ideas. For example, they embed modifiers (participles, appositives, adjectives, and adverbs) into sentences to deliver more information effectively and efficiently.

Let's suppose, for example, that you have a set of information that contains several actions performed by the same person.

Example

Myrna glanced at the clock repeatedly.

She gathered her books and coat in her arms.

She waited impatiently for the schoolbell to ring.

To write out those three activities as if they are all main or coordinate ideas is not only wasting words (and the reader's time), it is inaccurate. The three actions may occur approximately at the same time, but they do not all hold exactly the same significance. The writer must ask, "What action do I want the reader to see as primary? Which actions are secondary (or subordinate) to the main one? Given my purpose, in what order should I place them to create the best effect on the reader?" Here are some options for rewriting the information by combining the three sentences into one:

Version 1

Glancing at the clock repeatedly, Myrna gathered her books and coat in her arms, waiting impatiently for the schoolbell to ring.

Version 2

Myrna waited impatiently for the schoolbell to ring, glancing repeatedly at the clock and gathering her books and coat in her arms.

Version 3

Gathering her books and coat in her arms and glancing at the clock repeatedly, Myrna waited impatiently for the schoolbell to ring.

Each version has one main idea. (In each case the main idea is in the clause that begins with "Myrna." Notice that the main idea is the same in the second and third versions; only its relation to the other actions has been changed by its position in the sentence.) Each version also contains two other clauses that modify the main clause. In each of those clauses the action is presented in an "-ing" form of the verb called a present participle. Discuss with your classmates the differences in the structure, meaning, and rhythm of each version. Which version do you prefer? Why do you find it preferable?

Let's study another set of information containing more than one item in the same word class. This time there are two things describing or renaming the same person.

Example

William Faulkner was a Southerner.

William Faulkner was the author of *The Sound and the Fury*.

Here are some options for rewriting the information by combining the two sentences into one:

Version 1

A Southerner, William Faulkner was the author of *The Sound and the Fury*.

Version 2

The author of *The Sound and the Fury*, William Faulkner was a Southerner.

Version 3

William Faulkner, author of *The Sound and the Fury*, was a Southerner.

In this example "Southerner" and "author" are two nouns which rename or modify the primary noun, "William Faulkner." In the first version "Southerner" is set apart from the main clause by a comma as an appositive. In the second and third versions "author" is set in apposition to "William Faulkner." The first time it precedes the main clause and the next time it comes as an interrupter between the noun (William Faulkner) and the verb (was). An appositive may appear directly before or directly after the noun it modifies.

Using the following sets of unconnected sentence ideas, practice combining the information from each set into a single sentence in which you give the ideas specific relationships to one another. In this exercise you will be developing sentences using present participles, past participles, and appositives as modifiers.

Exercise 3

Directions: Assume that the first sentence in each set contains the main idea. Embed into the main sentence the actions from the subsequent sentences.

Present participle (-ing verb form)
Example
The old lady stood under the oak tree.
She craned her neck.
She tilted her head.
She listened to the birds warbling.

Craning her neck and tilting her head, the old lady stood under the oak tree, *listening to the bird's warbling.*

1. He eyed the diamond pendant.
   He paused mid-stride.
   The diamond pendant sparkled in the candlelight.
2. Arthur broke his zipper.
   Arthur glanced at the clock.
   Arthur dressed hurriedly.
3. Meryl led the parade of midnight revelers.
   Meryl laughed.
   The revelers sang.
   The revelers danced in the streets.
4. The demolition experts leveled the eight-story building.
   The demolition experts detonated the charges.
   The demolition experts startled people for miles around.

Past participle
Example
The judge was peering over his glasses.
The judge had been lost in thought.
Lost in thought, the judge was peering over his glasses.

Example
The fugitive whirled hopelessly around.
The fugitive had been encircled by his pursuers.
The fugitive whirled hopelessly around, *encircled by his pursuers.*

Note: Past participles are verb forms which function as present participles do; the only difference is that *past* participles are the *past* tense of the verb, as the name suggests.)

1. The children played contentedly for hours on end.
   The children had been delighted with their new gift.
2. The sentry lay motionless in the cold, wet leaves.
   The sentry had been felled by a sniper's bullet.
3. The students dined at the town's finest restaurant.
   The students had been fed up with the school's food service.
4. Dalton's eyes searched the crowd for a familiar face.
   Dalton's eyes had been glazed over by the shock.

Appositives (nouns that rename other nouns)
Example
The city council member proposed a property-tax hike.
The city council member is a millionaire from North Hills.
The city council member, *a millionaire from North Hills,* proposed a property-tax hike.

Example
The soprano turned in a brilliant performance as Madame Butterfly.
The soprano is a senior music major.
Madame Butterfly is the lead role.
The soprano, *a senior music major,* turned in a brilliant performance as Madame Butterfly, *the lead role.*

1. The lecturer presented a novel interpretation of Lady Macbeth's character.
   The lecturer is a leading exponent of feminist literary criticism.

2. Dr. Bangs drank tonic water with a lemon twist while his colleagues drank martinis.
   Dr. Bangs is a rehabilitated alcoholic.
   His colleagues are heavy social drinkers.
3. For every game Pee Wee wore a blue ballcap as a lucky charm.
   Pee Wee was the captain of his team.
   The ballcap was his brother's championship cap.
4. Professor Wheedle wrote articles on the irrelevance of being relevant.
   Professor Wheedle was Chairperson of the Classics Department.

Now that you have practiced imitating certain sentence patterns using the information I have provided, develop those patterns in paragraphs yourself using your own information.

Examples for Exercise 4
Set of Information for the First Sentence

1.0 Marcus trembled with fear.
1.1 Marcus peered into the forest's darkness.
1.2 Marcus tried to remember the campsite location.

STEP 1: Combine the information into one sentence to serve as the main idea for paragraph.
Sentence 1: Trembling with fear and peering into the forest's darkness, Marcus tried to remember the campsite location.

STEP 2: Using the preceding sentence as the beginning idea for a story, create at least three more sentences to finish the story. First, write out in simple sentences a set of information for each sentence. Then combine the information into a single sentence. Use as many participles and appositives in the sentences as appropriate.

Set of Information for the Second Sentence

2.0 Marcus stumbled into marsh bogs.
2.1 Marcus got his boots wet.

2.2 Marcus lost the feeling in his feet.

Sentence 2: Stumbling into marsh bogs, Marcus got his boots wet, losing the feeling in his feet.

Set of Information for the Third Sentence

3.0 Marcus was an experienced backpacker.
3.1 Marcus knew he must not give in to fatigue or panic.
3.2 Fatigue and panic are the two greatest dangers to lost hikers.

Sentence 3: An experienced backpacker, Marcus knew he must not give in to fatigue or panic, the two greatest dangers to lost hikers.

Set of Information for the Fourth Sentence

4.0 Marcus crawled to the top of a knoll.
4.1 Marcus saw a flickering light below.
4.2 Marcus shouted for help.

Sentence 4: Crawling to the top of a knoll and seeing a flickering light below, Marcus shouted for help.

Set of Information for the Fifth Sentence

5.0 Marcus heard his companions return his call.
5.1 Marcus was a devoutly religious man.
5.2 Marcus thanked God for giving him the strength to survive the ordeal.

Sentence 5: Hearing his companions return his call, Marcus, a devoutly religious man, thanked God for giving him the strength to survive the ordeal.

Completed Paragraph:
Trembling with fear and peering into the forest's darkness, Marcus tried to remember the campsite location. Stumbling into marsh bogs, Marcus got his boots wet, losing the feeling in his

feet. An experienced backpacker, Marcus knew he must not give in to fatigue or panic, the two greatest dangers to lost hikers. Crawling to the top of a knoll and seeing a flickering light below, Marcus shouted for help. Hearing his companions return his call, Marcus, a devoutly religious man, thanked God for giving him the strength to survive the ordeal.

Exercise 4

Directions: 1. Combine into one sentence the set of information given for the first sentence. 2. Then, developing your own information and combining it into sentences, compose a paragraph to complete the story begun in the first sentence.

Paragraph One
Set of Information for the First Sentence

1.0 Darlene wanted to compete in the Olympics.

1.1 Darlene had a thoroughbred jumper.

1.2 Darlene trained with her horse everyday.

Sentence 1:

Set of Information for the Second Sentence

2.0
2.1
2.2

Sentence 2:

Set of Information for the Third Sentence

3.0
3.1
3.2

Sentence 3:

Set of Information for the Fourth Sentence

4.0
4.1
4.2

Sentence 4:

Completed Paragraph One:

Paragraph Two
Set of Information for the First Sentence

1.0 Brooke wanted to buy a home computer.
1.1 Brooke saved money from her paper route and baby-sitting jobs for half the cost.
1.2 Brooke bargained with her parents to borrow the balance.

Sentence 1:

Set of Information for the Second Sentence

2.0
2.1
2.2

Sentence 2:

Set of Information for the Third Sentence

3.0
3.1
3.2

Sentence 3:

Set of Information for the Fourth Sentence

4.0
4.1
4.2

Sentence 4:

Completed Paragraph Two:

Paragraph Three
Set of Information for the First Sentence

1.0 "Beak" Wilson was a star guard.
1.1 "Beak" Wilson was a popular student.
1.2 "Beak" Wilson visited the Counseling Center for severe depression.

Sentence 1:

Set of Information for the Second Sentence

2.0
2.1
2.2

Sentence 2:

Set of Information for the Third Sentence

3.0
3.1
3.2

Sentence 3:

Set of Information for the Fourth Sentence

4.0
4.1
4.2

Sentence 4:

Completed Paragraph Three:

Paragraph Four
Set of Information for the First Sentence

1.0
1.1
1.2

Sentence 1:

Set of Information for the Second Sentence

2.0
2.1
2.2

Sentence 2:

Set of Information for the Third Sentence

3.0
3.1
3.2

Sentence 3:

Set of Information for the Fourth Sentence

4.0
4.1
4.2

Sentence 4:

Completed Paragraph Four:

In addition to using participles and appositives to modify information in main clauses, writers also use absolute phrases or
clauses. An absolute phrase or clause contains information sometimes referred to as an "aside" or as a "parenthetical remark."
Take this sentence, for example:

> Jeffrey executed a perfect jacknife dive, *his legs straight and
> his hands touching his feet just before plunging into the
> water.*

In this sentence the main idea is presented in the first clause
and the remainder of the sentence after the comma is an absolute
clause used to modify the main idea. Although it may seem atypi-
cal to have such a long absolute clause, I use it as an example
to show you that length of clause is no measure of what is a
main or what is a subordinate idea.

Directions: Study the following example of a sentence with
an absolute clause which is developed from information in three
simple sentences. Then practice writing this type of sentence
modifier.

Exercise 5

Example
Mark climbed out of the pool.
Mark's teeth were chattering.
Mark's lips were blue.

Mark climbed out of the pool, *his teeth chattering and his lips blue.*

1. The belly dancers circled around him.
   The belly dancers' hips undulated.
   The belly dancers' eyes moved suggestively.
2. We were delayed for more than an hour.
   The freeway was jammed.
3. Barton looked absolutely ghoulish.
   His eyes were set deep in their sockets.
   His skin had a bluish-white pallor.
4. The car slowed to a halt on a desolate stretch of Interstate 95.
   The fuel indicator pointed to "E."
   The engine sputtered and died.

The next exercise presents you with the opportunity to design various combinations of participles, appositives, and absolutes used to modify the same sentence.

Exercise 6

Directions: Combine information in each set of sentences into a single sentence, creating at least two kinds of modifiers in each finished sentence.

Example

J. B. Dalton ended his hour-long concluding argument to the jury.
J. B. Dalton was the murder defendant's attorney.
J. B. Dalton's suit was wrinkled and damp with perspiration.

His suit wrinkled and damp with perspiration, J. B. Dalton, *the murder defendant's attorney,* ended his hour-long concluding argument to the jury. (absolute and appositive)

Example

The marathon runner collapsed after crossing the finish line.
The marathon runner finished among the top 10.
The marathon runner was a 26-year-old school teacher.

Finishing among the top ten, the marathon runner, *a 26-year-old schoolteacher,* collapsed after crossing the finish line. (participle and appositive)

1. Dannemeier lurked about the coffeeshop the entire day.
   Dannemeier was an undercover narcotics agent.
   Dannemeier looked like a low-life drifter.
   Dannemeier wore dark glasses, a ratty sweatshirt, frayed bluejeans, and worn-out sneakers.
2. The dancer floated effortlessly across the stage on tiptoe.
   The dancer's arms extended skyward.
   The dancer was a Russian emigré.
   The dancer thrilled the audience.
3. Professor Peach diagrammed the complicated circuitry for the class.
   Peach was Associate Professor of Electrical Engineering at State University.
   Professor Peach saw that the entire class was confused by the book's description of the circuitry.
4. Farley gobbled the cookies.
   Farley acted like Sesame Street's ravenous cookie monster.
   Farley was the Dunes' two-year-old.
   Farley's hands stuffed the cookies into his mouth.

The following exercise once again asks you to experiment with creating sentences containing the types of modifiers presented in this section: participles, appositives, and absolutes. Follow the directions carefully because the process is reversed.

Exercise 7

Directions: 1. Write out four sentences in each of which you combine at least two different types of modifiers. 2. Then *decombine* each sentence; in other words, write all of the information from each sentence in simple sentences, one idea to a sentence.

Example

One coatsleeve missing and his pantlegs in shreds, Cameron walked unsteadily away from his totally demolished car, *an '82 Trans Am.* (absolute and appositive)

Cameron walked unsteadily away from his totally demolished car.

Cameron has an '82 Trans Am.

Cameron's coatsleeve is missing.

Cameron's pantlegs are in shreds.

MAKING SENTENCE STRUCTURE AND SENSE: PART TWO

While the flexible structure of the English sentence presents writers with countless sentence pattern variations, there are three basic sentence types: the cumulative sentence, the periodic sentence, and the balanced sentence. Generally speaking, most contemporary writers use the cumulative sentence pattern; not only is it popular today because it is the least formal type, but the cumulative sentence pattern also permits writers to list a series of modifiers, an efficient and, frequently, a dramatic way of presenting a lot of information. (For example, the sentences in Part One of this chapter are forms of the cumulative sentence type.) However, you will find that you have more sentence pattern options available to you if you know how to write all three types. Therefore, read the following discussion carefully and practice imitating and creating these three basic sentence types.

The Cumulative Sentence

In the cumulative sentence information accumulates by degrees. A writer states a main idea outright and then modifies or qualifies it by adding words, phrases, or clauses. For example, look at these two cumulative sentences:

In high school Diane Keaton exaggerated everything, laughing big, walking like a truck driver, ratting her hair higher than anyone else, hiking her skirts higher, wearing black nylons against the school rule, and wearing a lot of lipstick.[2]

Chartres Cathedral is the bridge between the Romanesque and the Gothic worlds, between the world of Abelard and the world of St. Thomas Aquinas, the world of restless curiosity and the world of system and order.[3]

Sometimes the modifying details precede the main idea, as in this catalog-like sentence:

> The land of golden beaches, snowcapped alps, beautiful lakes, thermal wonderland, majestic fiords, emerald hills, Maori culture, giant snow-covered glaciers, and subtropical islands, New Zealand offers you a one-stop world tour.[4]

Occasionally the modifying details both precede and follow the main idea, as in this case:

> Short, thickset, pock-marked, dark as an Arab, the fellow lurched along like a crazy man—rushing, dawdling, waving his arms, muttering hoarsely, intensity blazing from his face.[5]

Look at the same, detailed description of the aging Beethoven presented in simple sentences:

> The fellow was short. The fellow was thickset. The fellow was pock-marked. The fellow was dark as an Arab. The fellow lurched along like a crazyman. The fellow was rushing. The fellow was dawdling. The fellow was waving his arms. The fellow was muttering hoarsely. Intensity was blazing from the fellow's face.

Don't you agree that the first version is the preferable one? I prefer it because it is easier to read (about half the length) and because it is dramatic. It describes Beethoven physically first: "Short, thickset, pock-marked, dark as an Arab," then it presents the dominant idea of his action: "The fellow lurched along like a crazy man—" followed by four additions to or modifiers of that action: "rushing, dawdling, waving his arms, muttering hoarsely," and ending with a comment on the quality of the look on his face: "intensity blazing from his face." The writer creates a dramatic effect with the cumulative sentence which the simple sentence version cannot match even though the information is presented in the same sequence. The next exercise presents you with the challenge of creating cumulative sentences from the sets of information provided.

Exercise 8: Making Cumulative Sentences

Directions: Practice making cumulative sentences by combining into one sentence the information from each of these sets of simple sentences:

1. The Oyster Bar is just about everything it should be.
   The Oyster Bar is honest.
   The Oyster Bar is straightforward.
   The Oyster Bar offers an unmatched variety of fish.
   The fish is prepared without gimmicks.
   The fish is quickly served.
   The serving is at easy going prices.[6]
2. Coach Belts are classic glove leather belts.
   Coach Belts are well constructed and beautifully detailed.
   Coach Belts are made in a range of men's and women widths and sizes.
   Coach Belts are designed in a crisp, traditional saddlery look.
   Coach Belts are distinguished by authentic, solid, brass hardware, classic harness buckles.
   Each buckle is individually cast in sand.[7]
3. Aerobic dancing is an activity.
   The activity combines things.
   Jogging is one of the things.
   Calisthenics is one of the things.
   Dancing is one of the things.
   A cheery attitude reminiscent of a high-school leaders' club is one of the things.
   Aerobic dancing is the latest health fad.[8]
4. Hong Kong is seldom more dazzling than during the Chinese New Year festivities.
   Markets are abustle.
   Junks and sampans are decked out with a confetti of flags.
   Temples are jammed and aglitter with pinwheels.
   Holiday lighting displays go up.
   Parks turn into holiday flower markets.

Paper shops churn out banners and posters.

The banners and posters say, "Business Prosperity," or "Success in Affairs."[9]

5. The period following Charles II's restoration in 1660 was an extraordinary age.

It was an age that prided itself on its enlightenment and elegance.

It was an age that prided itself on its emergence from the barbarities of the Gothic and absurdities of the Elizabethans.

Yet it was a coarse and cynical age.

It was a callous and corrupt age.

It was an age which nevertheless produced some of the greatest men in the history of English art, philosophy, and science.[10]

6. The Pacific is exciting.

The Pacific is mysterious.

The Pacific is exotic.

The Pacific is more than just an ocean full of islands.

The Pacific is an area of legend and adventure.[11]

7. Natives and tourists by the thousands mill on the promenades.

Natives and tourists by the thousands perch on the bulkheads.

Natives and tourists by the thousands dangle feet in the drink.

Natives and tourists by the thousands flirt on the benches.

Natives and tourists by the thousands lounge in the outdoor cafes.

Natives and tourists by the thousands savor the sounds and sweet airs.

Natives and tourists by the thousands turn Baltimore's Inner Harbor into a continuous celebration.[12]

8. The Piz Badile is situated in the most enchanting cirque of mountains that one could imagine.

The Piz Badile is situated in the Bondasca Valley in Ticino.

In the Bondasca Valley everything is wonderfully ordered,

from the depths of the valley to the slender summits of pale granite.

In the Bondasca Valley the villages of Promontogno and Bondo are real mountain villages.

The villages are a mixture of Swiss orderliness and Italian fantasy.

The villages are not ugly, hybrid growths of upstart towns.

Ugly, hybrid growths of upstart towns are often the case with mountaineering and skiing centres.[13]

9. Hired dwarfs clowned to contribute to something.

Wrestlers grunted and pounded each other to contribute to something.

Storytellers told tales to contribute to something.

Dancing girls performed slow dances and wild acrobatic stunts to contribute to something.

The something is the many-sided entertainment of an acient Egyptian banquet.[14]

10. Islam is the youngest of man's great universal religions.

Islam is the simplest and most explicit of man's great universal religions.

Islam is also one that venerates an all-powerful God.

Islam's adherents encompass nearly one-seventh of the world's total population.[15]

The Periodic Sentence

Like a good mystery novel the periodic sentence holds the reader in suspense by withholding the main idea until the end. Just as the novel's mystery unfolds gradually, so, too, does the main point in a periodic sentence evolve until it reaches a climax at the end. Look at these examples:

Let every nation know, whether it wishes us well or ill, that we shall pay any price, bear any burden, meet any hardship, support any friend, oppose any foe to assure the survival and the success of liberty.[16]

From the toddler who dreads the dark to the businessman who tenses up on plane trips, all of us have our share of fears.[17]

Aside from Bertolucci's *Last Tango in Paris,* which I haven't seen, the most talked about movie in America today is neither a major-studio Hollywood release nor a critically acclaimed import from Europe but is instead a cheapie, hard-core, porno flick called *Deep Throat.*[18]

If the information in this last periodic sentence were delivered in a straightforward, undramatic way, without any forward movement to a climax, it might read this way.

Aside from Bertolucci's *Last Tango in Paris,* which I haven't seen, *Deep Throat,* a cheapie, hard-core, porno flick is the most talked about movie in America today, and it is neither a major-studio Hollywood release nor a critically acclaimed import from Europe.

While this second version presents the same information, it lacks the first version's suspense; suspense often stimulates readers to read more eagerly.

Try your hand at recognizing and composing suspense-filled periodic sentences by working through the following exercises.

Exercise 9: Making Periodic Sentences

PART ONE. Directions: Read aloud the pairs of sentences and circle the number of the periodic sentence in each pair.

1.1 I guess the answer is that I find myself unable to see anything but Samuel Beckett's two sad tramps forever waiting under that wilted tree for their lives to begin at the end of the road we are following with such self-assured momentum.

1.2 The answer is, I guess, that I find myself unable to see anything at the end of the road we are following with such self-assured momentum but Samuel Beckett's two sad tramps forever waiting under that wilted tree for their lives to begin.[19]

2.1 In 1963, deciding it was time to move on, and after taking German at Harvard summer session, Irving enrolled at the Institute of European Studies in Vienna.

2.2 Irving enrolled at the Institute of European Studies in Vienna in 1963, after deciding it was time to move on and after taking German at a Harvard summer session.[20]

3.1 In the city of the future everyone lives underground, everything is run by a computer in Danville, Illinois, and there are funnel-like buildings and pancake-shape cars.

3.2 In the city of the future, which is depicted as having funnel-like buildings and pancake-shape cars, if I recall, everything, supposedly, runs by a computer in Danville, Illinois and everyone—well, everyone who is anyone, at least—lives underground.[21]

4.1 Drinking a demitasse of expresso at a sidewalk cafe, I suddenly realized, as I looked up and down the street, that one would never see, no matter where one traveled, a more elegant city than Paris.

4.2 Drinking a demitasse of expresso at a sidewalk cafe and looking up and down the street, I suddenly realized that one would never see a more elegant city than Paris, no matter where one traveled.

5.1 Bach is not just a stern-faced architect of 200-year-old musical monuments, but a man of festive spirit and playful nature as well, who is at home in our own idiom as well as the traditional.

5.2 Not just a stern-faced architect of 200-year-old musical monuments, but a man of festive spirit and playful nature as well, Bach is at home in our own, as well as the traditional, idiom.[22]

6.1 We are waiting for the game to begin on an afternoon in mid-May, sitting in shadow with a sunlit, grassy, baseball diamond before us.

6.2 An afternoon in mid-May, sitting in shadow with a sunlit, grassy, baseball diamond before us, we are waiting for the game to begin.[23]

7.1 For vacationers, the Japanese province of Kyushu's resorts, national parks, playgrounds, shrines, historic sites, and luxuriant flora—all bathed in a delightful climate—offers a wealth of scenery.

7.2 The Japanese province of Kyushu's resorts, national parks, playgrounds, shrines, historic sites, and luxuriant flora—all bathed in delightful climate—offers a wealth of scenery for vacationers.[24]

8.1 To hear and recreate the sound and sense of his original is always the task of the translator, whether of the impressionist or literalist camp.

8.2 Whether of the impressionist or literalist camp, the translator always has as his task to hear and recreate the sound and sense of his original.[25]

9.1 Our first childhood memories are fragmentary and mysterious, as though veiled by a lifting fog.

9.2 Fragmentary and mysterious, as though veiled by a lifting fog, are our first childhood memories.[26]

10.1 Because society expects it of them, and even when their instincts are against it, people often rush—headlong—into marriage.

10.2 People often rush headlong into marriage even when their instincts are against it because society expects it of them.

PART TWO. Directions: Make a periodic sentence out of each of the following loosely constructed sentences.

Example

The space shuttle Columbia performed flawlessly on its third mission, roaring into the Florida sky just an hour behind schedule on a date fixed two months ago.

(revised as a periodic sentence)

Roaring into the Florida sky on its third mission just an hour behind schedule on a date fixed two months ago, the space shuttle Columbia performed flawlessly.[27]

1. He claimed he enjoyed shoveling snow if he had a companion and if the temperature did not dip too low.

2. The kitten surveyed the scene below with growing suspicion from a perch on the tree's uppermost branch.

3. The television cameras ventured into the locker room of the victorious Pittsburgh Pirates to witness the predictable jollity at the end of the game.[28]

4. I have been intending for the last forty years to write a book about malapropisms, the only subject on which I consider myself an expert.[29]

5. The First Amendment was scarcely heard of for a century and a half in our nation's history and now it seems to be in the papers everyday—government secrets, reports' sources, school libraries, obscenity, and access to courtrooms.[30]

6. Our hand-formed solid crystal apple has become a classic, flawless in its clarity, purity, and absence of color, absorbing and reflecting its surroundings.[31]

7. Kranjska Gora ranks as Yugoslavia's number one winter resort, nestled in a heavenly setting in the Julian Alps where Austria, Italy, and Yugoslavia meet.[32]

8. Many qualities have earned the Steinway piano a rich reputation wherever the beauty of music is valued, the responsiveness of its touch, the fullness of its sound, and the subtlety of its tonal range.[33]

9. The Detroit Symphony has fallen on hard times, like the auto industry, its future seriously jeopardized by management problems and financial difficulties.[34]

10. Saul Bellow's *The Dean's December* is an infuriatingly uneven book that veers, not without visible effort, from drear to dazzle.[35]

The Balanced Sentence

The balanced sentence presents two similar ideas in parallel words, phrases, or clauses. Generally short, this artful sentence type delights readers with the surprise of the dual pattern in structure and meaning. Because of its wit, length, and epigrammatic form, the balanced sentence is often used in formal writing. Employ balanced sentences in your writing whenever their formal structure fits the content or occasion of your essay. Study how these examples work:

Let us never negotiate out of fear. But let us never fear to negotiate.[36]

By doubting we come to questioning, and by questioning we perceive the truth.[37]

If Gladstone fell into the Thames, that would be a misfortune, and if anyone pulled him out, that, I suppose, would be a calamity.[38]

Let him who has given a favor be silent; let him who received it tell it.[39]

Exercise 10: Balanced Sentences

Directions: Using the preceding sentences as models, write out five balanced sentences.

Example

The composer succeeded in writing emotionally moving music, but he remained emotionally unmoved by his success.

The next two sets of exercises give you opportunities for reviewing and practicing the elements of sentence sounds and sense which have been presented in this chapter.

Exercise 11

PART ONE. Directions: Combine each set of sentences into one sentence.

Example

The camel is the great burden-bearer.
The camel is one of the ugliest animals of all.
The camel is one of the meanest animals of all.
The camel is one of the most useful animals of all.

The camel, the great burden-bearer, is one of the ugliest, meanest, and most useful animals of all.

Example

Soviet arsenals have expanded.
The arsenals are of weapons.
The weapons are nuclear.
The expansion is to a point where a surprise Soviet nuclear attack can lay waste the U.S. arsenals.

The expansion is to a point where a surprise Soviet nuclear attack can destroy our vastly inferior military capability.

The expansion is to a point where a surprise Soviet nuclear attack can leave practically unscathed the USSR as an unrivalled world power.

Soviet nuclear weapons arsenals have expanded to a point where a surprise Soviet nuclear attack can lay waste the U.S. arsenals, destroy our vastly inferior military capability, and leave practically unscathed the USSR as an unrivalled world power.[40]

1. Shorthand is a method of writing.
   The writing is rapid.
   The writing is in symbols instead of words.
2. The Scottish terrier is a small dog.
   It has short legs.
   It has a chunky body.
   It was first raised in the Scottish Highlands in the 1800s.
3. Sunburn is an inflammation of the skin caused by overexposure to the sun.
   Sunburn is common.
   Sunburn is painful.
   Sunburn bears testimony to bad judgment.[41]
4. Computer chips have integrated circuitry.
   The chips are tiny.
   The chips are silicon.
   The chips are half the size of a fingernail.
   The circuitry is powerful enough to book seats on jumbo jets.
   The circuitry is powerful enough to cut complex swatches of fabric with little waste.
   The circuitry is powerful enough to help children learn to spell and play chess.[42]
5. Members of the underclass are responsible for most crime in most communities.
   They are the arsonists.
   They are the purse snatchers.
   They are the drug addicts.

They are the defeated people.

They plague society.[43]

6. Ansel Adams' photographs present visions of the American West.

The photographs are of snow-covered peaks in the morning sun.

The photographs are of storm clouds rolling through a mountain pass.

The photographs are of moonrise over a New Mexico landscape.

The visions are intimate.

The visions are majestic.[44]

7. Denny McMahon was a fellow hockey player.

McMahon could do everything I could not do.

McMahon could stickhandle without staring at the puck.

McMahon could skate backwards without ever falling.

McMahon could hit vicious slap shots.

McMahon could circle the rink counterclockwise without appearing staggering drunk.

McMahon could pass accurately.

McMahon could fake out the defenseman or goalie everytime in one-on-one situations.[45]

PART TWO. Directions: Combine each set of sentences into three different sentence patterns. Circle which of the three patterns you prefer and explain the reasons for your preferences.

Example

The toddler darted out of its grandfather's grasp.

The toddler slid under the table.

The toddler squeezed between two chairs.

The toddler was pleased with itself.

1. Pleased with itself, the toddler darted out of its grandfather's grasp, sliding under the table and squeezing between two chairs.

2. Darting out of its grandfather's grasp, the toddler, pleased with itself, slid under the table and squeezed between two chairs.

3. Sliding under the table and squeezing between two chairs, the toddler darted out of its grandfather's grasp, pleased with itself.

Example

The dog barked at the mailman.
The dog was large.
The dog was spotted.
The dog was following a daily ritual.
The barking was loud.
The barking was constant.
The mailman smiled.
The mailman never slackened his pace.

1. Following a daily ritual, the large, spotted dog barked loudly and constantly, at the mailman who smiled and never slackened his pace.
2. The large, spotted dog, following a daily ritual, barked loudly and constantly at the smiling mailman who never slackened his pace.
3. Barking loudly and constantly at the smiling mailman who never slackened his pace, the large, spotted dog followed a daily ritual.

1. Ron lifted up Maria's letter.
   Ron was shaking.
   The lifting was slow.
   The letter was crumpled.
   The letter was damp with tears.
2. The guest ate the doughnuts.
   They were sugar doughnuts.
   There were six doughnuts.
   The eating was ravenous.
   The guest looked around.
   The looking was furtive.
3. Barbara putted the golf ball.
   Barbara was confident.
   The putt was strong.

The putt was straight.
The putt overran the hole.
4. The stranger stood before the mirror.
The stranger combed her hair.
The stranger chewed gum.
The stranger appeared unaware of our presence.
5. The window exploded into chunks.
The explosion was from heat.
The heat was intense.
The chunks were small.
The chunks were crystal.
The chunks littered the entire car's interior.
6. David washed the dishes.
David was joking.
David was whistling.
The dishes were from dinner.
7. The neighbor hung the clothes on the line.
The neighbor bent over.
The neighbor stretched up.
The neighbor worked without pausing.
8. Carol adjusts her necklace.
The necklace is gold.
The necklace is her favorite.
The necklace was a birthday present from a friend.
Carol smiles contentedly.
9. The horse was a bay.
The horse strutted.
The horse whirled on its hind legs.
The horse snorted the dust.
The horse swished its tail.
The horse's actions were regal.
10. The boy had black hair.
The boy grimaced.
The boy swatted at flies.
The swatting was menacing.
The swatting was aimless.

This last exercise gives you an opportunity to practice creating your own variations of the sentence patterns you have been identifying and imitating in the preceding exercises.

Exercise 12

Directions: Combine the following sets of sentences into two separate paragraphs. Let the first serve as the opening paragraph of a story and the second as the closing paragraph. Then, you create the middle of the story, one that moves logically from the beginning to the final sections.

Set of Information for the Introductory Paragraph

1.0 Cassie tiptoed up the steps.
1.1 The steps were to the porch.
1.2 The steps were white marble.
1.3 The steps were moonlit.
2.0 Cassie's hand was shaking.
2.1 She reached for the doorknob.
2.2 The doorknob was brass.
2.3 The doorknob was antique.
2.4 She jerked her hand back.
2.5 The jerk was when she heard her father's voice.
2.6 Her father's voice was within.
3.0 Cassie heard her father lecture her mother.
3.1 Her father said, "That young lady has broken the rules for the last time."
3.2 The saying was vehement.
3.3 The saying was with finality.
4.0 Cassie could hear her own raspy breathing.
4.1 Cassie could hear her thumping heart.
4.2 The thumping was loud.
4.3 Cassie could hear her thoughts.
4.4 Her thoughts were, "I can't go in there. Maybe I can crash at Marie's or Earl's till this blows over."

Completed Introductory Paragraph:

Set of Information for the Concluding Paragraph

1.0 Cassie looked around the livingroom.
1.1 The look was as if she had been away from home five years not five weeks.
2.0 Her face was forlorn.
2.1 Her face was drawn.
2.2 Her eyes darted from her father to her mother.
2.3 Her father was a Victorian man.
2.4 Her mother was kindhearted.
2.5 Her mother was understanding.
3.0 Cassie twisted a handkerchief in her hands.
3.1 Cassie searched for the right words.
3.2 The words were to describe her odyssey.
3.3 The odyssey was agonizing.
3.4 The odyssey was liberating.
3.5 The odyssey taught her the meaning of the word "home."

Completed Concluding Paragraph:

Share your completed story with a group of your classmates. You will, of course, be interested to discuss each other's version of the story detail. But also examine the various sentence structures you used, discussing how these structures affect the story's meaning and its effect upon the reader.

CONCLUDING NOTES ON STRUCTURE AND SENSE

The three sentence patterns we've looked at—cumulative, periodic, and balanced—are rather formal structurally; therefore, composing them requires a great deal of planning, writing, and rewriting. Also, because they are emphatic patterns, experienced writers usually employ them in conclusions or other places where dramatic effect will be useful. Writers often use less formal variations of these patterns and, sometimes, combinations of them. As I said earlier, the cumulative sentence appears more frequently in contemporary prose than the other two patterns, because it is the least formal and because listing a series of items is an efficient—and sometimes dramatic—way of delivering a lot of information.[46]

I know of no writer who says, "I'll begin this essay with a balanced sentence." Or, "I think what this paragraph needs is a sentence with an appositive and two participal clauses." Neither does a basketball player say, "Now, I'm taking a jump shot." Or, "The bounce pass will really make this fast break work." Both the writer and the basketball player act spontaneously in their respective situations. However, each of them has to learn the fundamental activities of the game. Thus, while some of the sentence-combining exercises in this chapter present you with artificial drills (like practicing lay-ups and play designs), they provide you with a repertoire of sentence structures and sense from which you can make spontaneous selections when playing the writing game.

Finally, while the exercises in this chapter have been encouraging you to write longer and more complex sentences, do not infer that a piece of writing full of longer and more complex sentences is necessarily well written. As a general rule, vary the length of sentences in your writing. In other words, for the most part compose your ideas in complex sentences, clearly illustrating the relationships among ideas as effectively and efficiently as you can. But also use short sentences occasionally. They serve an important function. For example, they can change the rhythm of your prose. And they can be emphatic.

SENTENCE SENSE REVIEW

Completing this review exercise will help you know if you have a basic sense of correct sentences. Following is a brief definition of three common sentence faults: the sentence fragment, the comma splice, and run-together sentences. There are examples of each error and corrections of them. *Read the definitions, examples, and corrected versions carefully; then complete the exercises that follow.*

Sentence Fragment

A sentence fragment is a group of words set off as a complete sentence but which is incomplete. Usually, it is an error in punctuation rather than a problem of basic sentence sense. Sometimes, however, it results from an inability to recognize complete thoughts.

Examples

a. She wanted to help combat world famine. *Even if in just a small way.*

Corrected:

She wanted to help combat world famine even if in just a small way.

b. "Workaholics" crave new challenges. *Preferring always to have goals to strive for rather than achieving them.*

Corrected:

"Workaholics" crave new challenges, preferring always to have goals to strive for rather than achieving them.

c. Something in the human spirit wants to be free. *Regardless of the circumstances of its imprisonment.*

Corrected:

Something in the human spirit wants to be free regardless of the circumstances of its imprisonment.

d. The prosecutor failed to present sufficient evidence against the defendants. *Which would convince the jury that they were guilty beyond a reasonable doubt.*

Corrected:

The prosecutor failed to present sufficient evidence against the defendants which would convince the jury that they were guilty beyond a reasonable doubt.

e. The critics doubted that she had the artistic vision to fulfill her life's ambition. *To become an impresario.*

Corrected:

The critics doubted that she had the artistic vision to fulfill her life's ambition to become an impresario.

or,

The critics doubted that she had the artistic vision to fulfill her life's ambition: to become an impresario.

Comma Splice

A comma splice, or comma fault, occurs when a writer places a comma between two complete sentences rather than an appropriate end punctuation mark, like a semicolon (;) or a period (.).

Note: The term "comma splice" is a metaphor. To splice means to join together two separate things, two ropes, for example, or two electrical wires. It is an error in punctuation to join or splice two complete sentences together with a comma; they must remain separate units. The semicolon serves to indicate a full stop between the sentence units and also to show a close relationship between the sentence's ideas; some writers consider it a particularly stylish device.

Examples

a. The fighting is not over, it has just reached a lull.
   Corrected:
   The fighting is not over; it has just reached a lull.
   or,
   The fighting is not over. It has just reached a lull.
b. He raised geraniums by the dozens each summer, however, he never planted salmon-colored ones.
   Corrected:
   He raised geraniums by the dozen each summer; however he never planted salmon-colored ones.
   or,
   He raised geraniums by the dozen each summer. However, he never planted salmon-colored ones.
c. We planned a trip to Japan, we had just finished reading *Shogun* and wanted to see the homeland of the samurai warriors.
   Corrected:
   We planned a trip to Japan; we had just finished reading *Shogun* and wanted to see the homeland of the samurai warriors.
   or,
   We planned a trip to Japan because we had just finished reading *Shogun* and wanted to see the homeland of the samurai warriors.

d. We gazed in awe at the ice-covered mountains, they sparkled like crystal in the sunlight.

Corrected:

We gazed in awe at the ice-covered mountains; they sparkled like crystal in the sunlight.

or,

We gazed in awe at the ice-covered mountains, which sparkled like crystal in the sunlight.

e. It clamored out of the garage into the moonlight, scampered across the lawn, and slid down the embankment, then all we heard was the wind.

Corrected:

It clamored out of the garage into the moonlight, scampered across the lawn, and slid down the embankment; then all we heard was the wind.

or,

It clamored out of the garage into the moonlight, scampered across the lawn, and slid down the embankment. Then all we heard was the wind.

Run-Together Sentences

A writer creates run-together sentences by failing to place any appropriate end punctuation mark at the end of a complete sentence. Thus, it runs into the following sentence structure. Sometimes the error is called a run-on sentence, but it is more appropriately named a run-together sentence since the result is two sentence structures which run together.

Examples

a. We were stuck in traffic for 45 minutes no doubt we would miss the kickoff.

Corrected:

We were stuck in traffic for 45 minutes. No doubt we would miss the kickoff.

or,

We were stuck in traffic for 45 minutes; no doubt we would miss the kickoff.

or,

Because we were stuck in traffic for 45 minutes, no doubt we would miss the kickoff.

b. The rookie strode out to the mound his knees shook when he looked at the throng in the grandstand.

Corrected:

The rookie strode out to the mound. His knees shook when he looked at the throng in the grandstand.

or,

The rookie strode out to the mound; his knees shook when he looked at the throng in the grandstand.

or,

The rookie strode out to the mound and his knees shook when he looked at the throng in the grandstand.

c. I think my uncle must be crazy he wants to sell his house and move into a condominium.

Corrected:

I think my uncle must be crazy. He wants to sell his house and move into a condominium.

or,

I think my uncle must be crazy; he wants to sell his house and move into a condominium.

or,

I think my uncle must be crazy, *because* he wants to sell his house and move into a condominium.

Sentence Sense Exercise

Some of the following sentences are correct; some are incorrect. To check your ability to recognize sentence faults, read the sentences. Then next to the number corresponding to each sentence write "correct," if it is so, or "fragment," "comma splice," or "run-together," depending on the error. *For each incorrect sentence, write out a correct version.*

1. While growing to maturity, an apple is vulnerable to many potentially destructive forces. Insects, diseases, and even bruising.

2. Her face was etched with a deep tan, her eyes were a little bloodshot from hours of looking at the sun reflecting off the water.

3. Peacedale is one of the youngest towns in the region, nevertheless, it has a rich heritage.

4. In April the sports fishing season opens throughout New England and people's thoughts turn to fish. To eating the golden fried fillets, clams, and scallops and the succulent lobsters which will soon be sold at the little roadside stands.

5. Rose simply turned to her brother he mistook her action and bolted from the room.

6. Heather stirred the mixture, Ron, who was all thumbs, greased a baking pan.

7. Bet on the chestnut mare, she runs well on a muddy track.

8. Although it is an innovative structure, the basic design is functional.

9. Milton was the last person to do something because it was in fashion. True to family tradition.

10. He followed her everywhere that day. No matter where she went, she felt like a suspect under surveillance.

11. Terry's racquet was the perfect weight. Perfect for serving, perfect for net play, and perfect for backhand strokes.

12. Moving up and down the narrow basement stairway safely never crossed Jeff's mind, on the contrary, he ran up and down them, taking them two at a time.

13. Hand stenciling is a forgotten art. Which some craftspeople are reviving.

14. Enter the contest even if you don't believe you can win.

15. There is practically no way to break this toy. Except for the way Harold whacked it.

16. The question is just how much is enough, not how much do they think they can get.

17. Pistachio nuts, which are grown in California, are shipped to New Jersey for processing they claim labor is cheaper in New Jersey.

18. Bill hit a fly ball out to Melissa, she shaded her eyes from the sun and caught it one-handed, basket-style.

19. For hours he complained that he was hungry, although he still could not bring himself to eat the soup.

20. George flicked on all of the lights one at a time, Marilyn never stirred, even though the room was bright as midday.

The answer key to this exercise is printed at the end of the chapter, after the endnotes (p. 197). Compare your answers to those in the key. If you identified 18 or more of the sentences correctly, you have a good ability to recognize basic sentence faults. You may still find that you commit occasional sentence faults when writing, because being able to *recognize* faults when reading sentences does not always ensure that you will be able to *compose* faultless sentences. The more you practice, the more fault-free your sentence making will become.

What if you had difficulty identifying sentence faults? If you missed three or more answers, ask your instructor for further explanation and exercises for the particular error or errors with which you need help. Spending some extra time developing good sentence sense is a sound investment. Once you develop consistency in composing error-free sentences, you gain confidence as a writer. And confidence is a significant ingredient for success. Just ask some musician or athlete who had to spend extra time practicing the fundamentals of his or her music or sport.

NOTES

1. Adapted from Carol Tucker, "Robert Penn Warren," *Saturday Review,* July 1980.

2. Adapted from Jack Kroll, Kartrine Ames, and Janet Huck, "Thoroughly Modern Diane," *Newsweek,* 15 February 1982.

3. Adapted from Kenneth Clark, *Civilisation* (New York: Harper and Row, 1969).

4. Adapted from an advertisement in *Travel/Holiday,* March 1980.

5. Adapted from Brad Darrach, *Ludwig Von Beethoven: A Tragically Sundered Titan* (New York: Time, Inc., 1976).

6. Adapted from Herbert B. Livesey, "Seafood Sensation: Grand Central's Oyster Bar," *Travel & Leisure,* January 1982.

7. Adapted from an advertisement for Coach Belts in *The New Yorker,* 28 December 1981.

8. Adapted from "The Talk of the Town," *The New Yorker,* 28 December 1981.

9. Adapted from Karen Cure, "Welcoming the Year of the Monkey," *Travel/Holiday,* January 1980.

10. Adapted from F. E. Halliday, *An Illustrated Cultural History of England* (New York: Crescent Books, Craven Publishers, Inc., 1981).

11. Adapted from an advertisement by Judith Friedburg, "The Pacific—A Panorama," *Travel & Leisure,* February 1980.

196   *Writing Practice*

12. Adapted from Michael Demarest, "He Digs Downtown," *Time,* 24 August 1981.

13. Adapted from Gaston Rebuffat, *Starlight and Storm: The Ascent of the Six Great North Faces of the Alps,* trans. Wilfred Noyce and the Rt. Hon. Lord Hunt (New York: Oxford University Press, 1968).

14. Adapted from Lionel Casson, *Ancient Egypt* (New York, Time, Inc., 1965).

15. Adapted from *The World's Great Religions* (New York: Time, Inc., 1957).

16. John Fitzgerald Kennedy, "Inaugural Address," *Public Papers of the Presidents of the United States, John Fitzgerald Kennedy, 1961* (Washington, D.C.: United States Government Printing Office, 1962).

17. Adapted from Dan Kaercher, "Childhood and Adult Fears: New Tactics for Coping," *Better Homes and Gardens,* October 1981.

18. Thomas Meehan, " 'Deep Throat' Is Hard to Swallow," *Saturday Review,* March 1973.

19. Adapted from Theodore Roszak, *The Making of a Counter Culture* (New York: Doubleday & Company, Inc., 1969).

20. Adapted from R. Z. Sheppard, "Life Into Art," *Time,* 31 August 1981.

21. Adapted from Gerald Nachman, "Future Shock," *Newsweek,* 29 March 1982.

22. Adapted from a Honeywell advertisement, "The Joy of Bach," *The New Yorker,* 28 December 1981.

23. Adapted from Roger Angell, "The Sporting Scene," *The New Yorker,* 20 July 1981.

24. Adapted from Eugene Fodor, "The Real Japan," *Travel & Leisure,* August 1980.

25. Adapted from Albert Cook, "Preface," *Homer/The Odyssey: A New Verse Translation* (New York: W. W. Norton and Co., 1967).

26. Adapted from Curtis Cate, *George Sand: A Biography* (Boston: Houghton Mifflin Company, 1975).

27. Adapted from Jerry Adler, "Science: 'We're Kind of Busy Up Here,' " *Newsweek,* 5 April 1982.

28. Adapted from Carll Tucker, "The Back Door," *Saturday Review,* December 1979.

29. Adapted from Goodman Ace, "Top of My Head," *Saturday Review,* December 1979.

30. Adapted from Charles Rembar, "For Sale: Freedom of Speech," *The Atlantic Monthly,* March 1981.

31. Adapted from an advertisement for Steuben Glass in *The New Yorker,* 14 December 1981.

32. Adapted from Helmut and Gea Koenig, "Ski Yugoslavia," *Travel/Holiday,* December 1979.

33. Adapted from an advertisement for Steinway pianos, *Saturday Review*, January 1982.

34. Adapted from Scot Haller, ed., "The Insider," *Saturday Review*, January 1982.

35. Adapted from Helen Dudar, "The Graying of Saul Bellow," *Saturday Review*, January 1982.

36. John Fitzgerald Kennedy, "Inaugural Address," *Public Papers of the Presidents of the United States, John Fitzgerald Kennedy, 1961* (Washington, D.C.: United States Government Printing Office, 1962).

37. Kenneth Clark, *Civilisation* (New York: Harper & Row, 1969).

38. Benjamin Disraeli as quoted in Nancy McPhee, *Book of Insults*. (New York: Penguin Books, 1980).

39. Seneca, originally in Latin, trans. Charles Jurny, Jr. et al., *First Year Latin* (Boston: Allyn and Bacon, Inc., 1979).

40. *Bulletin of the Atomic Scientists*, September 1970, #35.

41. Adapted from Donald M. Vickery and James F. Fries, *Take Care of Yourself, A Consumer's Guide to Medical Care* (Reading, Mass.: Addison-Wesley, 1979), p. 61.

42. Adapted from Merrill Sheils with Wm. Cook, Michael Reese, Marc Frons, Phyllis Malamud, "And Man Created the Chip" *Newsweek*, 30 June 1980.

43. Adapted from Ken Auletta, "A Reporter at Large; The Underclass—Part I," *New Yorker*, 16 November 1981.

44. Adapted from Susan K. Reed "Ansel Adams Takes on the President," *Saturday Review*, November 1981, p. 32.

45. Adapted from Laurence Sheehan, "Let's Hear It for the Flying McMahons," *Yankee*, January 1982.

46. I am indebted to Francis W. Christensen's work for much of my understanding and discussion of the sentence, especially of the cumulative sentence. See Francis Christensen and Bonniejean Christensen, *Notes Toward a New Rhetoric*, 2nd ed. (New York: Harper & Row, 1978).

ANSWER KEY TO SENTENCE SENSE EXERCISES, PP. 193–194.

1. fragment
2. comma splice
3. comma splice
4. fragment
5. run-together
6. comma splice
7. run-together
8. correct
9. fragment
10. correct
11. fragment
12. comma splice

13. fragment
14. correct
15. fragment
16. correct

17. run-together
18. comma splice
19. correct
20. comma splice

7
TYPES OF WRITING

A PRELIMINARY NOTE

In addition to developing a storehouse full of various sentence structures, practicing writers acquaint themselves with different types of writing. Because the dual guidelines of writing purpose and audience require that writers be resourceful in how they present information, writers need to explore optional types of writing for each situation. The more writing types they have at their command, the greater chance they have of selecting an effective type for a given situation.

In the next several pages I present some of the basic types of writing commonly used in college writing situations. The types presented here are description, narration, exposition, comparison and contrast, analysis, and persuasion. While these are presented as "pure" types, writers use them most often in different combinations. So, do not regard these types as static models or as ends in themselves. Rather, study them in order to employ the techniques of these types as means to an end, in other words, as strategies for fulfilling your writing goals.

For example, think for a moment about the kinds of writing that may be assigned to you over the next few years. Students in literature and history courses discuss themes, events, and characters in human drama and analyze the texts which present them. Students of marketing or business management may read case studies of economic or entrepreneurial activities and recommend corporate actions. In journalism courses students report the facts of a news conference, a sports event, or a traffic accident; and they practice, in addition, estimating the implications of a Supreme Court decision, a social trend, or a federal fiscal policy. Science students describe the experiments they conduct and analyze the results. Social-work students compose client histories, and nursing students write patient summaries. Students of political science analyze governing institutions and the political behavior of people and argue this or that position on domestic and foreign policies. In each of these writing situations one type of writing may serve more effectively than another; still, it is more than likely that a combination of types will meet the needs of a given situation. Practice the writing types individually and in combination so that when the occasion arises, you can incorporate the most appropriate types in your writing as you draft, develop, and revise your topic. The next several pages provide you with opportunities to practice the basic writing types.

Writing is a Game of Show and Tell.

DESCRIPTION

In descriptive writing one paints a picture, showing a reader how something, someplace, or someone looks. Writing description takes a keen eye and the ability to select precisely the right concrete words. In some situations an "objective" description is the most appropriate, that is, a description focusing wholly on features of the subject itself uncolored by the writer's feelings or opinion about the subject described.

However, more often than not, writers describe something not only to show it to the reader, but also to make the reader "see" it in a certain way. For example, a travel writer uses the following paragraph to set the scene for nighttime fishing:

> It's a typical January evening. About an hour after sunset, in the blue-gray light of the rapidly approaching darkness, you are standing on Maine's Eastern River Bridge, midway between Dresden and Richmond. The biting cold of the night air grates against your skin, and your nose catches the acrid scent of wood smoke suspended above the river. The warm,

yellow glow of bare light bulbs seeps through the cracks of loosely constructed shacks anchored to the ice below. The otherwise quiet solitude enveloping you is split by an occasional piercing crack of tide-shifted ice, and your ears perceive the faint sounds of laughter and excitement in the distance.[1]

This writer recreates the experience for the reader by setting the reader in a specific place ("you are standing on Maine's Eastern River Bridge, midway between Dresden and Richmond") and by listing sense impressions:

> *sight:* "hour after sunset," "blue-gray light," "warm, yellow glow of bare light bulbs"
> *touch:* "biting cold," "night air grates against your skin"
> *smell:* "nose catches the acrid scent of wood smoke"
> *hearing:* "otherwise quiet solitude . . . is split by an occasional crack of tide-shifting ice," "faint sounds of laughter and excitement"

Notice, also, that this writer evokes a special mood by his word choice; study his use of verbs (action words) and modifiers (descriptive words) to see how he builds the sense of man battling against the natural elements. This writer's primary purpose is to give the reader the "feel" of this experience, to lure the reader up to Maine for the winter smelt fishing. His audience, readers of *Yankee* magazine, are New Englanders (by residence or sympathy) who might fish New England's waters or, at least, want to know about it vicariously.

Another travel writer creates a special atmosphere out of an autumn scene in Yellowstone Park:

> Autumn crisps the air, gilds the aspens, burnishes the cottonwoods, banishes the crowds. Wildlife, often timid in the tourist season, begin to reclaim their domain. Elk bugle in the woods, moose go courting in the wetlands, bears gorge themselves on berries for the long sleep, and buffalo herds draw closer to the warm vapors of the geysers, paying little heed to the few humans who intrude.[2]

By carefully selecting each verb, this writer has depicted animals reigning supreme in an idealized, natural world as pure as the

Garden of Eden before the fall of man. This writer's purpose in creating such an unspoiled natural scene is to entice urban dwellers out West to see the country's natural beauty (and, of course, to support the off-season tourist business). Making two lists of verbs reveals the writer's method of painting natural life as good, even noble, and man as bad, an exile or an intruder:

natural life	*man*
autumn	
crisps	
gilds	
burnishes	
banishes	man is banished
wildlife reclaim	
elk bugle	
moose go courting	
bears gorge themselves	
buffalo herds draw closer	humans intrude

Notice, also, that space is not circumscribed here. The reader does not view the scene from any particular mountaintop; rather, he or she is given a sense of the limitlessness of the lands, not bounded by anything, least of all man-made fences.

In the following paragraph a sports writer sets the scene for a college baseball game.

An afternoon in mid-May, and we are waiting for the game to begin. We are in shadow, and the sunlit field before us is a thick, springy green—an old diamond, beautifully kept up. The grass continues beyond the low chain-link fence that encloses the outfield, extending itself on the right-field side into a rougher, featureless sward that terminates in a low line of distant trees, still showing a pale, early-summer green. We are almost in the country. Our seats are in the seventh row of the grandstand, on the home side of the diamond, about halfway between third base and home plate. The seats themselves are more comforting to spirit than to body, being a surviving variant example of the pure late-Doric Polo Grounds mode, the backs made of a continuous running row of wood slats, divided off by pairs of narrow cast-iron arms, within which are slatted let-down seats, grown arthritic with rust and countless layers of gray paint. The rows are stacked so closely upon each other (one discovers) that a happening on the field of sufficient interest to warrant a rise or half-rise to one's feet is often made more memorable by a sharp crack to the kneecaps delivered by the backs of the seats just forward; in time, one finds that a dandruff of gray paint flakes from the same source has fallen on one's lap and score-card. None of this matters, for this view and these stands and this park—it is Yale Field, in New Haven—are renowned for their felicity.[3]

Make an assessment of the descriptive writing in the preceding paragraph by answering these questions and by listing the key words in the paragraph which relate to the questions:

1. Where is the scene?

2. Where is the writer located in the scene?

3. What is the time (of year and day)?

4. What concrete or sensory language is used?

5. What sense of space is conveyed?

6. What mood is created?

7. What special techniques does the writer use to create the scene and to elicit the feelings he does?

8. What is the writer's primary aim in composing this paragraph?

9. Who is the intended audience for this paragraph?

Discuss your responses with a group of classmates and draft a statement summarizing your assessment of the paragraph's purpose and method.

Writers also use concrete language and specific techniques of organizing information to describe people in particular ways. For example, Sandy, a student in my course, used the traditional top-to-bottom method of organizing her description of a character:

George is a cheerful-looking fellow, rather short in height. He comes to work each day wearing the same beige shirt, each sleeve haphazardly rolled up on his arm. His face is clean shaven, except for a short white moustache, tapering off into two neat curls. On occasion, he wears a banjo player's straw hat with a green band across the middle, under which waves of silvery white hair sweep evenly around his head. The pocket on his cotton shirt is fully stuffed, shooting off an array of pens, pencils, pads and a pair of eyeglasses. A weathered-out black belt supports his large brown pants over a barrel of a belly. His feet hold a pair of tired black work boots that yearn to be replaced. He's the type of man that everybody knows and likes, but nobody associates with, for one reason or another. At first glance, he seems unrefined, a bit rough around the edges. But look closer and you'll find a colorful human being, sensitive to others with a flair for life.

Compare Sandy's method of organizing details with the following one:

> He saw . . . a man of under size, his hands in his coat pockets, a cigarette slanted from his chin. His suit was black, with a tight, high-waisted coat. His trousers were rolled once and caked with mud above mud-caked shoes. His face had a queer, bloodless color, as though seen by electric light; against the sunny silence, in his slanted straw hat and his slightly akimbo arms, he had that vicious depthless quality of stamped tin . . . [His eyes were] two knobs of soft black rubber.[4]

This is the picture William Faulkner paints of his main character, Popeye, in the beginning of the novel *Sanctuary*. Faulkner follows no traditional method of presenting details: not top-to-bottom, bottom-to-top, outside-to-center, center-outward, left-to-right, nor right-to-left. Rather, he presents details in disorienting manner, moving from the general view of an undersized man to his hands (in his coat pockets), to his suitcoat, down to his trouser bottoms, to his shoes, up to his face, to his hat, down to his arms, and later up to his eyes. After presenting a few lines of dialogue, Faulkner returns to describe the now-squatting Popeye:

> He squatted in his tight black suit, his right-hand coat pocket sagging compactly against his flank, twisting and pinching

cigarettes in his little, doll-like hands, spitting into the spring. His skin had a dead, dark pallor. His nose was faintly aquiline, and he had no chin at all. His face just went away, like the face of a wax doll set too near a hot fire and forgotten. Across his vest ran a platinum chain like a spider web. . . . Popeye's eyes looked like rubber knobs, like they'd give to the touch and then recover with the whorled smudge of the thumb on them.[5]

This time Faulkner focuses more on Popeye's facial features, but here, again, notice the helter-skelter order in which Faulkner presents the details: from Popeye's suit, to his coat pocket, to his hands, up to his mouth ("spitting"), to his skin, to his nose, to his face (with focus on no chin), down to his vest, and up again to his eyes. Faulkner breaks away from the traditional ways of presenting spatial details, using a seemingly chaotic or random order of presentation; he does so as a means of emphasizing that this character is not properly put-together: his body parts seem to be at sixes and sevens. The specific features and details Faulkner gives further develop this idea the reader gets from the order in which they are presented.

Let's study the physical details Faulkner selects for the reader's two initial looks at Popeye:

First look	*Second look*
a man of undersize	tight black suit
cigarette slanted from chin	coat pocket sagging compactly
tight black suit	doll-like hands
trousers ⎫ mud-caked shoes ⎭	spitting
	skin—dead, dark pallor
face—queer, bloodless color as seen by electric light	nose—faintly aquiline
slanted straw hat	no chin
	face—falls away like a wax doll
slightly akimbo arms	platinum (watch) chain—like a spider web
eyes—two knobs of soft black rubber	eyes—rubber knobs—whorled smudge

The details show Popeye to be a distorted man, a perversion
of humanity. He is a man whose face has a queer, bloodless
color and whose skin has a dead, dark pallor. Notice that although
he is in sunlight, his face appears to be seen by electric (unnatural)
light. He is a man of undersize whose hands are doll-like, whose
eyes lack any brightness or human color ("soft, black, rubber
knobs"), whose nose is hooked like that of a bird of prey ("aquiline" = hooked beak like that of an eagle or a hawk), and whose
face seems melted away below the nose "like a wax doll set
too near a fire." (A protruding chin, or square jaw, often stands
for strength of character. Popeye seems to lack any chin whatso-
ever.) Furthermore, he is a man who is at odds; nothing about
him is erect or straight: "slanted straw hat," "cigarette slanted
from his chin [what chin?]," "slightly akimbo arms," "coat pocket
sagging compactly [there is a gun in it]." Indeed, Popeye turns
out to be a man who is inhumane and perverted. Faulkner presents Popeye as such at first sight to the reader by the specific
details he selects and by his unique method of presenting them.

Thus, from the preceding examples it should be evident that
writers have a particular purpose and audience in mind when
they describe how something, someplace, or someone looks. *Writing purpose and audience provide the criteria for selecting
and arranging the details of the description.* The following
exercises first ask you to sort through descriptions to find the
writers' purposes and intended audiences; second, you are chal-
lenged to write descriptions yourself for particular purposes and
audiences.

Exercises in Description

1. Study the following descriptions; list and categorize the details
of each selection. (You may use one of the methods I used with
the preceding examples.)

A single knoll rises out of the plain in Oklahoma, north and
west of the Wichita Range. For my people, the Kiowas, it is
an old landmark, and they gave it the name Rainy Mountain.
The hardest weather in the world is there. Winter brings bliz-
zards, hot tornadic winds arise in the spring, and in summer
the prairie is an anvil's edge. The grass turns brittle and
brown, and it cracks beneath your feet. There are green belts

along the rivers and creeks, linear groves of hickory and pe-
can, willow and witch hazel. At a distance in July or August
the steaming foliage seems almost to writhe in fire. Great
green and yellow grasshoppers are everywhere in the tall
grass, popping up like corn to sting the flesh, and tortoises
crawl about on the red earth, going nowhere in the plenty
of time. Loneliness is an aspect of the land. All things in
the plain are isolate; there is no confusion of objects in the
eye, but *one* hill or *one* tree or *one* man. To look upon that
landscape in the early morning, with the sun at your back,
is to lose the sense of proportion. Your imagination comes
to life, and this, you think, is where Creation was begun.[6]

I am standing on the Pont des Arts in Paris. On one side of
the Seine is the harmonious, reasonable facade of the Institute
of France, built as a college in about 1670. On the other bank
is the Louvre, built continuously from the Middle Ages to
the nineteenth century: classical architecture at its most splendid and assured. Just visible upstream is the Cathedral of
Notre Dame—not perhaps the most lovable of cathedrals, but
the most rigorously intellectual facade in the whole of Gothic
art. The houses that line the banks of the river are also a
humane and reasonable solution of what town architecture
should be, and in front of them, under the trees, are the open
bookstalls where generations of students have found intellectual nourishment and generations of amateurs have indulged
in the civilised pastime of book collecting. Across this bridge,
for the last one hundred and fifty years, students from the
art schools of Paris have hurried to the Louvre to study the
works of art that it contains, and then back to their studios
to talk and dream of doing something worthy of the great
tradition. And on this bridge how many pilgrims from America, from Henry James downwards, have paused and breathed
in the aroma of a long-established culture, and felt themselves
to be at the very centre of civilisation.[7]

My hotel was called the Hotel des Trois Moineaux. It was a
dark, rickety warren of five storeys, cut up by wooden parti-
tions into forty rooms. The rooms were small and inveterately
dirty, for there was no maid, and Madame F., the *patronne*,
had no time to do any sweeping. The walls were as thin as
matchwood, and to hide the cracks they had been covered

with layer after layer of pink paper, which had come loose and housed innumerable bugs. Near the ceiling long lines of bugs marched all day like columns of soldiers, and at night came down ravenously hungry, so that one had to get up every few hours and kill them in hecatombs. Sometimes when the bugs got too bad one used to burn sulphur and drive them into the next room; whereupon the lodger next door would retort by having *his* room sulphured, and drive the bugs back. It was a dirty place, but homelike, for Madame F. and her husband were good sorts. The rent of the rooms varied between thirty and fifty francs a week.[8]

Paddy was my mate for about the next fortnight, and, as he was the first tramp I had known at all well, I want to give an account of him. I believe that he was a typical tramp and there are tens of thousands in England like him.

He was a tallish man, aged about thirty-five, with fair hair going grizzled and watery blue eyes. His features were good, but his cheeks had lanked and had that greyish, dirty-in-the-grain look that comes of a bread and margarine diet. He was dressed, rather better than most tramps, in a tweed shooting-jacket and a pair of old evening trousers with the braid still on them. Evidently the braid figured in his mind as a lingering scrap of respectability, and he took care to sew it on again when it came loose. He was careful of his appearance alto-gether, and carried a razor and bootbrush that he would not sell, though he had sold his "papers" and even his pocketknife long since. Nevertheless, one would have known him for a tramp a hundred yards away. There was something in his drifting style of walk, and the way he had of hunching his shoulders forward, essentially abject. Seeing him walk, you felt instinctively that he would sooner take a blow than give one.[9]

State in a few sentences the writing purposes for each of these selections. Then comment on the writers' choice and arrangement of details. For example, using Kenneth Clark's description in the second selection, can you sketch a map of the region around the Pont des Arts in Paris? What spatial order does Clark use?

2. Select a familiar object, person, or scene on your campus.
a. Without naming the subject you have chosen, write a descrip-

tion of it or him or her for your classmates. Your purpose in writing this description is to enable your readers to recognize the subject—not all at once, but by degrees. b. Using the same subject, write the description for graduates of your school. With the same writing purpose, do you need to change any details or the arrangement of them? c. Finally, describe the same subject for students who will enter your school next semester. Your purpose here is different from the previous "recognition" purpose: this time you want to make the new students feel welcome by presenting them with a familiar sight they will see upon arriving at campus. Before writing this third description, think carefully about what changes in detail or arrangement you may have to make.

3. Describe your hands. First, list the physical characteristics and any noteworthy features of your hands. Then write a description of your hands from each of these perspectives:

a. as indicative of your work or career;

b. as seen through the eyes of a physician, a manicurist, or a palmist; and

c. as manifestations of your personality.

Expand one of these descriptions into a full essay. For example, the following is an essay Dawne wrote. She began drafting a description of her hands as they reveal her personality, but discovered a new purpose when revising: to use the description of her hands as a means of discussing something of her relationship to her mother.

I am fond of calling my hands my best feature; in fact I entertain hopes of acquiring my own personal *scam:* a hand modeling career—they would grace any man's scruffy neck.

My mother will tell any man that next to her eldest daughter's wide blue eyes and full lips, her best feature is her hands. They are lovely, well-formed, slender hands, she says, unlike her own which are bitten and gnarled. Not surprisingly—as her daughter has no children and she has had six, with hands of varying quality. Her daughter watches, noticing no wrinkles, no scars, no calluses on her mother's pearly skin.

My mother will bite her nails as she says that her mother,

whom I've never met, has just such delicate hands; odd, as she uses them shucking black-eyed peas and frying hush puppies most of the time.

My hands are tiny with long, tapered fingers, almost perfect, that my mother checks every holiday for an equally perfect diamond. My skin, should anyone stroke it, is not as flawlessly smooth as it looks—I religiously wash with pure Swiss Buttermilk soap to avoid irritating its singular delicacy. It gives my skin a sweet, buttery scent—elusive, but familiar.

My fingernails are of different lengths, some abnormally long, thus broken at the base but never bitten and rarely covered with gauche lacquer. At times, when vanity dictates how I spend precious free minutes, I paint them but upon the first chip of the coating I immediately remove the offending red stuff with lemon-scented oil. Oh, but painted nails look mean striping a naked back.

My mother hates dirt under the nails and will notice it on a strange woman quicker than baldness or absent limbs; therefore, I wash my hands many times a day and have often left a room in acute anxiety over some clot of dried scum under my nails—unidentifiable, and better left so.

My hands complement a fragile crystal goblet but they also wield a 10-inch French knife skillfully. Most of the time. I do have a small round scar on the tip of my left index finger. I lost control of my knife once, and neatly sliced my flesh through the nail and the pumpernickle. I didn't notice the wound until the blood dripped onto the mirror-clean stainless steel table. Never slice bread with a French knife. I have a close-up slide of my stitches to remind me of that rule in living color. One slim finger, cream colored, save for a clotted, brown C etched on its face, lying docile on a slab of blue metal.

NARRATION

If a writer paints a picture in descriptive writing, in narrative writing he or she makes the picture move. The essential element in narration is temporal order; the writer describes action in a time sequence. Thus, writing narration requires a good sense of timing and the ability to connect one item to another in a sequence.

Of course, the commonest form of narration is storytelling. From childhood to adulthood you have heard or read stories. You may also have told or written a few. If so, you may have some sense of how to sequence action, in other words, how to link separate actions together chronologically. You may also realize that writers of narrative—especially nonfiction writers—have specific purposes for telling a story. Using the following selections, I will discuss how a writer achieves certain effects through narration.

One student in my class, Jayne, wrote about her experience driving up Mount Washington, New England's tallest peak:

> We begin the ascent by car up the Mount Washington road without any knowledge of what is ahead. The narrow dirt road winds around the mountain for miles. It is, however, paved at the bad curves for safety and better traction. Trees line the road for the first few miles and our journey is like a drive in the country. The thick foliage obscures our view of the surrounding mountains and scenery.
>
> After a few miles, a feeling of fearful anticipation begins to overcome us. Passing cars have only inches of room between themselves. The road becomes steeper and very winding. And it appears as though there isn't enough room for cars to pass each other without driving over the edge. The trees begin to thin out and offer travelers little or no protection against this.
>
> Soon, however, a panoramic view unfolds from behind the obstruction of trees. Brilliant fall colors of reds, oranges, and yellows adorn the trees now far below us. As though standing at attention, the mighty mountains seem to arise in splendor. The air is crisp and refreshing; we feel the tranquility and serenity which abounds in the midst of such majestic mountains.
>
> Our final destination, the summit of Mount Washington, is covered in crystalized ice. Puffy white clouds embrace the nearby mountain peaks, and they give the illusion we could walk across them. The spectacular view is endless and absolutely unforgettable!

Jayne's purpose is to express the feelings of fear and awe as well as admiration of the scene, rather than to focus on the action of the ascent itself. Therefore, she composes sentences using more modifiers (descriptive words) and fewer verbs (action words).

On the other hand, a sportswriter, reporting on a light heavyweight championship boxing match, pays little attention to the scenery, preferring to emphasize the action and its direct consequences. Take, for example, William Nack's description of the sixth-round slugging between Matthew Saad Muhammad and Dwight Braxton:

> Saad Muhammad lurched along the ropes. Braxton pursued. He buried a hook and a right to the body, then came up with a jarring left and right to the head. Saad Muhammad reeled. Another left and right drove him back, and still another sent him toppling against the ropes in Braxton's corner. Braxton pummeled him again, his short arms pumping like pistons. The suffering challenger tried to protect his head, but Braxton was in front of him and crashing punches home until referee Carlos Padilla mercifully waved him away at 1:23 of the round.[10]

To compare the differences in writing purposes and the ways those differences become evident in their choice of language, list Jayne's descriptive and action words separately; then list William Nack's descriptive and action words separately. Jayne's point of view is that of someone concerned about the danger of the ascent and excited to awe by the spectacle of the Mt. Washington environs. Nack's perspective is that of someone enamored of the power and impact of Braxton's punches.

Still, a writer can describe scenery, report action, and deliver supplementary information in the same passage as long as he or she pays attention to the balance of information and carries the reader carefully from one item to the next. Notice how this writer does just that as he describes a sport very different from boxing:

> A top-hatted groom sounds the coach horn. The horn is long and slender and its cry lifts over the countryside. Tugging at the reins, a powerful four-in-hand matched team of Holsteiners or Appaloosas or Clydesdales or Gelderlanders—perhaps $100,000 worth of horseflesh—awaits the orders from

their whip (the driver) sitting atop the carriage. Soon the carriage rumbles through the rolling countryside, across fields and streams, woodlands and roadways. The whip glances at the stopwatch, and beside him the referee scrutinizes the horses' gait; going too fast is penalized as severely as going too slow. When plunging across a water hazard—one of eight hazards spaced along the course—the carriage seems to teeter dangerously, and the grooms cling to its sides like sailors in a storm.

This is Columbus Day weekend in Hamilton, Massachusetts, scene of the Myopia Combined Driving Event, the nation's oldest (1975) and most prestigious event in one of the newest, most exclusive, and most anachronistic sports in the world.[11]

The writer supplies expository, or explanatory, information by inserting it unobtrusively within the narrative passage. The following information does nothing to forward the action of the narrative; it serves to explain or provide a context for the action.

1. "—perhaps $100,000 worth of horseflesh—"
2. "whip (the driver)"
3. "going too fast is penalized as severely as going too slow"
4. "—one of eight hazards spaced along the course—"

Of course, the last sentence of the passage is also entirely expository, explaining where and when the event took place. This writer's purpose is to report the action from the perspective of one most concerned about the challenge of the sport's course and rules.

Some writers compose "how-to" narratives. In other words, they write directions on how to perform this or that activity within the frame of the story. Take, for example, the right way to eat lobsters:

We took the lobsters, scalding hot in our hands, and broke them in two. We guzzled the hot tomalley right from the shells. Broke off the big-claws, put the ends in our mouths, tipped back our heads, worked the jaws of the claws, and let the hot juice run down our throats. I did not have to show

Lloyd. He knew how. He had eaten Maine lobsters before. His chin dripped in the firelight as my brother's and mine did. We cracked the thick claws in our teeth and got the sweet red meat out whole. We put the tailpieces between our palms held as if at prayer, cracked inward, laid the flanges wide, broken open clean as a whistle, lifted out a column of meat as large as a tholepin, stripped off the top strip and took out the dark thread of the colon, and shoved the whole business into our mouths till our mouths could hold no more. We knew just how to do it. We were old hands. We gorged ourselves on meat hot as the spruce embers and sweet as a boy's first love.[12]

This kind of writing is very close to the explanation of a process I will present in Part Two. The sentences "We knew just how to do it. We were old hands," serve as a comment to the reader: if you want to belong to the "in" crowd, eat lobsters as we do. The last line, a comment on the lobster meat and on the experience described, is a lyrical metaphor only a poet could compose.

Numerous writers have used narrative powerfully to effect one end or another. Two diverse writers are George Orwell and Annie Dillard. Here is a paragraph from Orwell's narrative essay, "Shooting an Elephant":

When I pulled the trigger I did not hear the bang or feel the kick—one never does when a shot goes home—but I heard the devilish roar of glee that went up from the crowd. In that instant, in too short a time, one would have thought, even for the bullet to get there, a mysterious, terrible change had come over the elephant. He neither stirred nor fell, but every line on his body had altered. He looked suddenly stricken, shrunken, immensely old, as though the frightful impact of the bullet had paralyzed him without knocking him down. At last, after what seemed a long time—it might have been five seconds, I dare say—he sagged flabbily to his knees. His mouth slobbered. An enormous senility seemed to have settled upon him. One could have imagined him thousands of years old. I fired again into the same spot. At the second shot he did not collapse but climbed with desperate slowness to his feet and stood weakly upright, with legs sagging and head drooping. I fired a third time. That was the shot that did for him. You could see the agony of it jolt his whole body and knock the last remnant of strength from his legs. But in falling he seemed to tower upwards like a hugh rock toppling, his trunk reaching skywards like a tree. He trumpeted, for the first and only time. And then down he came, his belly towards me, with a crash that seemed to shake the ground even where I lay.[13]

What are some of the effects Orwell creates within the narrative frame to make this paragraph so powerful? First of all, he manipulates the sense of time. Look, for example, at the sentences beginning, "In that instant, in too short a time," "at last, after what seemed a long time—it might have been five seconds, I dare say," and "At the second shot." Second, he exaggerates the action and the stature of the elephant: in a blow-by-blow description he delivers actions with the thoroughness of a slow-motion video replay, and he increases the mammoth size of the elephant with the similes "like a huge rock toppling" and "like a tree" and by his hyperbolic use of modifiers. One need read only this paragraph to infer Orwell's writing purpose for the entire essay.

Annie Dillard narrates and marvels at wondrous, though commonplace, natural activities which are for her manifestations of the invisible power within and beyond nature. In the following selection she tells how courting frogs can take a surprising turn.

A couple of summers ago I was walking along the edge of the island to see what I could see in the water, and mainly to scare frogs. Frogs have an inelegant way of taking off from invisible positions on the bank just ahead of your feet, in dire panic, emitting a froggy "Yike!" and splashing into the water. Incredibly, this amused me, and, incredibly, it amuses me still. As I walked along the grassy edge of the island, I got better and better at seeing frogs both in and out of the water. I learned to recognize, slowing down, the difference in texture of the light reflected from mudbank, water, grass, or frog. Frogs were flying all around me. At the end of the island I noticed a small green frog. He was exactly half in and half out of the water, looking like a schematic diagram of an amphibian, and he didn't jump.

He didn't jump; I crept closer. At last I knelt on the island's winterkilled grass, lost, dumbstruck, staring at the frog in the creek just four feet away. He was a very small frog with wide, dull eyes. And just as I looked at him, he slowly crumpled and began to sag. The spirit vanished from his eyes as if snuffed. His skin emptied and drooped; his very skull seemed to collapse and settle like a kicked tent. He was shrinking before my eyes like a deflating football. I watched the taut, glistening skin on his shoulders ruck, and rumple, and fall. Soon, part of his skin, formless as a pricked balloon, lay in floating folds like bright scum on top of the water: it was a monstrous and terrifying thing. I gaped bewildered, appalled. An oval shadow hung in the water behind the drained frog; then the shadow glided away. The frog skin bag started to sink.

I had read about the giant water bug, but never seen one. "Giant water bug" is really the name of the creature, which is an enormous, heavy-bodied brown beetle. It eats insects, tadpoles, fish, and frogs. Its grasping forelegs are mighty and hooked inward. It seizes a victim with these legs, hugs it tight, and paralyzes it with enzymes injected during a vicious bite. That one bite is the only bite it ever takes. Through the puncture shoot the poisons that dissolve the victim's muscles and bones and organs—all but the skin—and through it the giant water bug sucks out the victim's body, reduced to a juice. This event is quite common in warm fresh water. The frog I saw was being sucked by a giant water bug. I had been kneeling on the island grass; when the unrecognizable flap of frog skin settled on the creek bottom, swaying, I stood up and brushed the knees of my pants. I couldn't catch my breath.[14]

A Final Note on Description and Narration

You will probably receive few writing assignments that require you to write solely in the descriptive or the narrative modes. Most frequently you will combine descriptive and narrative writing in an essay composed primarily of an expository writing type. Begin deciding whether to use descriptive or narrative writing as you initially generate ideas and sketch them for drafting. To decide whether, and how, to use description or narration, ask yourself:

• Can I present any information in a picture or a story?
• What likely effect would this type of writing produce?
• Would a vivid picture in the first paragraph engage the reader's attention?
• Could I conclude my point with a dramatic, narrative ending?
• What is my specific reason (purpose) for writing description or narration?
• What feelings or thoughts do I want to evoke from the reader?
• What details will I select?
• What point of view or location will I adopt?
• What action words and descriptive words will I use?
• What time sequence do I want to use?
• Should I use any special effects such as humor, hyperbole (exaggeration), time warping, or metaphoric language?

After you have written a descriptive or narrative passage, read it aloud to a friend or into a tape recorder. Ask your friend to read it to you or play it back on the recorder; as you listen, close your eyes and "see" the picture or action you have created. If something seems amiss—this description, that action, or the timing, for example—revise until it "looks" right in your mind's eye.

Exercises in Narration

1. Select a simple, well-known story like one of those listed here and tell it to a small group of classmates.

"Goldilocks and the Three Bears"
"The Three Little Pigs and the Big Bad Wolf"
"Jack and Jill"

Discuss what you believe to be the point of the story. Then divide into subgroups and compose revisions of the story to fit one of these purposes:

a. to emphasize Goldilocks' naughtiness and the bears' surprise

b. to focus on Goldilocks' and the bears' actions

c. to underscore the "badness" of the wolf

d. to express the terror and then the craftiness of the pigs

e. (expand the story) to show that Jack was adventurous but foolhardy

f. (expand the story) to show that Jill was a simple-minded follower who could have saved herself with a little independent thinking

g. (expand the story) to show that Jack and Jill were aware of the perils of climbing the hill, but, desperate for water, they persisted until tragedy befell them.

Have each subgroup retell the story and discuss the various revisions. Finally, compose a journal entry in which you discuss the changes you made in the story to fit the new writing purpose.

2. Write a narrative passage, selecting a topic from Group A, a writing purpose from Group B, and an audience from Group C.

Group A: Topic	Group B: Purpose	Group C: Audience
1. course registration	1. to make someone's routine activities appear heroic	1. your parents
2. a campus political event		2. your boyfriend or girlfriend
3. a date	2. to emphasize your emotional response to the action	3. an acquaintance at another school
4. a segment of a campus sports event		4. foreign students interested in enrolling at your school
5. a traditional school social event	3. to manipulate time movement for a particular effect	
	4. to emphasize school spirit	
	5. to call for a change of policy (without stating it explicitly)	

Read your narration and discuss your writing decisions with a group of your classmates. Then write a journal entry in which you discuss narrative strategies you learned from completing this exercise.

3. Review the story you composed in the last chapter (See Exercise 12 pp. 187–188.) State your purpose in composing it as you did and explain whether your methods served well in

fulfilling that purpose. If you see better ways of doing it, make appropriate revisions. Finally, look at your methods for setting the time sequence and for making transitions. What can you do to improve them now that you've seen more examples of narration?

4. Read the following short narrative essay. It is the third chapter in John Steinbeck's novel, *Grapes of Wrath*. Steinbeck does not explicitly state his purpose, but it is implied, especially in the first and last paragraphs. Write out an explicit statement of Steinbeck's purpose and discuss his strategy of fulfilling it.

The concrete highway was edged with a mat of tangled, broken, dry grass, and the grass heads were heavy with oat beards to catch on a dog's coat, and foxtails to tangle in a horse's fetlocks, and clover burrs to fasten in sheep's wool; sleeping life waiting to be spread and dispersed, every seed armed with an appliance of dispersal, twisting darts and parachutes for the wind, little spears and balls of tiny thorns, and all waiting for animals and for the wind, for a man's trouser cuff or the hem of a woman's skirt, all passive but armed with appliances of activity, still, but each possessed of the anlage of movement.

The sun lay on the grass and warmed it, and in the shade under the grass the insects moved, ants and ant lions to set traps for them, grasshoppers to jump into the air and flick their yellow wings for a second, sow bugs like little armadillos, plodding restlessly on many tender feet. And over the grass at the roadside a land turtle crawled, turning aside for nothing, dragging his high-domed shell over the grass. His hard legs and yellow-nailed feet threshed slowly through the grass, not really walking, but boosting and dragging his shell along. The barley beards slid off his shell, and the clover burrs fell on him and rolled to the ground. His horny beak was partly open, and his fierce, humorous eyes, under brows like fingernails, stared straight ahead. He came over the grass leaving a beaten trail behind him, and the hill, which was the highway embankment, reared up ahead of him. For a moment he stopped, his head held high. He blinked and looked up and down. At last he started to climb the embankment. Front clawed feet reached forward but did not touch. The hind feet kicked his shell along, and it scraped on the grass, and on the gravel. As the embankment grew steeper and steeper, the more frantic were the efforts of the land turtle. Pushing hind legs strained and slipped, boosting the shell along, and the horny head protruded as far as the neck could stretch. Little by little the shell slid up the embankment until at last a parapet cut straight across its line of march, the shoulder of the road, a concrete wall four inches high. As though they worked independently the hind legs pushed the shell against the wall. The head upraised and peered over the wall to the broad smooth plain of cement. Now the hands, braced on top of the wall, strained and lifted, and the shell came slowly up and rested its front end on the wall. For a moment the turtle rested. A red ant ran into the shell, into the soft skin inside the shell, and suddenly head and legs snapped in, and the armored tail clamped in sideways. The red ant was crushed between body and legs. And one head of wild oats was clamped into the shell by a front leg. For a long moment the turtle lay still, and then the neck crept out and the old humorous frowning eyes looked about and the legs and tail came out. The back legs went to work, straining like elephant legs, and the shell tipped to an angle so that the front legs could not reach the level cement plain. But higher and higher the hind legs boosted it, until at last the center of balance was reached, the front tipped down, the front legs scratched at the pavement, and it was up. But the head of wild oats was held by its stem around the front legs.

Now the going was easy, and all the legs worked, and the shell boosted along, waggling from side to side. A sedan driven by a forty-year old woman approached. She saw the turtle and swung to the right, off the highway, the wheels screamed and a cloud of dust boiled up. Two wheels lifted for a moment and then settled. The car skidded back onto the road, and went on, but more slowly. The turtle had jerked into its shell, but now it hurried on, for the highway was burning hot.

And now a light truck approached, and as it came near, the driver saw the turtle and swerved to hit it. His front wheel struck the edge of the shell, flipped the turtle like a tiddly-wink, spun it like a coin, and rolled it off the highway. The truck went back to its course along the right side. Lying on its back, the turtle was tight in its shell for a long time.

But at last its legs waved in the air, reaching for something to pull it over. Its front foot caught a piece of quartz and little by little the shell pulled over and flopped upright. The wild oat head fell out and three of the spearhead seeds stuck in the ground. And as the turtle crawled on down the embankment, its shell dragged dirt over the seeds. The turtle entered a dust road and jerked itself along, drawing a wavy shallow trench in the dust with its shell. The old humorous eyes looked ahead, and the horny beak opened a little. His yellow toe nails slipped a fraction in the dust.[15]

5. Write a narrative passage about a natural event or action: a horse trotting, a spider weaving a web, a cat cleaning itself, a storm gathering force and spending itself, a bird building its nest, a stream flowing, and so on. Consciously model your narrative strategy after Steinbeck's, Dillard's, or Orwell's. Then rewrite the passage in the manner of a second author in that group. Write out an explicit statement of your writing purpose for each revision. Share your two versions with a group of your classmates and discuss how adopting a different narrative strategy necessitates revising the writing purpose.

6. a. Read the following narrative passage written by Pat Jordan about a young pitcher:

He stood on the pitcher's mound with a baseball in his hand— a tall, gangling boy of 12 in a little-league uniform that was so small for him, the pants legs barely reaching his knees, that he resembled a stick figure. I remember he had a long face, and pale skin, and that his eyes were wide and unblinking, like those of a trapped animal.

He did not look like a pitcher, not even a little-league pitcher. He had to pause a second before each pitch to remind himself how to put his foot on the rubber, and then how to pump, and kick, and lunge, and follow through so that he was squared off against the batter now only a few feet away. And as he went through his motion, step by awkward step, he watched himself to make sure he got it right, watched himself with such simple concentration, in fact, his brow knitting, that he seemed to forget entirely about the batter. He had probably been recruited to pitch by his coach, the manager of a local supermarket, because he was so much taller than the other boys his age, and his coach had felt his size would frighten batters in a way his talent—or, rather, his lack of talent—would not. But he frightened no one. On this clear summer day, in full view of his parents, a few dozen fans and myself, already a little-league star pitcher at 12, he could not retire even the tiniest of batters. The fans laughed at him at first, and then they began to feel sorry for him. "He's trying so hard," said a mother in the home-plate stands behind me.

With each succeeding base hit, the pitcher took more and more time between pitches, until he was virtually immobile on the mound, unable to deliver another pitch. He looked toward the bench for his coach, but his coach was bent over, his hands cupped around a match, lighting a cigarette. The pitcher's shoulders sagged and he forced himself to begin his mechanical delivery once again. The batter hit a ground ball toward the mound. The pitcher followed it with his eyes, but he could not make himself reach for it. The ball passed very close to his right foot and continued on into center field. The pitcher remained frozen in his follow-through for a split second, as if an idea were forming in his head, and then he fell to the ground, clutching first his left foot and then his right foot as he writhed in the dirt. His coach and his teammates rushed out to him and the umpire called time. They hovered over him for a few minutes—his coach, down on one knee, massaging his right foot—and then he stood up. With his arms draped over the shoulders of two smaller teammates, he hobbled off the mound to the applause of sympathetic fans. That applause seemed to me then, as it does now, to have stemmed not only from the fans' sense of relief that the pitcher was not seriously hurt but also from their sense of relief that they would no longer have to witness his humiliation.

The fans' sympathetic applause began to build as he crossed the first-base line. Only I was not so sympathetic. I yelled out, loud enough for all to hear, "That's one way of gettin' off the mound!" The fans around me booed and hissed, and somebody shoved me in the back.

"You ought to be ashamed," a woman's voice said. But I wasn't. I knew, even then, that I was right.[16]

b. Write a journal entry summarizing the action and the character presented. State what you think Jordan's purpose is.

c. Now write a narrative passage focusing on a single figure; select, as Jordan has, some particular quality of character that you want to emphasize through the style or actions of the character. Here are some topic suggestions: a bartender, a model, a quarterback, a mail deliverer, a security officer, a teacher, a child at play, a waiter or a waitress, a judge on the bench, a short-order cook, an artist, a secretary, an elderly person.

Set Forth an Idea and Develop it.

EXPOSITION

Exposition means to set forth ideas or facts about a topic and to give a detailed explanation of them; exposition in its pure form is distinguishable from description, narration and persuasion. Writing exposition requires sound thinking and clear written expression of that thinking. One must especially be able to distinguish between main and subordinate items, and between abstract ideas and concrete examples; and, further, one must be able to make effective connections between items of information. While there are several ways to write exposition, I will present these basic methods: using examples, showing a process, comparing and contrasting, defining terms, showing cause and effect, and classifying and analyzing.

Examples

A simple, straightforward, and concrete way to express your ideas on a topic is to begin by writing out your main idea in a general statement and then develop that generalization by listing specific illustrative examples.

This paragraph on manics, people who are abnormally excited and who have excessive feelings of well-being, illustrates the pattern of generalization and examples:

Manics love to gamble. They love the excitement of it. The racetrack, roulette wheel, cards, slot machines—whatever the game, the manic enjoys the rush and thrives on the tension, and he finds that this form of quick gratification suits his impatient temperament precisely. He has to wait all week for a paycheck, but only two minutes for a horse race. A manic has schemes to beat the dealer, the house, the track, or the numbers. He will manipulate for the sheer joy of manipulating, nonstop for twenty hours a day. He may—in headlong pursuit of success—cheat, lie, and steal without quite realizing what he is doing. In fact, when he gambles, he gets so caught up in his machinations, so stimulated by the wheeling and dealing, that he turns other people on, catches them up in his fantasies of instant millions and the Midas touch.[17]

The main idea, or generalization, is contained in the first three sentences and could be summarized this way: "Manics thrive on the excitement (the rush and tension) of gambling, finding that this form of quick gratification suits their impatient temperament precisely." The rest of the information in the paragraph consists of examples of manic gambling activities.

Here is a similarly organized paragraph which begins with a generalization and follows with supporting examples:

Few heroes lower their sights in the prime of their lives; triumph leads inexorably on, often to destruction. Alexander wept because he had no new worlds to conquer; Napoleon, overextended, sealed his doom in the depth of a Russian winter. But Charles Darwin did not follow the *Origin of Species* (1859) with a general defense of natural selection or with its evident extension to human evolution (he waited until 1871 to publish *The Descent of Man*). Instead, he wrote his most obscure work, a book entitled: *On the Various Contrivances by Which British and Foreign Orchids Are Fertilized by Insects* (1862).[18]

The examples the author lists are Alexander, Napoleon, and Charles Darwin. But, in this case the examples are not a parallel series; in other words, they are not all the same. Darwin is different. He is an exception to the general statement. The author sets up the development of this turning point or break from the generalization with the first word, "Few." At "But" the paragraph idea turns away from examples of the general rule to the exception (Darwin) and states a second generalization. The statement in parentheses and the last sentence present two specific examples in support of the second general statement. The idea development and examples in this paragraph could be illustrated this way:

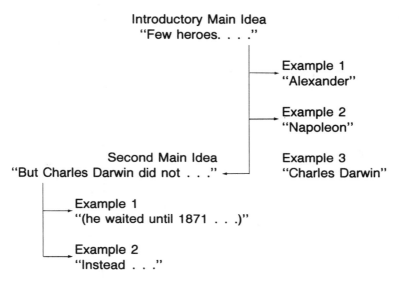

Introductory Main Idea
"Few heroes. . . ."

Example 1
"Alexander"

Example 2
"Napoleon"

Second Main Idea
"But Charles Darwin did not . . ."

Example 3
"Charles Darwin"

Example 1
"(he waited until 1871 . . .)"

Example 2
"Instead . . ."

Figure 7.1

This paragraph illustrates how one can effectively use the generalization-and-example method to present an idea as an exception to a rule; in fact, its author, Stephen Jay Gould, is a well-known scientist and award-winning writer who has made significant discoveries proving exceptions to the rules of evolution.

In this final example of beginning a paragraph with a generalization, the author is discussing Alfred Hitchcock's creation of the film image of Grace Kelly:

In three films Hitchcock created the Kelly woman—a creature whose impeccable exterior concealed a banked inferno of erotic and emotional drives. In "Dial M for Murder," as the wife whose silky husband (Ray Milland) plots to have her murdered, Kelly's passive vulnerability takes on a disturbing, erotic charge—innocence as spiritual masochism. "Rear Window" is more complex as Kelly plays a kind of super-Cosmopolitan girl out to get James Stewart into a marriage that he wants and fears. Kelly's ravishing movements—turning on the lights, sitting on Stewart's lap—become a ballet of tender entrapment. Best of all is "To Catch a Thief," in which Kelly is the rich girl fascinated by Cary Grant as both man and jewel thief. Maddeningly beautiful, simmering behind dark glasses and genteel silences, the quintessential Kelly emerges in her superbly witty seduction of Grant. Turning to say good night to him at her hotel room, her expression of subtly mocking desire freezes him in a connoisseur's amazement as she slides her white arms like Pavlova around his neck and gives him the kind of kiss that started the Trojan War.[19]

The writer presents as examples Grace Kelly's roles in three films: "Dial M for Murder," "Rear Window," and "To Catch a Thief." Notice that within his expository comments on each example, the writer includes a mini-narration, a brief summary of a plot segment; each narrative segment stretches longer than the previous one, showing how one can mix types of writing to develop ideas.

Writers need not feel obligated to begin every paragraph with the main idea. Provided that the connections are clearly made, the placement of main idea and examples can vary. Consider this reordering of a previous paragraph:

Alexander wept because he had no new worlds to conquer; Napoleon, overextended, sealed his doom in the depth of a Russian winter. Few heroes lower their sights in the prime of their lives; triumph leads inexorably on, often to destruction. But Charles Darwin did not follow the *Origin of Species* (1859) with a general defense of natural selection or with its evident extension to human evolution (he waited until 1871 to publish *The Descent of Man*). Instead, he wrote his most obscure work, a book entitled: *On the Various Contrivances by Which British and Foreign Orchids Are Fertilized by Insects* (1862).

Of course, placement of the main idea is not a matter of a writer's whim; a writer should place the main idea where it is most effective. What is preferable: a direct opening statement of the point, or the summarizing or dramatic effect of placing it last? You may notice the reason the main idea in the reordered paragraph fits well after the examples of Alexander and Napoleon and preceding Darwin is that the development of the main idea breaks or turns at that point.

A Note on Using Examples

You will probably find numerous writing occasions when it is appropriate to use examples to support or illustrate a point. As you jot down information during a thinking-strategy session, identify your main idea and examples which illustrate or support it. Before drafting, check to see that you have, in fact, identified the main point and that all of your examples illustrate that main point. Draw a tree or some other graphic design to check visually on the soundness of your thinking. Furthermore, as you draft, take care to make effective connections between your main idea and examples. Review appropriate sections in Chapters 2 and 3 if you need to refresh your memory on these matters.

Process

The most explicit way of illustrating an action, a process, or a task is by showing it in operation. As you have seen from the paragraph on lobsters in Part One of this chapter, process exposition is akin to narration. Both present activity in a time sequence. The basic difference between the two is that the purpose of process exposition is explicitly to instruct, demonstrate, or explain a step-by-step process; the purpose of narration, on the other hand, is to tell a story with the emphasis on character, action, scene, and meaning.

Recipes are passages of process exposition as are "how-to" books. Take, for example, one writer's directions to the reader with the problem of a clogged drain:

How to unclog a fixture drain: When a sink, lavatory, shower, or bathtub drains slowly or not at all, the usual cause is an accumulation of hair, grease, or other debris lodged somewhere near the drain.

First try cleaning it with a rubber force cup, sometimes called a plumber's friend or plunger. The best type of plunger for this job is one with a wide, flat face that enables it to make good contact with the near-flat fixture bottom.

Run an inch or two of water into the basin. Remove the stopper if there is one. Plug up the overflow opening with a wet cloth or have someone hold his hand tightly over it. This will keep the plunger pressure from by-passing the clogged area and blowing out of the overflow outlet. Tip the force cup up to expel its air and place it directly over the drain. Plunge it down and pull it up firmly and rhythmically to build up force. Then pull the plunger off the drain opening to draw up the stoppage.

You can also try doing this with a special compressed-air plunger that acts like a pump.

If plunging has not worked after several minutes, try a liquid chemical drain cleaner. If the stoppage is still there, use a sink auger, also called a plumber's snake. The auger is rotated into the drainpipe and will generally cut its way through the obstruction. Also a garden hose will sometimes do the job. Try it with and without water pressure.

If none of these work, remove the cleanout plug at the bottom of the trap. Some traps have no cleanout plugs and may themselves have to be removed. Others, called drum traps, used chiefly on tubs and showers, have screw-off covers accessible below the floor near the fixture. Insert the snake at the trap to remove debris. As a last resort, you may have to remove the trap to locate and clear out the clog.[20]

As with many cookbooks and "how-to" books, this passage was accompanied by a list of items necessary for performing the steps in the process in addition to pictures and graphic illustrations of specific operations within the process.

Some processes are so intricate (like tying shoelaces), invisible (like thinking), or so gradual in movement and so grand in scale (social change, for instance) that any graphic illustration is only symbolic; delineating and explaining the process effectively depends on exposition. Our bodily processes, the function of the liver, for example, are invisible to most of us, but medical scientists who have observed them with the aid of technology can explain them to us. Here is surgeon Richard Selzer explaining where alcohol goes in the human body and what its effects are on the liver and other organs:

The human body is perfectly suited for the ingestion of alcohol, and for its rapid utilization. In that sense we are not unlike alcohol lamps. Endless is our eagerness to devour alcohol.

Witness the facts that it is absorbed not only from the intestine, as are all other foods, but directly from the stomach as well. It can be taken in by the lungs as an inhalant, and even by the rectum if given as an enema. Once incorporated into the body, it is to the liver that belongs the task of oxidizing the alcohol. But even the sturdiest liver can handle only a drop or two at a time, and the remainder swirls ceaselessly about in the bloodstream, is exhaled by the lungs and thus provides the state police with a crackerjack method of detecting and measuring the presence and amount of alcohol ingested. Along the way it bathes the brain with happiness, lifting the inhibitory cortex off the primal swamp of the id and permitting to surface all sorts of delicious urges such as the one to walk into people's houses wearing your wife's hat. Happily enough, the brain is not organically altered by alcohol unless taken in near-lethal amounts. The brain cells are not destroyed by it in any kind of moderate drinking, and if the alcohol is withdrawn from the diet, the brain rapidly awakens and resumes its function at the usual, if not normal, level. One must reckon, nevertheless, with the hangover, which retributive phenomenon is devised to make the drinker feel guilty. In fact, it is not more than a nightmarish echo of the state of inebriation brought on by excessive fatigue and the toxic effects of congeners, the natural products of the fermentation process that give distinction to the taste of the various forms of alcohol.[21]

Selzer also talks about the use of the knife at the beginning of the surgical process:

One holds the knife as one holds the bow of a cello or a tulip—by the stem. Not palmed nor gripped nor grasped, but lightly, with the tips of the fingers. The knife is not for pressing. It is for drawing across the field of skin. Like a slender fish, it waits, at the ready, then, go! It darts, followed by a fine wake of red. The flesh parts, falling away to yellow globules of fat. Even now, after so many times, I still marvel at its power—cold, gleaming, silent. More, I am still struck with a kind of dread that it is I in whose hand the blade travels, that my hand is its vehicle, that yet again this terrible steel-bellied thing and I have conspired for a most unnatural purpose, the laying open of the body of a human being.

A stillness settles in my heart and is carried to my hand. It is the quietude of resolve layered over fear. And it is this resolve that lowers us, my knife and me, deeper and deeper into the person beneath. It is an entry into the body that is nothing like a caress; still it is among the gentlest of acts. Then stroke and stroke again, and we are joined by other instruments, hemostats and forceps, until the wound blooms with strange flowers whose looped handles fall to the sides in steely array.[22]

Selzer does not sound like the stoic professionals in green scrub suits you hear spouting medical jargon, does he? No, of course not. A highly literate and reflective person, Selzer has not written a book for fellow surgeons; he intends his book to be read by educated laypeople who appreciate his philosophical bent and fanciful flights into lyricism.

A Note on Explaining or Illustrating a Process

You may be called upon often to write essays explaining a process. For example, in a laboratory science course you may be asked to write the procedures you followed in conducting the experiments. You may find that combining descriptive writing and process exposition is an appropriate combination of writing types for such lab reports. Also, in a history course you might be asked to discuss the Reformation Movement in sixteenth-century Europe.

Finding a writing purpose for process exposition is rarely a problem: the purpose is usually obvious. The challenge of writing effective process exposition lies in how to achieve the purpose. Answer these questions when you are beginning to write about process:

- What steps are involved?
- What can I assume the reader knows about the process?
- What sequence enables the reader to understand (or to complete) the process most easily?
- How much information must I include to make the directions or explanation) clear?
- What connections or transitions should I use between steps?

Finally, for another example of giving directions for a simple process, reread the directions for making a cube (pp. 34–38); for an example of the explanation of a process already completed, reread Ellen's revision analysis (pp. 119–125).

Compare and Contrast

One way of familiarizing your friends with a relatively unknown, up-and-coming ball player you know about is to compare him to a well-known, established player. To assess the advantages and disadvantages of heating a home with a woodstove, you can compare it to heating with oil, gas, coal, or solar energy. If you want to show the distinctively conservative views of one of your state's Senators, compare them to those of a liberal Senator.

Note: I use "compare" to mean showing both the similarities and the differences between two or more things or people. Instead of saying "compare and contrast," many teachers will simply use "compare," as I have, to mean both.

The first concern of the comparison writer is to select items which can be compared effectively for a given purpose and audience. You have heard the cliché, "You cannot compare apples and oranges." But of course you can. And you can compare them with effective results if, in fact, your purpose is to compare one type of fruit with another. However, if your purpose is to compare one variety of apple with another, then oranges are an inappropriate selection. Or, suppose that you are explaining the game of football to a group of European exchange students. They will probably find your explanation much more understandable if you compare football to soccer than if you compare it to basketball. And, whereas comparing video games to billiards is fine for the over-30 crowd, it is much less satisfactory for a group of grade schoolers.

Selecting appropriate qualities or characteristics to compare is another of the writer's concerns. If a writer's purpose is to compare the overall performance of a VW Rabbit with that of a Plymouth Horizon, then comparing interior fabric designs and color options is clearly less appropriate than comparing such things as turning ratios, zero-to-60 acceleration times, and suspension systems. Also, just as it is inappropriate to compare the functions and memory capacity of two computers without considering the cost of each, so, too, a comparison of one nation's productivity with another's imports is meaningless.

A third matter of concern is how to organize the various items of information for the most effective comparison or contrast. Recall that Kyle organized his comparisons category by category rather than whole subject versus whole subject. (See pp. 66ff.) Whether you organize your information on a whole-subject-to-whole-subject comparison or on a category-by-category comparison, keep items parallel in each section. (See Figure 7.2.)

Whole subject by whole subject:

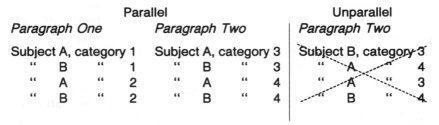

Parallel		Unparallel
Paragraph One	*Paragraph Two*	*Paragraph Two*
Subject A	Subject B	Subject B
Characteristic 1	Characteristic 1	Characteristic 4
" 2	" 2	" 1
" 3	" 3	" 3
" 4	" 4	" 2

Category by category:

Parallel		Unparallel
Paragraph One	*Paragraph Two*	*Paragraph Two*
Subject A, category 1	Subject A, category 3	Subject B, category 3
" B " 1	" B " 3	" A " 4
" A " 2	" A " 4	" A " 3
" B " 2	" B " 4	" B " 4

Figure 7.2

Category-by-category comparison can be an especially effective method of organization when the writer wants direct and brief comparisons of a series of characteristics as in this selection:

To-day, in the United States, two radically different plans for the support and conduct of higher institutions of learning are in process of development: the one that of the private university, the other of the university supported and controlled by the state. The first finds its notable examples mainly amongst the older universities of the East, the second in the universities of the Central and Western states. While these last are younger, their growth has been rapid, not only in the number of instructors and students, but in facilities and income.

In the Eastern States, where the older universities have for a century and more supplied the demands of higher education, no great state institutions have grown up. In the central West, on the other hand, where the state universities were founded just as the railroads were built, to supply not a present but a future want, there are few strong and growing private universities. In fact, there are in almost every Western state private colleges and universities whose development has been practically stopped, and which must in the end become feeders to the great state universities. . . .

These two systems of universities rest upon fundamentally different views as to the support of higher education. The one assumes that this support will come by the free gift of citizens of the commonwealth, the other assumes that the support of higher education no less than that of elementary education is the duty of the state. The one system appeals to the generosity of the individual citizen, the other appeals to the sense of responsibility and the patriotism of the whole mass of citizens. The one establishes a set of higher institutions which may or may not be in harmony with the elementary schools of the municipality or of the state; the other establishes a set of institutions which are an integral part of that system, and its crown. The one furnishes a system of instruction in which tuition fees are high and tending constantly to grow higher, the other furnishes a system of instruction practically free. The one had its origin in essentially aristocratic distinctions, whatever may be its present form of development, the other is essentially democratic in both its inception and its development.[23]

On the other hand, whole-subject-by-whole-subject comparison is the better organizational method when the writer wants to go into detail about the qualities or characteristics of each subject. Take, for instance, the following well-known comparison of the spider and the wasp:

THE SPIDER AND THE WASP

In the feeding and safeguarding of their progeny insects and spiders exhibit some interesting analogies to reasoning and some crass examples of blind instinct. The case I propose to describe here is that of the tarantula spiders and their arch-enemy, the digger wasps of the genus Pepsis. It is a classic example of what looks like intelligence pitted against instinct—a strange situation in which the victim, though fully able to defend itself, submits unwittingly to its destruction.

Most tarantulas live in the tropics, but several species occur in the temperate zone and a few are common in the southern U.S. Some varieties are large and have powerful fangs with which they can inflict a deep wound. These formidable looking spiders do not, however, attack man; you can hold one in your hand, if you are gentle, without being bitten. Their bite is dangerous only to insects and small mammals such as mice; for man it is no worse than a hornet's sting.

Tarantulas customarily live in deep cylindrical burrows, from which they emerge at dusk and into which they retire at dawn. Mature males wander about after dark in search of females and occasionally stray into houses. After mating, the male dies in a few weeks, but a female lives much longer and can mate several years in succession. In a Paris museum is a tropical specimen which is said to have been living in captivity for 25 years.

A fertilized female tarantula lays from 200 to 400 eggs at a time; thus it is possible for a single tarantula to produce several thousand young. She takes no care of them beyond weaving a cocoon of silk to enclose the eggs. After they hatch, the young walk away, find convenient places in which to dig their burrows and spend the rest of their lives in solitude. The eyesight of tarantulas is poor, being limited to a sensing of change in the intensity of light and to the perception of moving objects. They apparently have little or no sense of hearing, for a hungry tarantula will pay no attention to a loudly chirping cricket placed in its cage unless the insect happens to touch one of its legs.

But all spiders, and especially hairy ones, have an extremely delicate sense of touch. Laboratory experiments prove that tarantulas can distinguish three types of touch: pressure against the body wall, stroking of the body hair, and riffling of certain very fine hairs on the legs called trichobothria. Pressure against the body, by the finger or the end of a pencil, causes the tarantula to move off slowly for a short distance.

The touch excites no defensive response unless the approach is from above where the spider can see the motion, in which case it rises on its hind legs, lifts its front legs, opens its fangs and holds this threatening posture as long as the object continues to move.

The entire body of a tarantula, especially its legs, is thickly clothed with hair. Some of it is short and wooly, some long and stiff. Touching this body hair produces one of two distinct reactions. When the spider is hungry, it responds with an immediate and swift attack. At the touch of a cricket's antennae the tarantula seizes the insect so swiftly that a motion picture taken at the rate of 64 frames per second shows only the result and not the process of capture. But when the spider is not hungry, the stimulation of its hairs merely causes it to shake the touched limb. An insect can walk under its hairy belly unharmed.

The trichobothria, very fine hairs growing from dislike membranes on the legs, are sensitive only to air movement. A light breeze makes them vibrate slowly, without disturbing the common hair. When one blows gently on the trichobothria, the tarantula reacts with a quick jerk of its four front legs. If the front and hind legs are stimulated at the same time, the spider makes a sudden jump. This reaction is quite independent of the state of its appetite.

These three tactile responses—to pressure on the body wall, to moving of the common hair, and to flexing of the trichobothria—are so different from one another that there is no possibility of confusing them. They serve the tarantula adequately for most of its needs and enable it to avoid most annoyances and dangers. But they fail the spider completely when it meets its deadly enemy, the digger wasp Pepsis.

These solitary wasps are beautiful and formidable creatures. Most species are either a deep shiny blue all over, or deep blue with rusty wings. The largest have a wing span of about four inches. They live on nectar. When excited, they give off a pungent odor—a warning that they are ready to attack. The sting is much worse than that of a bee or common wasp, and the pain and swelling last longer. In the adult stage the wasp lives only a few months. The female produces but a few eggs, one at a time at intervals of two or three days. For each egg the mother must provide one adult tarantula, alive but paralyzed. The mother wasp attaches the egg to the paralyzed spider's abdomen. Upon hatching from the egg, the larva is many hundreds of times smaller than its living but helpless victim. It eats no other food and drinks no water. By the time it has finished its single Gargantuan meal and become ready for wasphood, nothing remains of the tarantula but its indigestible chitinous skeleton.

The mother wasp goes tarantula-hunting when the egg in her ovary is almost ready to be laid. Flying low over the ground late on a sunny afternoon, the wasp looks for its victim or for the mouth of a tarantula burrow, a round hole edged by a bit of silk. The sex of the spider makes no difference, but the mother is highly discriminating as to species. Each species of Pepsis requires a certain species of tarantula, and the wasp will not attack the wrong species. In a cage with a tarantula which is not its normal prey, the wasp avoids the spider and is usually killed by it in the night.

Yet when a wasp finds the correct species, it is the other way about. To identify the species the wasp apparently must explore the spider with her antennae. The tarantula shows an amazing tolerance to this exploration. The wasp crawls under it and walks over it without evoking any hostile response. The molestation is so great and so persistent that the tarantula often rises on all eight legs, as if it were on stilts. It may stand this way for several minutes. Meanwhile the wasp, having satisfied itself that the victim is of the right species, moves off a few inches to dig the spider's grave. Working vigorously with legs and jaws, it excavates a hole 8 to 10 inches deep with a diameter slightly larger than the spider's girth. Now and again the wasp pops out of the hole to make sure that the spider is still there.

When the grave is finished, the wasp returns to the tarantula to complete her ghastly enterprise. First she feels it all over once more with her antennae. Then her behavior becomes more aggressive. She bends her abdomen, protruding her sting, and searches for the soft membrane at the point where the spider's legs join its body—the only spot where she can penetrate the horny skeleton. From time to time, as the exasperated spider slowly shifts ground, the wasp turns on her back and slides along with the aid of her wings, trying to get under the tarantula for a shot at the vital spot. During all this maneuvering, which can last for several minutes, the tarantula makes no move to save itself. Finally the wasp corners it against some obstruction and grasps one of its legs in her powerful jaws. Now at last the harassed spider tries a desperate but vain defense. The two contestants roll over and over on the ground. It is a terrifying sight and the outcome is always the same. The wasp finally manages to thrust her sting into the soft spot and holds it there for a few seconds while she pumps in the poison. Almost immediately the tarantula falls paralyzed on its back. Its legs stop twitching; its heart stops beating. Yet it is not dead, as is shown by the fact that if taken from the wasp it can be restored to some sensitivity by being kept in a moist chamber for several months.

After paralyzing the tarantula, the wasp cleans herself by dragging her body along the ground and rubbing her feet, sucks the drop of blood oozing from the wound in the spider's abdomen, then grabs a leg of the flabby, helpless animal in her jaws and drags it down to the bottom of the grave. She stays there for many minutes, sometimes for several hours, and what she does all that time in the dark we do not know. Eventually she lays her egg and attaches it to the side of the spider's abdomen with a sticky secretion. Then she emerges, fills the grave with soil carried bit by bit in her jaws, and finally tramples the ground all around to hide any trace of the grave from prowlers. Then she flies away, leaving her descendant safely started in life.

In all this the behavior of the wasp evidently is qualitatively different from that of the spider. The wasp acts like an intelligent animal. This is not to say that instinct plays no part or that she reasons as man does. But her actions are to the point; they are not automatic and can be modified to fit the situation. We do not know for certain how she identifies the tarantula—probably it is by some olfactory or chemo-tactile sense—but she does it purposefully and does not blindly tackle a wrong species.

On the other hand, the tarantula's behavior shows only confusion. Evidently the wasp's pawing gives it no pleasure, for it tries to move away. That the wasp is not simulating sexual stimulation is certain because male and female tarantulas react in the same way to its advances. That the spider is not anesthetized by some odorless secretion is easily shown by blowing lightly at the tarantula and making it jump suddenly. What, then, makes the tarantula behave as stupidly as it does?

No clear, simple answer is available. Possibly the stimulation by the wasp's antennae is masked by a heavier pressure on the spider's body, so that it reacts as when prodded by a pencil. But the explanation may be much more complex. Initiative in attack is not in the nature of tarantulas; most species fight only when cornered so that escape is impossible. Their inherited patterns of behavior apparently prompt them to avoid problems rather than attack them. For example, spiders always weave their webs in three dimensions, and when a spider finds that there is insufficient space to attach certain threads in the third dimension, it leaves the place and seeks another, instead of finishing the web in a single plane. This urge to escape seems to arise under all circumstances, in all phases of life, and to take the place of reasoning. For a spider to change the pattern of its web is as impossible as for an inexperienced man to build a bridge across a chasm obstructing his way.

In a way the instinctive urge to escape is not only easier but often more efficient than reasoning. The tarantula does exactly what is most efficient in all cases except in an encounter with a ruthless and determined attacker dependent for the existence of her own species on killing as many tarantulas as she can lay eggs. Perhaps in this case the spider follows its usual pattern of trying to escape, instead of seizing and killing the wasp, because it is not aware of its danger. In any case, the survival of the tarantula species as a whole is protected by the fact that the spider is much more fertile than the wasp.[24]

ALEXANDER PETRUNKEVITCH

Of course, writers can intentionally break away from the traditionally accepted ways of writing, as the selection from Faulkner's *Sanctuary* illustrated (see p. 204). Here's a spoof on simplistic categorizing which also plays fast and loose with some of the traditional wisdom I have just outlined as concerns for the comparison writer. As you chuckle along, see if you can spot the error of the writer's ways.

There are two kinds of people in this world—those who insist that there are two kinds of people in the world and those who don't. As we were saying, there are two kinds of people in this world: the uptight and the loose. Face it; you're either one or the other.

How can you tell which you are? Uptight people take themselves seriously, and they hope you're taking them seriously as well. Neatness counts, but it's not everything. Some slobs are uptight, while some fancy dressers are loose. Loose people have a style that Alexander Haig would never understand.

The quintessential uptight and loose characteristics are hard to nail down. So let's start with a few examples. Some subjects nearly classify themselves. For example, Debbie Harry is loose, while Debby Boone is uptight. Pete Rozelle—uptight; Al Davis—loose. The Reverend Jerry Falwell—uptight; the Reverend Ernest Angley—loose. Get it?

Sometimes it's not so easy. Beware of deceptive labeling: John Anderson pretends he's loose but is uptight. Teddy Kennedy pretends he's uptight, but he's loose. Nancy Friday is uptight, even though she talks dirty about men. Al Goldstein is loose.

Flash Gordon is loose, but Superman's a white-knuckle flier. Rodney Dangerfield is uptight on the outside but loose on the inside. Doc Severinsen is the reverse. Robert Blake thinks he's loose, but he's really uptight. Robert Redford is loose, but he tries to hide it. G. Gordon Liddy used to be uptight but won't be reclassified as loose until he either gives up his first initial or starts using his first name. Sorry, G., but rules are rules.

Speaking of rules, *all* dogs, as a rule, are loose, except for Benji, who is uptight. All cats are uptight, except for Morris, who is loose. B. Kliban stationery, towels, toilet paper, etc., are all uptight. B. Kliban is loose.

The Rug Rule: Men who wear toupees are uptight. Howard Cosell is no exception. Willard Scott is.

Magazines are loose. Newspapers are loose on page one and uptight on the editorial page. The First Amendment crowd sorts out as follows:

Uptight	Loose
The New York Times	*The Wall Street Journal*
William F. Buckley's column	William F. Buckley on *Firing Line*
U.S. News & World Report	*Newsweek*
Ms.	*Savvy*
Cosmo	*Redbook*
Women's Wear Daily	*W*
Highlights for Children	*Ranger Rick's Nature Magazine*
National Geographic	*GEO*

TV is basically uptight, but there are some free spirits. Robert Hughes is loose as Toulouse but not so short. Fellow PBS-er Carl Sagan is as airtight as his scientific theories. All anchor men except for David Brinkley are uptight. All weathermen are loose. Dan Rather wants to be loose but isn't. Ted Koppel looks too much like Yoda to be classified. Board-room pitchman Lee (Factory to You) Iacocca is uptight; James Garner is loose. (Perhaps he'd be uptight, too, if he had to sell Chryslers instead of Polaroid cameras.) *M*A*S*H* is uptight (even though half the cast is in stitches). Phil Donahue, J. R. Ewing and the Ingalls are uptight. Andy Rooney, Larry Hagman and the Waltons are loose.

Loose Charlie's Angels: Kate Jackson, Tanya Roberts, Jaclyn Smith, Cheryl Ladd.

Uptight Charlie's Angels: Farrah Fawcett, Shelley Hack, Lady Diana Spencer.

Uptight Hall of Fame: Paul Lynde, the Ayatollah Khomeini, Jean Harris, Caspar Weinberger, Jesse Helms, Tom Snyder, Gay Talese.

Loose Hall of Fame: Miss Piggy, Johnny Carson, Willard Scott, Buddy Hackett.

Smokenders, Weight Watchers and est are all uptight. Don Juan the Yaqui sorcerer is loose. W. Clement Stone is uptight, but Obi-Wan Kenobi is loose. Uptight: sex advice from *Dear Abby*. Loose: Sex advice from the tantric master Bhagwan Shree Rajneesh.

Uptight Newtons: Fig, Olivia, Wayne.

Uptight: All famous women named Nancy. Also guns and vacuum cleaners.

Loose: The Rolling Stones.

Uptight: *Rolling Stone.*

Presidents who golf, have kitchen cabinets, hold meetings in bathrooms, show you their scars or split logs are loose. Presidents who carry their own luggage, jog, talk to mirrors or split logs to slay the killer trees are uptight.

Downstairs neighbors who bang on the ceiling with broom handles are uptight, as are neighbors who leave anonymous notes about your garbage. Uptight neighbors: Mister Rogers, Mexico, George Jefferson. Loose neighbors: Ed Norton and Canada.

Valuable Assets: Goldie Hawn is loose. Minnie Pearl and Ruby Dee are loose. Neil Diamond is uptight.

Typecasting: Loretta Lynn and Sissy Spacek are loose.

It's How You Play the Game That Counts: Dick Vermeil, Bowie Kuhn and Dave Kingman are uptight. George Brett, Mean Joe Greene and Terry Bradshaw are loose.

Christine Jorgensen did it for love, but Reneé Richards did it to win—that's uptight.

Uptight: Pope John Paul II kissing your sister.

Loose: Father Guido Sarducci kissing your sister.

Are They Uptight or Just Close? Jane Fonda is uptight, but she taught Tom Hayden how to be loose. Garry Trudeau is loose, but Jane Pauley is uptight, except when she takes her guitar to work. Liz and John Warner are uptight; he taught her everything he knows.

Loose Lips: Miss Rona.

Screwloose: Devo.

Footloose: Fred Astaire.

Loose dates: January 1, February 2, February 29, April 1, October 31.

Uptight dates: April 15, November 11, December 7, Blind.

To sum up, here's a handy guide to help you chart the rest of the world along its uptight/loose axis:

Uptight	Loose
New York City	Austin, Texas
Miami	Key West
Woody Allen playing Woody Allen	Woody Allen playing clarinet
Lisa Birnbach	Charles Gaines and George Butler
The Official Preppy Handbook	*Pumping Iron*
The French	The Italians
The New York Yankees	The Oakland Athletics
American Express	Visa
Guns	Butter
MacNeil	Lehrer
Ron Reagan, Jr.	Jack Ford
Tax lawyers	Tax accountants
The Sears Tower	The Leaning Tower of Pisa
Betty Crocker	Famous Amos
Ma Bell	Taco Belle
El Salvador	Aruba
Cocaine	Marijuana
Keith Jarrett	Chick Corea
Jogging	Walking
Halston	Ralph Lauren
Frank Borman	Freddie Laker
Barbra and Barry	Peaches and Herb
Rice	Pasta
Bucket seats	Back seats[25]

Another variety of comparison exposition is the extended metaphor, a comparison of two dissimilar things. The metaphor-writer's purpose, in addition to giving the reader a pleasant surprise, is to compare common qualities in the two different subjects. (To review an earlier discussion of metaphor as a thinking strategy, see pp. 42ff.)

An American writer of the last century, Henry David Thoreau, wrote *Walden,* a book about his way of living and his observations about life while at Walden Pond; in a chapter entitled "Brute Neighbors" he narrates a life-and-death struggle between red and black ants.

> I took up the chip on which the three [ants] I have particularly described were struggling, carried it into my house, and placed it under a tumbler on my window-sill, in order to see the issue. Holding a microscope to the first-mentioned red ant, I saw that, though he was assiduously gnawing at the near fore-leg of his enemy, having severed his remaining feeler, his own breast was all torn away, exposing what vitals he had there to the jaws of the black warrior, whose breast-plate was apparently too thick for him to pierce; and the dark carbuncles of the sufferer's eyes shone with ferocity such as war only could excite. They struggled half an hour longer under the tumbler, and when I looked again the black soldier had severed the heads of his foes from their bodies, and the still living heads were hanging on either side of him like ghastly trophies at his saddle-bow, still apparently as firmly fastened as ever, and he was endeavoring with feeble struggles, being without feelers and with only the remnant of a leg, and I know not how many other wounds, to divest himself of them; which at length, after half an hour more, he accomplished. I raised the glass, and he went off over the window-sill in that crippled state. Whether he finally survived that combat, and spent the remainder of his days in some Hotel des Invalides, I do not know; but I thought that his industry would not be worth much thereafter. I never learned which party was victorious, nor the cause of the war; but I felt for the rest of that day as if I had had my feelings excited and harrowed by witnessing the struggle, the ferocity and carnage, of a human battle before my door.[26]

It may not be obvious until the last line that this passage is a metaphor, although Thoreau implies it throughout by his hyperbolic description of the "foes" and their "war." You have seen another more direct, extended metaphor previously; recall Ellen's essay comparing writing to preparing for a costume ball (p. 130).

A Note on Writing Comparisons

Teachers frequently assign comparison-and-contrast topics because asking a student to explain or define something by comparing it to something else is such a useful way of getting the student to make distinctions among and judgments about disparate ideas. So you will find uses for this form of exposition quite often.

When you compare and contrast subjects, recall these suggestions:

- *Subjects:* Select subjects appropriate to the purpose and audience. Only pair apples with oranges if they fit your purpose. And select items familiar to your readers.
- *Categories:* Make categories of appropriate qualities and characteristics. Check to see that your comparisons are logically sound.
- *Organization:* Carefully structure a balanced presentation of the information. Design a symmetrical pattern of organization and follow it.

Define

Stating the specific meaning of a word, an object, or a concept is fundamental to much academic writing. A writer defines words or concepts precisely in order to clear up any ambiguity or vagueness in the reader's mind. Much of a college education is devoted to developing one's ability to think carefully and thoroughly about complex ideas and issues. To develop the cognitive skills necessary for this heady work requires a good deal of practice. One must learn to make fine distinctions between different items in the same category, such as descriptive writing from process writing, jazz from new-wave music, endomorphic from ectomorphic body types, an atheist from an agnostic, a rebel from a conformist, or a middle-of-the-roader. The dictionary not only contains definitions of words, but it also provides a model for how to write clear, precise word definitions. When new things come along with new names, they must be defined. Take jargon words, for instance. Jargon words are idiomatic or abbreviated terms developed by people in highly specialized fields of work. In order to familiarize novices with, let's say, computer functions, components, and concepts knowledgeable computer users must define the jargon words. Here's a list of computer jargon words and abbreviated terms defined in dictionary-definition format.

1. *ASCII.* (Pronounced "asky.") Stands for American Standard Code for Information Interchange. A standard code which assigns specific bit patterns to the *alphanumeric* characters on your keyboard. Example: the letter "E" is coded as "1000101."

2. *BASIC.* Stands for Beginner's All-Purpose Symbolic Instruction Code. The most popular micro, or personal computer, language. Some others include Pascal, Ada, Logo, C, FORTRAN, (FORmula TRANslation), and COBOL (COmmon Business Oriented Language).

3. *Baud.* (Pronounced "baed.") Bits per second: "The modem has a transmission rate of 300 baud."

4. *Board* or *card.* Rectangular, usually green, piece of hardware inside the machine that the chips and circuits are mounted on. Several boards can be attached to a chassis called a *plannerboard.* Well-designed boards are said to have good *architecture.*

5. *Boot.* To load a program.

6. *Bug.* Any defect or malfunction in hardware or software.

7. *CP/M.* Stands for Control Program for Microcomputers. The most popular disk operating system for eight-bit machines.

8. *cps.* Characters per second: "a 120 cps printer."

9. *CRT.* Cathode Ray Tube. The screen on the computer, also called a *monitor.* The more *pixels*—individual points of light—it has, the easier on the eyes. Also called *high resolution.*

10. *Documentation.* Software, or hardware manuals. With any luck, they're *user-friendly,* that is, easy to understand. Hardware that's designed with human comfort in mind is *ergonomic.*

11. *Dot matrix printer.* The kind of printer that makes typefaces composed of tiny dots. A *letter quality* printer uses either a *daisy wheel* or *thimble* mechanism to make a typewriter-style typeface.

12. *Dual processor.* A system or board having both an *8-bit* and a *16-bit* microprocessor. The 8-bit chips, which "ac-

cess" eight bits of information at a time, are the industry standard, and most software on the market is written for them, but they support a maximum RAM of only 64K. The newer 16-bits are faster and can handle up to 1,024K—one *megabyte*—of RAM. The dual processor provides the best of both worlds.

13. *I/O.* Input-output devices that can be hooked up to your printer, such as the modem that connects your telephone line or a printer. Also called *peripherals.*

14. *Intelligent terminal.* A personal microcomputer that works as a standalone machine, as opposed to a *dumb terminal* that's one of many terminals hooked up to a giant *mainframe* computer.

15. *Interface* or *port.* Pluglike part of the computer where the peripherals are attached. A *parallel* printer hooks up to a parallel interface (also called *Centronics parallel,* after the company that invented it), and receives all the bits of a byte simultaneously from a computer. *Serial* printers—which receive the bits in sequence—need a serial port, as do modems. Another name for the standard serial port is the *RS-232C.* When a computer and a peripheral interface properly and transmit data, it's a *handshake.*

16. *MHz.* MegaHertz. Refers to the speed of microprocessors in millions of cycles per second. When the performances of the two different machines are compared, the test is a *benchmark.*[27]

Some terms and concepts are so new, so full of history, or so complex that defining them adequately to a lay audience requires an extended definition. Here are two examples:

Bits and Bytes. The most basic unit of computing is also the most confusing, and the one that makes mathophobes think they'll never get it. But all you really have to know is that the logic behind computers is *binary*—based on the number two—rather than on the comfortably human fingers-and-toes decimal system.

The computer measures information in *bits* (short for binary digits), which consist of only two signals, represented mathematically as 0's or 1's. It takes a string of eight of them to comprise a *byte*, the equivalent of a letter or other single typewriter character. In the guts of the computer, those 1's and 0's are really just electronic pulses, negative or positive, like the little gates that opened or shut in the movie "Tron." What computer languages do is to translate human commands into mathematics that more directly communicate with this "machine language."

Since you can buy ready-made programs (*software*) of all kinds, it isn't necessary to learn any computer languages if you don't want to. Nor is it necessary to understand computers at the innards level, any more than you have to know which neurons are fired in your brain when you scratch your nose. It *is* helpful to realize that most of the computer-related numbers you hear bandied about are exponents of two. For example, a *kilobyte*, or K, isn't 1,000 bytes, although people refer to it that way as a shorthand convenience—it's 1,024 bytes, or 2 to the tenth power.[28]

SYMPHONIE FANTASTIQUE (*Fantastic Symphony*): a symphony by Hector Berlioz—one of the most important works of the nineteenth century. It was first performed in Paris in 1830, only three years after the death of Beethoven. With its defiance of Classical traditions, it was like the opening shot of the Romantic revolution. Almost everything about it was new and different. It has a story, or program. One theme is used throughout all the movements—Berlioz called it an *idée fixe*, or obsession. The symphony has five movements instead of the Classical four, and its harmony is highly chromatic. Its orchestration uses every orchestral group to the fullest extent. The strings soar up above the winds, free of their bread-and-butter job of holding down the harmony. Even the percussion instruments (usually restricted to marking accents) are given solo passages, or help to hold harmony. Berlioz had the audacity to specify that the work needed "at least thirty violins."[29]

You may have noticed that in these two selections the writers employed process exposition, showing how the subject operates (or sounds) in process. At other times it is useful to compare or contrast the subject with something else:

In America, ricotta is made from pasteurized cows' milk. In Italy, ricotta is made from unpasteurized ewes' milk. Needless to say, there is a difference in flavor. American ricotta is bland and tasteless, and one has to work with it to make it taste like something. Italian ricotta is rather sweet and, although very delicate, has a most distinctive flavor. Anyone who has savored the delight of fresh ricotta in Italy knows what I mean. The Italian ricotta is also looser and has a better texture. One has to use more cheese, more eggs and more seasonings when using American ricotta in a recipe to get close to the taste of the original.[30]

While writers commonly define by making distinctions between two similar things, like American ricotta cheese and Italian, they also define subjects by contrasting them with something dissimilar. For example, a writer could define "cooperation" by contrasting it with "competition," or define "table" by contrasting it with "chair," or "window," or "bed." In each of these cases, the writer intends to define the meaning or the qualities of the subject by showing them in literal contrast to meaning or qualities the subject does not possess.

However, a writer may also define a subject by comparing it with something dissimilar with the intention of pointing out similar meaning or qualities in the two. This is the method in the case of metaphors and similes. Look at the way Lewis Thomas defines "warts":

Warts are wonderful structures. They can appear overnight on any part of the skin, like mushrooms on a damp lawn, full grown and splendid in the complexity of their architecture. Viewed in stained sections under a microscope, they are the most specialized of cellular arrangements, constructed as though for a purpose. They sit there like turreted mounds of dense, impenetrable horn, impregnable, designed for defense against the world outside.

In a certain sense, warts are both useful and essential, but not for us. As it turns out, the exuberant cells of a wart are the elaborate reproductive apparatus of a virus.

You might have thought from the looks of it that the cells infected by the wart virus were using this response as a ponderous way of defending themselves against the virus, maybe even a way of becoming more distasteful, but it is not so. The wart is what the virus truly wants; it can flourish only in cells undergoing precisely this kind of overgrowth. It is not a defense at all; it is an overwhelming welcome, an enthusiastic accommodation meeting the needs of more and more virus.[31]

Thomas uses two different similes, one to describe the wart as it looks to the naked eye and another quite different one to describe how it looks through a microscopic lens.

Defining concepts is a major challenge for every writer. Because concepts—like poverty and love—are abstract rather than concrete, they have no physical characteristics by which to describe them. However, poverty has visible effects and acts of love are describable. So that once a writer has given an abstract definition of a concept, he or she can further develop the meaning of the term by showing its effects or illustrating it in a process. Let's look, for example, at the idea of anxiety. Simply and abstractly defined, anxiety is a type of worrying, usually a concern over some upcoming event. There are, however, effects or symptoms of anxiety which may be described: a restlessness or an agitation of the mind, a tenseness in the chest or cramping stomach muscles. Furthermore, there are specific kinds of anxiety (like test anxiety and math anxiety), the particulars of which can be detailed by showing someone exhibiting symptoms of such anxiousness. So, while a writer must be able to explain the abstractness of a concept, he or she can also describe its physical effects or visible presence in a process. For instance, here's how one writer illustrated the nature of math anxiety:

The first thing people remember about failing at math is that it felt like sudden death. Whether it happened while learning word problems in sixth grade, coping with equations in high school, or first confronting calculus and statistics in college, failure was sudden and very frightening. An idea or a new operation was not just difficult, it was impossible! And instead of asking questions or taking the lesson slowly, assuming that in a month or so they would be able to digest it, people remember the feeling, as certain as it was sudden, that they would *never* go any further in mathematics. If we assume, as we must, that the curriculum was reasonable and that the new idea was merely the next in a series of learnable concepts, that feeling of utter defeat was simply not rational; and in fact, the autobiographies of math anxious college students and adults reveal that no matter how much the teacher reassured them, they sensed that from that moment on, as far as math was concerned, they were through.

The sameness of that sudden death experience is evident in the very metaphors people use to describe it. Whether it occurred in elementary school, high school, or college, victims felt that a curtain had been drawn, one they would never see behind; or that there was an impenetrable wall ahead; or that they were at the edge of a cliff, ready to fall off. The most extreme reaction came from a math graduate student. Beginning her dissertation research, she suddenly felt that not only could she never solve her research problem (not unusual in higher mathematics), but that she had never understood advanced math at all. She, too, felt her failure as sudden death.[32]

A second example is the following extended definition of "nun"; notice that the writer's purpose is to explain the term from the perspective of people's general perception or image of nuns rather than to set forth a nun's job description or her particular role in the Catholic Church.

The image of the nun is a potent and a clear one. Curiously anachronistic, an image that attaches to the past, the nun appears in the mind's eye clothed in long black veil, enshrouded in white linen and black cloth. The image figures in pornography and jokes; it is a recognizable symbol to people who have never spoken to a nun in their lives. What does it stand for, and why does it continue to pervade? Perhaps its power derives from its embodiment of the idea of the unsexual woman, the woman whose identity does not come to her from her relation to men. The nun has implicitly in her choice of vocation rejected not only sex but motherhood, and the domestic life. And yet the associations that we bestow on nuns are simply a heightening of our ideas about the nature and behavior of women. We imagine them traveling in pairs, not knowing how much it costs to ride the subway, engrossed in a perfumed comtemplative cloud, or we see them as ravaging viragoes:

Sister Mary Ignatius now on Broadway terrorizes children from the depths of her pent-up sex. It is not so different from what we imagine of our mothers; the curiosity is that, although the reality of the nun's life is so patently different from that of the mother's, our responses to them are so much the same.[33]

A Note on Writing Definitions

Since a large amount of your higher education involves your learning new facts, words, and concepts, you will undoubtedly be writing numerous definitions. Sometimes you may be called upon to match words with their definitions, to write out short definitions, and to define terms or concepts in essays or papers of several hundred words. Here are some suggestions for when you are writing definitions:

• Rely on the dictionary for basic definitions and for models of the form for writing short definitions. (Ask the reference librarian to point out to you the dictionaries of special terms in various fields of study.)

• List as many appropriate qualities and characteristics as you can.

• Compare or contrast the subject with similar items or ideas, or with dissimilar items or ideas, by using metaphors or similes.

• Make distinctions clearly.

• Use other types of expository writing as appropriate: description, process, and so on.

• If the subject is an abstract concept, after you have defined its abstract qualities or characteristics, think of physical effects or visible processes you can describe as a way of elaborating the definition.

Cause and Effect

Writing exposition that identifies certain circumstances, processes, or actions, and specifies what made them happen or set them going is cause-and-effect writing. In a world full of incalculable phenomena it is a demanding intellectual task to sort through a number of possible causal agents to identify the right one or, as in many cases, the right ones, and to establish the order of their relation to an effect. For example, what caused the American Civil War? Was it the issue of slavery? Or were conflicts over the differing types of regional economies more to blame? Were other disputes of the day contributing factors: for instance, whether to strengthen the national government and regional demands for special-interest legislation? For another example, why does one individual prefer heterosexuality and someone else in the same family prefer homosexuality? Is human sexual identity a determinant of biology, psychology, or some combination of both?

Writing sound cause-and-effect exposition requires patient trial-and-error thinking, precise ordering of main cause and subordinate causes, and full, clear explanations of the causal relations presented. Look, for example, at this discussion of why people get fat:

People get fat because they consume more calories than they expend, and any exceptions to that rule would not only be a medical phenomenon but a violation of the laws of thermodynamics. But that insight does not fully explain why some people get fat on the same amount of food that keeps others thin, nor, for that matter, why some people feel the urge to eat more than they need. . . .

So some researchers have concluded that a person's weight is not merely the arbitrary point at which his greed happens to intersect his laziness, but the product of a dynamic process of fine-tuning appetite and metabolism. They suggest that the body has a "setpoint," a mechanism for stabilizing weight for long periods within a fairly narrow range—a range which may, but frequently does not, correspond to what Giorgio Armani thinks you should weigh. Dip below this setpoint, and your body nags you to get on with your noshing; go too far above it, and a subtle hormonal shift reminds you of how much fun it is to jog in the sleet.[34]

What was assumed to be the
cause ——————————————→ consuming more calories
of obesity, (the *effect*)   than expending

failed to account for *effects*
which were exceptions —————→ Some people getting fat on
to that cause.   the same amount of food
                                        which kept others thin, *and*
                                        why some people feel the
                                        urge to eat more than they
                                        need

Therefore, some researchers
believe
that obesity, (the *effect*)
has a different *cause.* —————→ A "setpoint" mechanism that
                                        regulates appetite and
                                        metabolism

Just as medical researchers analyze data to establish causal relations in our bodies, so political scientists assess and write about causal relations in the body politic. Take this writer's concern over a possible change in federal policy that would legalize "homework," industrial or clerical work performed in homes:

Unions are justifiably horrified by the idea of a return to homework, which was widespread in the 19th century. Because it would be hidden in private homes and apartments, no wage regulations could be enforced nor would wages have the same meaning as in a normal workplace, since the homeworker would have to cover all the overhead, and probably supply her own sewing machine, typewriter, or other equipment. Worse still, homework could reopen the door to child labor. Near the turn of the century, poor women and their children worked upward of 14 hours a day to fill their piecework quotas in New York City's garment and hat industries.[35]

The three detrimental effects of legalizing homework, as the writer sees it, would be that

1. no wage regulations could be enforced;

2. wages would actually mean less since laborers would supply all overhead and equipment; and

3. the door would be reopened for child labor.

Notice that the writer provides sufficient reasoning to support each of her assertions which she lists from least horrifying to most.

A Note on Determining Effects and Their Causes

In science courses you may assess the actions and reactions of agents and catalysts; in social science courses you may trace a social trend through media "hype" to its source in local customs; in literature courses you may study the tragic dilemmas of Hamlet or Oedipus, seeking in fate or character flaw the reasons for these dilemmas. When you are called upon to determine the causes of certain effects, refer to these suggestions:

- If the effect is not distinguished from the surrounding information, identify it by looking for a result or current state.
- Using trial-and-error thinking, sort through each piece of information that could be a potential cause of the effect.
- If several items have some causal relation to the effect, organize them according to their order of significance.
- Write sufficient explanations of causal relations. Explain, for example, if one cause creates an effect which itself becomes a cause of a subsequent effect.
- Draw a flow chart to help sort primary causes from secondary causes and to determine if there are multiple effects. See Figure 7.3.

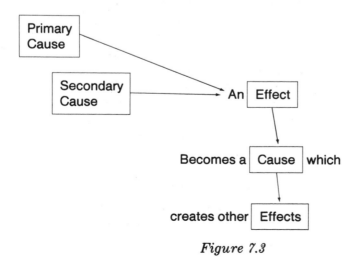

Figure 7.3

Classify and Analyze

Like illustrating, comparing, defining, and showing as cause or effect, classifying is another method of arranging information. Writing classification exposition challenges the writer to design appropriate categories for items in a set of information, to sort those items correctly into the categories, and to describe, explain, or analyze the items in each category.

Classification is sometimes very much like comparison in that certain qualities of items are compared. For example, the selection on uptight and loose people (pp. 239–242) compares and contrasts two basic types of people; it could also be labeled classification exposition because it sorts people into categories: The Rug Rule, Loose Charlie's Angels, Valuable Assets, and so on. However, that article lacks a significant element which distinguishes classification exposition: analysis. After sorting information into categories, the classifying writer explains or analyzes the qualities of items in each category. For an example, read this selection on types of wood used to build a piano:

> The wood that is transformed into a Steinway model D is of several different kinds, each with its own characteristics and purposes. Yellow poplar, which is soft and relatively cheap, is used as the "core wood" of such flat, tablelike parts as the piano's top; it is veneered with mahogany to give an attractive appearance. Maple is used where extreme hardness is necessary—for example, in the pin block, also called the wrest plank, which must hold tuning pins tight against the tension of the strings, and in the action, whose hundreds of tiny moving parts must be machined to precise tolerances. Sitka spruce, light in weight and high in strength, is used for structural cross braces; also, because it has long, parallel fibers that vibrate freely, it is used in the soundboard, the thin panel inside the case that amplifies the vibrations of the strings and projects their sound into the air.[36]

The writer categorizes the woods according to types, describes each type's physical characteristics, and explains how each one functions in the piano's structure. (In doing this, the writer uses descriptive and process exposition.) Notice that this writer's purpose—to identify the varieties of wood and to describe each one and explain its function—is significantly different from the writer of the uptight-and-loose-people piece which was primarily to identify people as one or the other; only in relatively few cases is there any explanation of the categorization of someone as uptight or loose.

In the next selection, a discussion of types of geometry, the writer takes a set of at least seven types and reduces them to three categories:

> There are many types of geometry—informal, formal, Euclidean, non-Euclidean, coordinate, experimental, etc. Nevertheless the various geometries can be grouped under three basic headings: experimental geometry, informal geometry, and formal geometry.
>
> Experimental geometry (or physical geometry) deals with properties of physical objects. For example, we can measure the surface area of an object or the volume of a container; and by means of a sufficient number of such measurements, we are able to arrive at a general formula for finding areas or volumes of all objects of a given shape. Therefore we can say that experimental geometry is a geometry of physical experiments and inductive reasoning.
>
> Formal geometry, however, treats properties of a general nature, not only physical objects, but geometric entities—concepts that we can only imagine. We begin with premises, called *postulates* or *axioms*, regarding these entities, and deductively prove theorems. Formal geometry is a geometry of deductive reasoning.
>
> Informal geometry lies somewhere between experimental geometry and formal geometry. Experimental geometry provides evidence for informal geometry, and informal geometry becomes formal geometry through the application of deductive logic and set theory. Informal geometry relies heavily on intuition and drawings to discover geometric facts.[37]

This writer observed a sound practice for classification writing: reducing the items to as few categories as possible. Creating too many categories often confuses readers. Using fewer categories also means including more items in each category, thus allowing more possibilities for examples and analysis within each. So, limit the number of categories to as few as possible when you can.

However, sometimes the number of categories is already given, as in the case of champagnes:

The word champagne, strictly speaking, applies *only* to a specific wine, made in a specific region of France, by a specific process, from only certain specific varieties of grapes. Many countries have recognized this terminology and have given different names to their wines that are made by the same method, such as Germany (Sekt), and Italy (Spumante). But in the United States, any sparkling wine, white or red, may be called champagne if it is made by the same bottle-fermented process as the original French champagne and bears on its label the region of its origin, such as California, New York State, etc., where the wine was made. Any kind of grapes may be used for American champagne.

All champagne is a blend, and certain official rules and regulations protect the public from a fraudulent wine. Because of the special way in which it is made, champagne is one of the very rare wines for which the brand name is more important than that of the vineyard or district the wine came from. The names used to classify champagne are *vintage champagne, non-vintage champagne* and B. O. B.

Vintage champagne need not be made *entirely* from the wines of a single, especially good year, but it *must* be made *in large part* from these wines, which are blended with wines from other years. No producer is allowed to sell as the champagne of a certain vintage more wine than he produced in that particular year; in other words, he cannot stretch a certain vintage with wine of lesser years. No vintage champagne may be shipped until it is three years old, and before shipping it has to be approved by a special interprofessional committee of experts.

Non-vintage champagne is almost always a blend of the wines of less good plus good years, the latter improving the quality of the first, which, alone, could not be sold. Non-vintage champagne bears the name of the French *shipper*, and this name is your guarantee. In practice, this means that in the case of the dozen-odd best champagne shippers, the wine is very good indeed. There are also smaller houses which produce a most creditable wine.

B. O. B. champagne, which stands for Buyer's Own Brand, is the least expensive kind; it is the champagne sold by a *retailer* under his own brand name. It is as good as the champagne the retailer bought in the first place, and is suitable for large-scale occasions like parties. It can be good, but never great.

Tête de Cuvée is a brand of champagne put out by some houses, which is supposed to be even better than their vintage champagne, usually made only from the first and most delicate pressing of the finest grapes or from special grapes. It is more expensive and sometimes worth the money; other times, not.

Blancs de Blancs are wines made entirely from white grapes, as distinguished from the usual way of making champagne from red grapes or a blend of white and red. (The juice of all grapes is white; the color is in the skin of the grapes.) *Blancs de Blancs* are supposed to be lighter wines, but this is a matter of personal opinion about a rather recent fashionable development in champagne making.[38]

Notice how the writer has organized the preceding essay:

Para. #1	Champagne—strictly defined	
	Examples of other sparkling wines	Sekt Spumante U.S. "champagne"
Para. #2	Elaborated definition and listing of three categories: vintage, non-vintage and B.O.B.	
Para. #3	Vintage champagne	In each category, the contents are described and some production procedures are discussed.
Para. #4	Non-vintage champagne	
Para. #5	B.O.B.	

Para. #6   Tete de cuvée
Para. #7   Blancs de Blancs

Although he does not include the last two categories in the list of bonafide champagnes in paragraph two, the writer adds them at the end. You may have also noticed that the writer has listed the types of champagne in descending order of quality. Finally, the last four sentences in paragraphs four through seven contain this connoisseur's estimate of the wine's relative quality.

A Note on Classifying and Analyzing

While classification exposition can be as simple and practical as listing cars and their primary characteristics under the headings full-size, mid-size, compact, and subcompact, usually in academic writing classification exposition is used to sort and assess in detail several complex items in a set of information. It could be used, for example, to address such issues or questions as the following:

Identify the major kinds of cardiac diseases and their treatments.

What literary devices does Eudora Welty use in *Losing Battles?* Describe them and their functions in the novel.

Discuss several types of corn hybrids developed in the Midwest this decade. Arrange them into three groups according to your own criteria, describing the features of each group.

Define the term "urban dweller," using examples that range selectively across the spectrum of classes and occupations. What characteristics do the various types have in common?

If you face a writing assignment like one of those preceding, and you determine that classification exposition is an appropriate type of writing to fulfill it, consider the following points:

• If you need to create categories, limit the number to as few as possible and take care to label them appropriately.

• Sort the various items of information into categories; check on the accuracy of your choices for inclusion.

• List the qualities of the items contained in each category.

• Arrange your categories in some order (best to worst, simplest to most complex) as appropriate to your writing purpose.

Exercises in Exposition

1. Reread the paragraph on manics (pp. 223–224) and write a similar paragraph, developing an idea by listing examples. Here are some sample ideas:

- My mother (or father) is a professional worrier.
- Deadlines give procrastinators their reasons for living.
- Campus politicians thrive on controversy.

2. How to make an omelette: Write a process essay explaining to a novice cook how to make an omelette. The various steps in the process are listed here, but—alas—they are scrambled. Put the steps in the proper sequence and also draw up separately a list of required ingredients and utensils. If you are good at sketching, create any illustrations you feel would be helpful.

- Fold the other edge in reverse over the first fold.
- Pour the beaten eggs into the melted butter and shake the pan, holding it with one hand.
- Season the eggs with salt and pepper; it is better to season each egg separately.
- Break five eggs into a porcelain or glass bowl.
- With your other hand immediately stir the eggs with a fork over high heat.
- Roll up the omelette: fold over one third of the omelette, working from the side of the pan with the handle, toward the open side.
- Serve the omelette and enjoy. Serves 4 to 6.
- Heat two tablespoons of butter in a skillet; let it melt but not brown.
- Cook the omelette according to taste: very moist, medium or well-done.
- Beat the eggs just enough to blend them, but no more.
- While the omelette is cooking, tap the skillet against the stove from time to time so that the omelette will not stick to the pan.[39]

3. Rewrite Selzer's paragraph on the knife as you believe a professor of surgical techniques would lecture his interns. (Sug-

gestion: For openers, call the knife a scalpel.) Share your version with a group of classmates. Explain your reasons for the revisions you made.

4. Compare and contrast an analogical clock (one with hands) to a digital one; discuss their functions in addition to the conceptual similarities and differences.

5. Write a short essay (500 words) comparing and contrasting your neighborhood, hometown, or city when you were a child to it as it is today. (If you have moved from your childhood home, compare it to your new place of residence.)

6. Write an essay of 500 to 1000 words on one of the following topics:

- Yourself as a learner in high school (or earlier) as compared to now;
- Some aspects of the status of women in American society;
- Two of your closest friends (or two members of your family);
- Freedom and responsibility as they pertain to you right now.

7. Reread the list of computer jargon words defined (pp. 245–247). With a group of your classmates, add as many more computer jargon words as you know; write out definitions for them.

8. In a large group brainstorming session draw up a list of campus jargon words. Divide the words among subgroups and draft definitions. Have the subgroups share their definition drafts with the large group; make revisions to the drafts as appropriate. Publish your jargon dictionary in the school newspaper or on a handout sheet.

9. Reread the selection on the images of a nun. Over the next week or so write journal entries on your childhood perceptions of some authority figure: a schoolteacher or principal, a member of the police, a priest, minister, or nun, an adult in your family, a storekeeper, and so on. After you have developed sufficient material write an essay portraying that figure as you saw him or her, or depicting your childhood images of him or her.

10. Write a statement directed to your former teachers, explaining why you have enrolled in college. Include in your discussion what factors influenced you.

11. Suppose that you are to present a talk to a sociology class classifying and analyzing the students at your school. Write an essay of 500 to 750 words about the types of students attending

your school. To avoid using stereotyped categories (unoriginal, trite, or hackneyed classifications), think carefully about people's characteristics and practices as a guide to your designing of category titles.

FOR FURTHER READING, WRITING AND STUDY

1. Read *The Preppy Handbook* and write an assessment of it as an example of classification exposition.

2. Work with a group of your classmates to design your own boardgame, named and modeled after the writing course in which you are currently enrolled:

OBJECT: To complete the course with the best grade you can achieve.

MATERIALS:

A game board (paint over it or glue on your newly designed top; write on the squares the course requirements, "bonus" and "sorry" card selections, and so on)

A pair of dice (for rolling to determine the number of spaces to move)

Bonus cards (to pick, telling you of good grades on writing assignments, of ways to improve by rewriting, of exemptions from some requirements because of high ability, and so on)

Sorry cards (to pick, telling of paper deadlines missed, of problem-filled rough drafts, of extra homework assignments, and of low grades on papers)

A spinner (an optional accessory which could be used to give players the opportunity to switch sorry cards for bonus cards, or to receive help [points] from the Writing Center to improve writing abilities)

RULES: Design the rules based on the required work in your course and on its "rules."

Note: Designing a successful boardgame takes considerable planning. One way to organize this work is to divide the tasks between various subgroups in your class. Each group should meet frequently over a several-day period, making notes, sketching designs and drafting ideas. Then, in a collaborative effort, the groups can put the game together. After a few trial runs to help you improve this or that aspect, you are ready to play.

ASSESSMENT: After playing the game write journal entries evaluating various elements of the game: How well were terms defined? Were the directions clear and in an appropriate sequence? And, finally, was it fun?

3. Suppose for reasons of fiscal austerity your school was forced to drop a major athletic program or to close an important academic program. Write an article for your school paper detailing the effects of such an action.

4. Read *Grapes of Wrath* entirely and write a paper discussing how the central idea of Chapter Three (pp. 219–221) relates to the main action and meaning of the novel.

5. In the second selection of the first exercise of this chapter Kenneth Clark mentions the American novelist, Henry James, as one of the pilgrims to Paris, the center of civilization. No doubt Clark was familiar with James's writings about the region. If you wish to study a classic descriptive essay, read James's essay on the Cathedral of Notre Dame at Chartres (near Paris); it is printed in *Portraits of Places* (Boston: James R. Osgood & Co., 1884). If, by chance, your library does not have that book, you can find the original version of the essay in a more recently published book: Henry James, *Parisian Sketches*, eds. Leon Edel and Ilse Dusoir Lind (New York: New York University Press, 1957). If both books are available, you might find it instructive to compare the two versions to see what revisions James made.

Be a pilgrim to a building of significant architectural merit in your region. Write an essay in which you discuss the building's history in addition to describing its physical features. If you need assistance in finding information, speak to a reference librarian or inquire at the local historical society office.

6. Read the following selection on machines that can walk and identify what type (or types) of writing it contains.

Many machines imitate nature: a familiar example is the imitation of a soaring bird by the airplane. One form of animal locomotion that has resisted imitation is walking. Can it be that modern computers and feedback control systems make it possible to build machines that walk? We have been exploring the question with computer models and with actual hardware.

So far we have built two machines. One has six legs and a human driver; its purpose is to explore the kind of locomotion displayed by insects, which does not demand attention to the problem of balance. The other machine has only one leg and moves by hopping; it serves to explore the problems of balance. We call the first kind of locomotion crawling to distinguish it from walking, which does require balance, and running, which involves periods of flight as well. Our work has helped us to understand how people and other animals crawl, walk and run.

Unlike a wheel, which changes its point of support continuously and gradually while bearing weight, a leg changes its point of support all at once and must be unloaded to do so. In order for a legged system to crawl, walk or run, each leg must go through periods when it carries load and keeps its foot fixed on the ground and other periods when it is unloaded and its foot is free to move. This type of cyclic alternation between a loaded phase, called stance, and an unloaded phase, called transfer, is found in every form of legged system. As anyone who has ridden a horse at a trot or a gallop knows, the alternation between stance and transfer can generate a pronounced up-and-down motion. We believe legged machines can be built that will minimize this motion.[40]

7. Read "The Lessons of Beekeeping" and write an essay addressing these questions: Of what type or types of writing is it made? What is the author's primary purpose? What secondary purposes might he have? For example, which goal do you think is primary: entertainment or analysis of behavior? Or is something else primary?

THE LESSONS OF BEEKEEPING

With bees or professors, the first principle is smoke

I have long been a believer in the proposition—now unfashionable—that hobbies or jobs should be strictly functional, and undertaken because they further one's ambitions. For example, my Ph.D. dissertation, on Medieval ecclesiastical politics on the eve of the Reformation, was extremely useful in one job I held as aide to the mayor of Boston. More recently I took up beekeeping as a method of improving my performance as an academic administrator. Although I am not an experienced beekeeper, I have already picked up some invaluable guidance.

1. The first principle is smoke. Beekeepers build a small fire in a hand-held bellows contraption. A few puffs of smoke before approaching bees has a singularly calming effect on them. Before any faculty discussion, I suggest a puff or two on the neglect and diffidence, if not outright venality, of a higher level of administration.

2. Never approach the bees frontally. Beekeepers always work from the back of a hive. Dealing with an issue directly often leads to a good stinging.

3. Do not labor under the delusion you can avoid being stung. Be philosophical about it: "The poison of the honeybee is the artist's jealousy" (Blake). Also be sensible: arrange to have a small test for allergies ahead of time. Some people suffer severe reactions to a sting or two, and must retire from the business precipitously with considerable embarrassment.

4. Bees are ill-tempered and likely to sting in windy and wet weather. It has to do with the fact that they are not working to gather nectar and pollen and thus become surly. On the other hand, good management and good weather (*i.e.,* luck) can lead to a bountiful harvest.

5. It is an error to succumb to the temptation of thinking that you can compensate for a sting by squashing the offender. I say this is an error because it does not take into account a fundamental principle: some bees have tenure. They are called queens.

6. Be careful when you mess with queens. A queen lives in a hive, which is a wooden box with an internal structure which looks rather complex, but is really quite simple. Inside this box are combs where honey is stored, the queen lays eggs, and the worker bees nurse the eggs and larvae, called brood, into maturity. Attempting to do in a queen is serious business. It is often difficult to find the queen. Or the queen may be fiercely protected by the workers. Removing a queen can be counterproductive because introducing a replacement queen into a hive has risks. A new queen can be set upon by the workers, and rejected or (since queens are somewhat delicate without workers to tend and feed it) die prematurely.

7. Swarming is seasonal and to be expected. This is a rather complicated process by which a queen, in a cluster of workers, takes off for new quarters. Capturing swarms is a quick way

to build up your operation. Back at the old hive, an interesting process occurs after swarming. The hive creates several queen cells. (Queens are made, not born.) Strangely enough, the first queen to hatch goes around and destroys all the unhatched or partially hatched aspiring queens.

8. In working with a hive, avoid abrupt and jerky movements. A fluid and gentle style, combined with smoke and work from the rear (assuming good weather) permits one to take a hive apart with hardly a stir or a buzzing.

9. Be sure to keep on the alert for outbreaks of American foulbrood disease. European foulbrood disease may be a lot worse, but it is much more rare.

10. Dream a little. Bees have a practice that commends itself to contemplation. Drones, whose sole purpose is to hang around and mate with that rarity, a virgin queen, are routinely driven out of the hive by the workers at the onset of winter. Given the stringent budget environment of turn-of-the-year honey stores, this example of productivity assessment and cost-effective goal-oriented action is inspiring to many people. Think and perhaps even talk a bit about this, but remember you should not aspire to the brutal efficiency of a hive of bees.

11. Don't take on more hives than you can handle readily. This requires hiring help, and the costs of the whole thing begin to get out of hand.

12. Have fun reading trade journals, where you can find all the latest information about killer bees, artificial insemination of queens, drone management, and recipes for success— just about none of which are applicable to your situation.

In all, it's a good business, if you have good weather.[41]

MICHAEL J. KELLY

This is an example of combined writing types. Paragraph by paragraph, analyze the writing types used here. For example, sketch a graphic illustration of the idea development in at least one of the paragraphs. Finally, write an explanation of how the writer used various writing types to make his point and to relate effectively to the audience.

8. Read E. M. Forster's "Voltaire and Frederick the Great," which is reprinted here:

Two hundred years ago a Frenchman paid a visit to a German. It is a famous visit. The Frenchman was delighted to come to Germany, his German host delighted to welcome him. They were more than polite to one another, they were enthusiastic, and each thought, "I am sure we are going to be friends for ever." Yet the visit was a disaster. They still talk about it in Germany today, and they say it was the Frenchman's fault. And they still talk about it in France. And I'm going to talk about it now, partly because it makes such a good story, and partly because it contains a lesson for us all, even though it did happen two hundred years back.

The Frenchman was Voltaire. People today sometimes think of Voltaire as a person who sneered at everything, and made improper jokes. He was much more than that, he was the greatest man of his age, indeed he was one of the greatest men whom European civilisation has produced. If I had to name two people to speak for Europe at the Last Judgment I should choose Shakespeare and Voltaire—Shakespeare for his creative genius, Voltaire for his critical genius and humanity. Voltaire cared for the truth, he believed in tolerance, he pitied the oppressed, and since he was a forceful character he was able to drive his ideas home. They happen to be my own ideas, and like many other small people I am thankful when a great person comes along and says for me what I can't say properly for myself. Voltaire speaks for the thousands and thousands of us who hate injustice and work for a better world.

What did he do? He wrote enormously: plays (now forgotten); short stories, and some of them are still read—especially that masterpiece, *Candide.* He was a journalist, and a pamphleteer, he dabbled in science and philosophy, he was a good popular historian, he compiled a dictionary, and he wrote hundreds of letters to people all over Europe. He had correspondents everywhere, and he was so witty, so up-to-date, so on the spot that kings and emperors were proud to get a letter from Voltaire and hurried to answer it with their own hand. He is not a great creative artist. But he is a great man with a powerful intellect and a warm heart, enlisted in the service of humanity. That is why I rank him with Shakespeare as a spiritual spokesman for Europe. Two hundred years before the Nazis came, he was the complete anti-Nazi.

I am so fond of him that I should like to add he had a perfect character. Alas, he hadn't! He was a bundle of contradictions and nerves. Although he loved truth he often lied. Although he loved humanity he was often malicious. Though generous he was a money-maker. He was a born tease. He had no dignity. And he was no beauty to look at either—a gibbering monkey of a man, very small, very thin, with a long sharp nose, a bad complexion and beady black eyes. He overdressed, as little people sometimes do, and his wig was so large that it seemed to extinguish him.

That is the Frenchman who sets out for Berlin on June 13, 1751; the German whom he is about to visit is Frederick the Great, King of Prussia.

Frederick is one of the founders of modern Germany, and Hitler has made a careful study of him. He plunged Europe into wars to advance his ambitions. He believed in force and fraud and cruelty, and in doing everything himself. He had a genius for organising, he preferred to employ inferior men, and he despised the human race. That is the dividing line between him and Voltaire. Voltaire believed in humanity. Frederick did not. "You don't know this damned race of men," he once exclaimed. "You don't know them. I do." He was a cynic, and having had a very unhappy childhood he felt till the end of his life that he had not been properly appreciated; and we know how dangerous such men can be, and what miseries they can bring upon themselves and others.

But there was another side to Frederick. He was a cultivated, sensitive gentleman. He was a good musician, he had read widely, and he had made a careful study of French. He even composed a number of French poems—they are not good, still they serve to show that to him German wasn't everything. He was, in this way, more civilised than Hitler. There was no Nordic purity nonsense about him. He did not think that Germany was destined to rule the world: he knew that the world is a very complicated place, and that we have to live and let live in it; he even believed in freedom of speech. "People can say what they like as long as I do what I like" was the way he put it. One day, as he went through Berlin he saw a caricature of himself on a wall, and all he said was: "Oh— hang it down lower so that it can be seen better."

The visit began in a whirl of compliments. Voltaire called

Frederick "The Solomon of the North," Frederick declared that of all his victorious titles the most precious was Possessor of Voltaire. He made his guest a court official, housed him royally, gave him a handsome salary, and promised an extra salary to his niece, Madame Denis, if she would come to keep house for him. (We shall hear more of poor Madame Denis in a minute.) Witty conversation, philosophic discussion, delicious food—Frederick liked good food, though he was careful to get it cheap. Everything seemed perfect—but! Not long after his arrival, Voltaire wrote a letter to a friend in France in which the ominous little word "But" keeps occurring.

"The supper parties are delicious. The King is the life of the company. But. I have operas and comedies, reviews and concerts, my studies and books. But, but. Berlin is fine, the princesses charming, the maids of honour handsome. But." We can interpret this But. It is the instinctive protest of the free man who finds himself in the power of a tyrant. Voltaire, for all his faults, was a free man. Frederick had charm and intelligence. But—he was a tyrant.

The visit went very slowly. Voltaire did several tiresome things. He got mixed up in a shady financial transaction, he quarrelled with another Frenchman who was in the king's service, he drank too much chocolate, and when the king rationed him he revenged himself by taking the wax candles out of the candlesticks and selling them. All very undignified. And—worst of all—he laughed at the king's French poems. Frederick, like Hitler, fancied himself as an artist, and he had often employed his guest to polish his verses up. Now he was told that the tiresome little monkey was poking fun at him and quoting him all over the place—a serious matter this, for some of the poems were imprudent, and intended for private circulation only. The Solomon of the North was vexed. He thought: "No doubt my visitor is a genius, but he is making more trouble than he's worth, and he's disloyal." And Voltaire thought: "No doubt my host is a mighty monarch, but I would rather worship him from a distance." He left Berlin, after a stay of two years, which had gradually become more and more uncomfortable for both parties.

But that is not the end. The real bust-up was yet to come. It occurred at Frankfurt, where Voltaire was waiting for Madame Denis to join him. Frankfurt did not belong to the King of Prussia. He had no legal authority there at all, but he had his "Gestapo" and he worked through them to interfere with personal liberty. He discovered that Voltaire had taken away from Berlin (it seems by accident) a copy of the wretched French poems, flew into a passion and ordered Voltaire's luggage to be searched. As always, he employed second-rate people and they went too far. They not only searched Voltaire's luggage but they imprisoned him and bullied him night and day in the hope of extracting information which would please their royal master. It is an incredible affair, a real foretaste of Nazi methods. Voltaire tried to escape; he was stopped at the gates of Frankfurt and dragged back, and Madame Denis, who now arrived to join her uncle, was also arrested and ill-treated. Madame Denis was a stout, emotional lady, with some pretensions as an actress. She was not one to suffer in silence and she soon made Europe ring with her protests. Voltaire's health broke down and he feigned to be more ill than he really was: he ran from his tormentors into an inner room and gasped, "Will you not even allow me to be sick?" His secretary rushed up to assist him, and Voltaire, while making all the motions of vomiting, whispered in his ear, "I am pretending! I am pretending!" He loved fooling people; he could be mischievous even in his misery, and this is to me an endearing trait.

Frederick saw things had gone too far. Voltaire and his niece were released, and in later years the two great men corresponded almost as enthusiastically as before. But they were careful not to meet and Voltaire at all events had learnt a lesson. Berlin had taught him that if a man believes in liberty and variety and tolerance and sympathy he cannot breathe the air of the totalitarian state. It all may seem nice upon the surface—but! The tyrant may be charming and intelligent—but! The machinery may work perfectly—but! Something is missing: the human spirit is missing. Voltaire kept faith with the human spirit. He fought its battle against German dictatorship two hundred years before our time.[42]

The essay's title suggests the obvious subjects of comparison, but what other, larger issues are being compared? (*Note:* Forster wrote the essay in 1941.) Draft an outline or a graphic illustration of the dual comparisons Forster makes in the essay.

PERSUASION: THE FRIENDLY ART

Persuasive writing—in its most formal sense—has as its purpose to urge or convince someone to do something. In a less formal sense, however, we call any writing persuasive which intends to change someone's mind about something. This purpose sets persuasion apart from description, narration, and exposition. However, some people contend that all writing is a form of persuasion; in other words, whether writers are describing something, telling a story, or setting forth an idea, their purpose is to persuade the reader to see it from their point of view. To some extent, I would agree.

So how can we distinguish persuasive writing from other kinds? By determining the primary writing intention. For example, if a sports writer composes a graphic, blow-by-blow account of a boxing match in order to entertain and report a sporting news event, we would classify the writing as description, narration, and exposition. On the other hand, if he or she composes the account to show the brutality of sport in order to convince people to support a ban on professional boxing in their state, we would call the writing persuasive, even though it contains elements of descriptive, narrative, and expository writing.

Let's test this method of distinguishing between types of writing; read this essay by Barbara Lazear Ascher which appeared in *The New York Times* "Hers" column:

A CLOSE MARRIAGE SHOULD NOT MEAN INDIVIDUALITY'S END

In his essay "Three Good Women," Montaigne writes of women who committed suicide with their husbands. Only in the case of Paulina, wife of Seneca, did the attempt fail. But, says Montaigne, such failure does not diminish her honor, virtue and devotion, "showing by the pallor of her face how much of life had flowed away through her wounds."

He tells of Pliny the Younger's neighbor, who suffered from an incurable disease and whose wife persuaded him to leap with her from their window into the sea. She promises that he will die in her arms. "But for fear that the closeness of her embrace might be loosened by the fall and by terror, she had herself tightly bound and attached to him around the waist."

And Arria, who takes her life to encourage her husband, Paetus, to do likewise after his imprisonment by the Emperor Claudius. Plunging her husband's dagger into her breast and then placing the bloodied weapon into his hand, she exhorts him, "Believe me, the wound that I have made does not pain me, but the wound that you are to give yourself, that O Paetus, pains me."

Was this the pain that led to Cynthia Koestler's recent suicide? There is no telling. No Latin historian was standing by to bring us the final story. As of this writing we know only that Arthur Koestler was suffering from leukemia and Parkinson's disease "but that his wife was not known to have had any grave ailment." (I suppose a broken heart does not qualify as a grave ailment.) Their close friend Melvin Lasky tells us that "their marriage was almost impossibly close; her devotion to him was like no other wife's I have ever known."

I fear for devoted wives. I refuse to idealize these women and their endings. I cannot see death as the proper outcome of a good marriage. I cannot see self-sacrifice as a standard of devotion. I am sorry, Montaigne, but I cannot see that to qualify for "goodness" I must tie myself to the waist of another in the plunge for death or life. I understand that loving is giving of the self. I will not be persuaded that that includes giving up the self.

Of "impossible closeness' I would say, Beware. When two hearts beat as one, one of those hearts is in hiding.

A man in the business of finding hiding hearts, a specialized detective of sorts, a psychoanalyst, described the process of analysis as "the longest goodbye." I would describe all loving as the longest goodbye. Starting with our parents, who taught us of gravity and our own perimeters, who painted the world of experience in the vibrant finger paints of words. "Me," "you," "exciting," "fun," "happy," "sad"—real feelings in a real world painted in primary colors and illuminated by a spotlight. We were given a self and bade goodbye.

And in our adult lives the passion of our couplings comes in part from the knowledge that we are close, we are bound, we merge and say goodbye.

Every morning as we part for work or wave a child off to school, we are murmuring small goodbyes, often without a twinge of the heart. This is practice built into the system, preparation for what is to come—that final and most fearsome of farewells.

Some fear the final farewell so completely that they refuse ever to live as separate individuals, to practice their goodbyes. They refuse to take part in the drill, to march up and down the heart's cutting edge. So frightened are they of separation that they attempt to blend their own boundaries with those of their beloved. They believe that by moving side by side they will become one. That eventually, like the tigers in "Little Black Sambo," their frenzied attachment will melt them down into a common ghee. They would have it that they can weave a numbing cloth to bind the heart, that they can place their hearts in purdah.

And there are those who will not enter into intense relationships, will not open themselves to another, who are afraid of intimacy because "it will hurt too much when it ends." They say goodbye before they have ever said hello.

The best marriages I have known have been between people whose greetings are joyous and farewells sad, whose individuality is cherished and encouraged. Their mergings are limited to their lovemaking, to which they bring fearless, eager and vulnerable selves. Afterward they dust off the sharp edges of their lines of demarcation and go about their lives.

They are like the crowds that gather on beaches and mountaintops to watch the sunset. They act as if they don't know how this show ends. They approach with wonder. Their quiet comments can be heard as darkened sky gives way to rose, to violet, to yellow. But then there is silence and stillness when the show ends, when night has finally and irrevocably swallowed day. The curtain has come down, but the audience remains for one moment of numbed disbelief. Then they stand up, straighten their skirts, adjust their ties and move out into the night.

Just more practice. We keep coming to the sunsets to remind ourselves that there will never be another quite like it, to feel the ache and to relearn that grief eventually spreads out against the sky, softens and dissipates.

What happened, Cynthia Koestler? How did you forget

this? Or did you never practice? Did you truly believe that you would be left forever in darkness when the brilliance of your husband's light flickered and was snuffed? Did your disease feel as fatal as his actually was? At what point are we so bound in life that death for one must mean death for the other? Even orchids, attached as they are to trees, flesh to bark, pollen to sap, continue to bloom after their tree is rootless and dry.

I grieve for you, Mrs. Koestler. I think that upon autopsy it might be revealed that there are recesses of our hearts that match. I too have dreamed of lassoing the sun, of digging in my heels, of spurs kicking up the dust as I am dragged over the horizon. I too feel the draw of Pliny's neighbors' mutual plunge. The idea of final merging, of being bound waist to waist, is not without its appeal. Mine is also a powerful love. But somehow I see it differently.

I don't know where the medical examiner would find that the paths of our hearts changed course. Have I built a wall where yours is a sluice? Am I brook where you are slough? There's no telling.

But I must part company with Paulina, with Arria. I will not have my virtue rest on self-inflicted wounds. And I must part company with you, Mrs. Koestler, because I will not surrender myself in silence or in screams. I will take the plunge for life. But lest my resolve "be loosened by terror," I will bind myself about the waist with a fierce and stubborn knot and attach it to my own heart.[43]

BARBARA LAZEAR ASCHER

What kind of writing is this? Exposition: it sets forth information about Cynthia Koestler's suicide. Comparison: it compares Koestler's suicide to those of other "devoted wives" in history. Analysis: it categorizes people as able or unable to say goodbye to loved ones. Narration: it tells the metaphorical story of sunset watchers. Of course, it contains elements of all of these kinds of writing, and more. But, primarily, it is persuasion. On what do I base my judgment? I believe Ascher first implies her purpose in the fifth paragraph. (Notice, by the way, the rhetorical emphasis on the self—I—in Ascher's patterning each of the paragraph's seven sentences identically.) Then she reiterates her purpose in the final paragraph (where there is also a reiteration of the pattern of rhetorical emphasis on the self). I believe Ascher not only wants to retell the stories of so-called devoted wives like Cynthia Koestler, Paulina, and Arria; but she also—and primarily—wants to persuade other women to her position that the will for individual life after the loss of a mate should outweigh any notion, however virtuous it may seem, to follow him to the grave by suicide.

The Appeals of the Friendly Art

Writers have many means of persuading readers to see things their way. For example, they can appeal to the readers' sense of logic, to their moral sense, or to their emotions. What appeal would you say Ascher uses in her essay? "A logical appeal," seems like a good answer at first; after all, Ascher carefully analyzes the reasons for the devoted wives' suicides. However, the metaphorical narrative of the sunset watchers (paragraphs 13 and 14) is a significant part of Ascher's argument and it stands as a brilliant emotional appeal ("to feel the ache and to relearn that grief eventually spreads out against the sky, softens and dissipates"). Her concluding paragraphs, also, weave logical reasoning with a romantic call to living on after her spouse's death ("I will bind myself about the waist with a fierce and stubborn knot and attach it to my own heart"); her call to live is moral and emotional in the same way as her opposition's primary appeal for committing suicide is moral and emotional ("honor, virtue, devotion"). So, finally, I believe that one must concede that Ascher uses both logical and emotional appeals.

Certainly, anyone who has read or heard Martin Luther King, Jr.'s rhetorically resplendent speech, "I Have A Dream," knows how enduring and effective an appeal to the audience's emotions and morality can be. And yet, noted rhetoricians argue for the preeminence of King's "Letter from Birmingham Jail" because it is built on clear, carefully reasoned logic and is devoid of any trace of passion. Thus, the question of what kind of persuasive appeal a writer should use depends—as do other choices a writer makes—on the audience and the writing intention. With respect to audience the persuasive writer should ask the following questions:

- Are the readers likely to favor or oppose my position?
- Are they well informed on the topic?

• What examples or reasons will clarify the issue and which may confuse it in the readers' minds?

• What tone of voice will sound sufficiently authoritative and assertive without alienating or antagonizing the readers?

• How can I be fair to the opposition's position without giving the readers any reason to favor it?

• To what should I appeal in the readers—their sense of logic, their morality, their emotions or some combination?

With these questions in mind read the following selection, the opening paragraphs of an article from *Ms.* magazine:

Biology has always been used as a curse against women. From Darwin to Desmond Morris, from Freud to Robin Fox, from animal behaviorists who consider themselves open-minded but "realistic," to the sober professors of ethology, the message has rarely changed: men are biologically suited to their life of power, pleasure, and privilege, and women must accept subordination, sacrifice, and submission. It's in the genes. Go fight city hall.

Since the late 1960s, there's been an explosion of evidence showing the remarkable variety and adaptability of animal behavior. But even though we have more, not less, scientific evidence of female autonomy and power than we did 15 years ago, there's been little change in what most people *think* biology tells us.

The view of females as biological seconds still infests much of behavioral biology. Even the new kid on the Darwinian block, *socio*biology, attempts to scientize the old misogyny by positing specific sex-linked genes for such behavior as dominance and submission. Thus biology becomes not only destiny but personality as well.

Though this is the mainstream of contemporary biological thought, it is not, fortunately, the only stream in town. Divergent views have recently begun to question the astoundingly naive assumption that only males act and have begun to observe what females of different species actually do with their lives. The results for female primates—our closest relatives—are startling.[44]

Collaborating with a group of your classmates, list the character-istics that you believe define the *Ms.* readership and assess how well you believe the author of this selection performed on the preceding questions on gauging the audience.

Along with a sound sense of the audience, persuasive writers have to know their writing intentions and how to present them. The questions they must ask themselves are very similar to those on audience, except that now writing purpose is the fulcrum on which the balance hangs:

- What is my main point?
- What information is it essential to impart in order to make my main point?
- What appeal (logical, moral, emotional) is the best strategy for my purpose?
- What examples and reasons will most effectively support my position?
- What acknowledgment should I give to the opposition's posi-tion? How can I turn such acknowledgment to my advantage?

Cleveland Amory, animal's best friend, is at verbal war with hunters; he uses their arguments and data strategically for his purposes in the following selection from an essay entitled, "Sup-port Your Right to Arm Bears:"

Hunters are fond of protesting that they have never been responsible for the endangerment of any species. It is a diffi-cult argument to maintain. In the first place, it seems a reason-able assumption that the animals did not shoot each other. In the second place, although loss of habitat and changing environmental pressures were obviously responsible for much endangerment, the fact remains that the Endangered Species Act of 1973 begins, and I quote, "The two major causes of extinction are hunting and destruction of natural habitat." And in the Endangered List itself—all the way from the Aleu-tian Canada goose to the Mexican duck—one of the chief prob-lems remaining is that hunting is still allowed by the Bureau of Sport Fisheries and Wildlife.

In the third and final place, take the tables extracted from the Red Data Book of the International Union for the Conservation of Nature. These, as Roger Caras has pointed out, clearly demonstrate that, in the case of literally dozens and dozens of animal species, hunting has been not just "a major factor" in the endangerment, but the *only* major factor—and it has been listed as such. These species include such strange "game" as the giant armadillo, the Indochinese lar gibbon and the glacier bear—the latter's "reasons for decline" being listed in the U.S. Endangered Species Act as "over-hunting as a curio." Other equally curious game animals for which hunting is listed as the only major factor are the Amazonian manatee and the Syrian and Somali wild asses. The list also includes such prize "trophies" as the grizzly bear, the Bali tiger, the rhino, the snow leopard and the giant otter.[45]

How do you rate Amory's performance on the questions on writing intention?

A Final Note on Persuasion

Persuasion is a subtle art. It requires a good deal of finesse to develop effective strategies of persuasion for various topics and audiences. For some people, persuasion is their job: advertising and marketing analysts, politicians, consumer advocates, editorial writers, and trial lawyers, to name a few. So, it is likely that you will find occasion to write persuasively in several college courses. Certainly, you must be well informed about the topic in order to persuade people to your views on it. And while you cannot expect to become an expert on every topic you might want to write persuasively about, you do need to become sufficiently well informed about the subject to make knowledgeable judgments and to draw sound inferences (tentative conclusions based on partial information). When you are called upon to write persuasively, refer to the questions in this section.

Exercises in Persuasion

1. Develop a persuasive essay for parents of adolescents on the topic "What About Video Games and Your Child?" You may want to refer to the information on video games in Chapter 2 (pp. 36–38), but you will also want to gather information from other sources. For example, an issue of *IEEE Spectrum* contains

three articles that present more technical information than many popular magazines: *IEEE Spectrum,* December 1982, pp. 20–33. Ask your reference or periodical librarian if your library subscribes to this journal. Or, if you have an engineering department or school, inquire there.

2. Read Philip Slater's article "Men and Madness: Some Thoughts on the Violence Factor."

I've been thinking lately about the insanity defense. People are quite reasonably upset about it: so many well-to-do murderers acquitted because they "didn't know what they were doing." But what interests me is how such a strange practice came to exist in the first place. By this I don't mean its legal precedents, or its liberal rationale. I mean the deeper social forces that have held it in place and made it seem normal and acceptable.

There are always lots of reasons for any social practice, and the insanity defense is no exception. But I am particularly impressed with how cozily it nestles into the structure of the traditional male role. Most violent crimes are committed by men, and this obsessive legal wrangling about whether the defendant was in control of himself or not is a very male preoccupation. It is often pointed out that the core of the traditional male role is an unwillingness to take responsibility for feelings. Men do this in two ways: by denying that feelings have anything to do with their behavior, and by dissociating themselves from any feelings that do make an untoward appearance.

Men often claim, for example, to act solely from "rational motives." These usually turn out, on inspection, to involve some sort of competitiveness or greed (impulses that are themselves rooted in chronic anxiety and self-doubt). Thus in our society if a man kills for money or power, he's considered wicked but rational. If he kills for any other reason, we call it a "senseless" killing (it makes no sense to us), and there's a fighting chance (if he's rich) that the jury will decide he's crazy.

Men maintain this illusion of emotionlessness (which we might call the Vulcan Illusion, after Mr. Spock) with the aid of language and technology. When we examine their content, for example, foreign-policy papers—so imposingly "rational"

on the surface—all reduce to something like: "If I can't play
in your sandbox, you can't play in mine!" or "You hit me
first!" And we are sending purely technical messages with
our roaring motors, shrieking tires, and rasping appliances?
Would we have to impress each other so noisily with our machines if we didn't feel small, and weren't ashamed to admit
it? Could nuclear weapons have been developed without the
emotional fuel of despair and self-hatred?

When feelings become too powerful to deny or disguise,
men often say, "I didn't know what I was doing" or "I wasn't
myself," which is the burden of the insanity defense. It says
a man isn't responsible for any activity that isn't based on
greed or competition. By the same token, alcohol has always
been the preferred macho drug: it allows a man to express
feelings without owning them ("It was just the whisky talkin',
Johnny").

Awkward feelings can also be projected onto women. "Hell
hath no fury like a woman scorned," men say, although this
legendary feminine vindictiveness pales before its masculine
counterpart. Hardly a day passes without some man or boy
hacking up his sweetheart for letting him down gently. The
truth is that men don't handle "scorn" at all well, mainly
because they don't allow themselves to express their hurt,
vulnerable feelings directly. Usually, they try to disguise them
as anger, or just bury them and look grim. Sometimes they
count on women to decode and allay these hidden feelings
for them. Perhaps this is why popular male movie stars, from
Bogart to Eastwood, so often portray men who seem clinically
depressed. It gives their female fans something to work toward ("*I* could make him happy"). Close-ups of male actors
feature the Poignant Look perfected by Dustin Hoffman and
Al Pacino—a look that says: "I can't *express* any vulnerable
feelings—like any *real* man I'm emotionally constipated—but
you can *see* them here, way in the back of my eyes." Novels
and dramas in which a man at first seems crusty, cold, or
just plain nasty, but proves ultimately to have his heart in
the right place, are still another way of shoring up that creaky
social contraption we call the traditional male role.

There is an iron law that whenever you invent an awkward
social custom that twists human nature out of shape, you
have to create a hundred more to compensate for the emotional
mess it makes. There's also a law that if you don't take respon-

sibility for a feeling, you find yourself spending an inordinate amount of time discussing and analyzing and arguing about it. We love to probe the knot of unexpressed feeling and cracking repression that drives a man to violence. The *effect* seems to interest us less. We want to know how that macho mechanism broke down so we can patch it up again.

But, do we still want to patch it up? We've learned that "rational" men too often deal with matters of emotional significance by burying them—deep in the ground or under the ocean—hoping that some woman will find a way to handle them at some future date. If not, they reason, they can always say they didn't know what they were doing.

There is some evidence that this system is now falling into disrepute. Cynics may claim that disillusionment with the insanity defense began when it was extended to cover cases of extreme premenstrual tension. But I would suggest that it is just one of many signs that the traditional male role is beginning to lose its fascination.[46]

Would you classify this as persuasive writing? Slater does not urge the reader to take any specific action. Is one implied? State his purpose. If this is not persuasive writing, what type is it?

Write a persuasive essay in which you imply (that is, suggest but do not state explicitly) that the reader do something as a result of reading your views. *Note:* If you want to write on the topic of premarital sex, refer to the information on the topic in Chapter 3 (pp. 66ff).

3. Read Martin Luther King, Jr.'s speech, "I Have A Dream." Then select a topic for a persuasive essay and write it, modeling your strategy after the emotional and moral appeals of King's speech.

Or,

Read Martin Luther King, Jr.'s essay, "Letter from Birmingham Jail." Then select a topic for a persuasive essay and write it, modeling your strategy after the logical appeal of King's essay.

SEEING WRITING TYPES IN THE CONTEXT OF PROCESS

Like exercises in thinking strategies (Chapter 2) and exercises in structuring sentences (Chapter 6), exercises in writing types are a means to an end. A writer practices using the Star method in order to develop more efficient and thorough means for producing writing ideas. Similarly, he or she practices connecting and combining sentence elements in order to learn how to build better sentence structures in which to express those ideas. So, too, the writer practices describing, narrating, explaining, and persuading in order to compose more effective forms of presenting the ideas.

No writer I know begins by saying, "I am going to write an essay of definition exposition." Why not? Because writing germinates as unconnected, formless ideas. Only as those ideas begin to evolve into some mature form can a writer see a purpose and know what type of expression to use in attaining that purpose for a particular audience. Certainly writers should rehearse various forms of expression, but they should not prescribe a form before they know the writing purpose for which they need to select a form.

Sometimes a writer unconsciously selects a writing type in a spontaneous reaction to a writing assignment. For example, topics such as "Tell About a Time When You Learned Something Important About Yourself" or "Compare Free Will and Determination" suggest writing types. At other times a writer may consciously decide on one type of writing only after working through some drafts to discover a writing purpose. That is the way I selected narration as the type for my essay, "Lake O' the Woods." (Reread my remarks on pp. 90–91.) Thus, the criterion for selecting a writing type is writing purpose, whether the writer discovers that purpose already in an assigned topic or discovers it during the drafting process.

After deciding to use a particular writing type in part of an essay or as a way of achieving the entire writing purpose, the writer integrates the development of the writing type into the process of drafting and revising, all of which is guided by his or her sense of purpose and audience. In this way the writer weds form and content into a union.

NOTES

1. Stephen O. Muskie, "When the Smelt Are Running," *Yankee*, January 1982, p. 31.
2. G. S. Bush, "Yellowstone," *Travel & Leisure*, January 1982, p. 47.
3. Roger Angell, "The Web of the Game," *The New Yorker*, 20 July 1981, p. 96.

4. William Faulkner, *Sanctuary* (New York: Random House), p. 5.

5. Ibid., p. 6.

6. N. Scott Momaday, *The Way to Rainy Mountain* (New York: Ballantine Books, 1970), p. 5.

7. Kenneth Clark, *Civilisation* (New York: Harper and Row Publishers, 1969), p. 1.

8. George Orwell, *Down and Out in Paris and London* (New York: Harcourt Brace Jovanovich, 1961), p. 6.

9. Ibid., pp. 149–150.

10. "The Might of Dwight, A Saad End," *Sports Illustrated*, 16 August 1982, pp. 28–29.

11. Edgar Allen Beem, "Sport of Princes," *Yankee*, October 1982, p. 122.

12. Robert Coffin, *Yankee Coast* (New York: Macmillan Company, 1947), p. 19.

13. *A Collection of Essays* (Garden City, New York: Doubleday and Company, 1954), pp. 160–161.

14. Annie Dillard, *Pilgrim at Tinker Creek* (New York: Bantam Books, 1975), pp. 5–7.

15. John Steinbeck, *The Grapes of Wrath* (New York: Viking Press, 1939), pp. 20–22.

16. Pat Jordan, "Pitchers' Duel," *Playboy*, July 1981, pp. 115, 118.

17. Ronald R. Fieve, *Moodswing: The Third Revolution in Psychiatry* (New York: William Morrow and Company, 1975), p. 71.

18. Stephen J. Gould, *The Panda's Thumb: More Reflections in Natural History* (New York: W. W. Norton, 1980), p. 19.

19. Jerry Adler with Scott Sullivan and William Echikson, "Portrait of a Lady," *Newsweek*, 27 September 1982, p. 37.

20. *Reader's Digest Complete Do-it-yourself Manual* (Pleasantville, New York: The Reader's Digest Association, Inc., 1973), p. 216.

21. Richard Selzer, *Mortal Lessons: Notes on the Art of Surgery* (New York: Simon & Schuster, 1974), p. 68.

22. Ibid., p. 92.

23. Henry S. Pritchett, "Shall The University Become a Business Corporation?" Reprinted in Louise Desaulniers, ed., *Highlights From 125 Years of the Atlantic* (New York: The Atlantic Monthly Company, 1977), pp. 221–222.

24. Alexander Petrunkevitch, "The Spider and the Wasp," *Scientific American* 187 (August 1952), pp. 20–23.

25. "Uptight and Loose," *Playboy*, July 1981, pp. 144–145.

26. Henry David Thoreau, *Walden* and *Civil Disobedience*, Owen Thomas, ed. (New York: W. W. Norton, 1966), pp. 153–154.

27. Lindsay Van Gelder, "Instant Techie Handbook," *Ms.*, February 1983, p. 40.

28. Ibid., p. 36.

29. Norman Lloyd, *The Golden Encyclopedia of Music* (New York: Golden Press, 1968), p. 574.

30. James Beard et al., *The Great Cooks Cookbook* (New York: Ferguson/Doubleday, 1974), p. 86.

31. Lewis Thomas, *The Medusa and the Snail: More Notes of a Biology Watcher* (New York: Viking Press, 1979), pp. 76–77.

32. Sheila Tobias, *Overcoming Math Anxiety* (New York: Norton Publishing Co.), pp. 44–45.

33. Mary Gordon, "The Unexpected Things I Learned From the Woman Who Talked Back to the Pope," *Ms.*, July/August 1982, p. 65.

34. Jerry Adler with Mariana Gosnell, "What It Means To Be Fat," *Newsweek*, 13 December 1982, p. 84.

35. Barbara Ehrenreich and Karin Stallard, "The Nouveau Poor," *Ms.*, July/August 1982, p. 224.

36. Michael Lenehan, "The Quality of the Instrument: Building a Steinway Grand Piano," *The Atlantic Monthly*, August 1982, p. 34.

37. John M. Peterson, *Basic Concepts of Elementary Mathematics* (Boston: Prindle, Weber and Schmidt, Inc., 1971), pp. 245–246.

38. Raymond Oliver, *La Cuisine: Secrets of Modern French Cooking*, trans. and eds. Nika Standen and Jack Van Bibber (New York: Tudor Publishing Company, 1969), p. 819.

39. Adapted from Oliver, p. 120.

40. Marc H. Raibert and Ivan E. Sutherland, "Machines That Walk," *Scientific American*, January 1983, p. 44.

41. Michael J. Kelly, "The Lessons of Beekeeping: With bees or professors, the first principle is smoke," *The Chronicle of Higher Education*, 6 November 1978, p. 48.

42. E. M. Forster, *Two Cheers for Democracy* (New York: Harcourt Brace Jovanovich, 1979), pp. 167–171.

43. Barbara Lazear Ascher, "Hers," *The New York Times*, 17 March 1983.

44. Naomi Weisstein, "Tired of Arguing About Biological Inferiority?" *Ms.*, November 1982, p. 41.

45. *Man Kind? Our Incredible War on Wildlife* (New York: Harper & Row, 1974), p. 15.

46. Philip Slater, *Ms.*, October 1982, p. 100.

AN AFTERWORD:
Writing That
Cannot Be Taught

Now what?

So, you have completed this composition course. Are you a Writer now? Chances are if you *think* of yourself as a Writer, you *are* one.

But suppose you do not yet have enough confidence in your abilities to see yourself as a Writer. Suppose that, although you did fairly well in the course, you still find each new writing assignment a struggle. Or, suppose that in the next few semesters you have no courses that require any significant amount of writing. Then, when you face essay examinations and other courses that do require papers, you have forgotten the strategies you found helpful this semester. Then what do you do?

No musician, dancer, or athlete can leave off practicing for several months and then perform effectively on command. The same is true of writers. To maintain a certain level of proficiency a writer must continue practicing. Otherwise, he or she may regress to a lower performance level in a relatively short period of time.

How well you maintain the level of proficiency you have developed in this course depends on your practicing some writing-to-learn exercises as a part of your routine study regimen. Naturally, if you enroll in another writing course, you will have another context in which to write: a teacher's instruction, assignments, and assessment; a community of writers; and deadlines—wonderful, awful deadlines.

Lacking the structure of another writing course, however, you can create your own writing context as you study for your courses. Just commit some time everyday for practicing basic reading, writing, and thinking exercises. Using the materials from your courses, you can:

- summarize readings
- freewrite on course topics
- keep a course journal
- rewrite class lecture notes
- draft hypothetical exam questions
- share and discuss your writing with other writers
- assess your new teachers as new audiences*

If you want to refresh your memory of the directions for these activities, look them up in the appropriate sections of this book.

I trust that you have found this course and textbook useful in learning to practice writing. I urge you to continue practicing as long as you continue wanting to learn. Continue your writing practice because being a Writer is more than just knowing a set of language skills.

Writers possess querying minds, develop ways of seeing patterns, practice the art of wedding content and form, and—most of all—have a sense of confidence as meaning makers. Furthermore, Writers continually write; they are, in fact, indistinguishable from the act of writing because they are always generating, drafting, incubating, and revising ideas. The Writer writing is like Yeats' blossoming tree and dancer dancing:

> O chestnut-tree, great-rooted blossomer,
> Are you the leaf, the blossom or the bole?
> O body swayed to music, O brightening glance.
> How can we know the dancer from the dance?[1]

---

* For a discussion of teachers as the trickiest audience of all, see Peter Elbow's *Writing With Power* (New York, Oxford University Press, 1980).

To a Writer, writing is a way of being, a way of doing, a way of knowing. To be such a Writer, a meaning maker, is to compose writing that cannot be taught. It can only be learned by writing practice and performance.

NOTES

1. William Butler Yeats, "Among School Children," M. L. Rosenthal, ed., *Selected Poems and Two Plays of William Butler Yeats* (New York: Macmillan, 1962) p. 117.

Index